I0819016

HOW TO RULE THE WORLD

HOW TO RULE THE WORLD

An Education in Power at

STANFORD UNIVERSITY

THEO BAKER

PENGUIN PRESS NEW YORK 2026

PENGUIN PRESS
An imprint of Penguin Random House LLC
1745 Broadway, New York, NY 10019
penguinrandomhouse.com

Insert credits:
Page 1: (*top*) Andrew Brodhead, Stanford University;
(*middle*) Jason Doiy via Getty Images;
(*bottom*) Linda A. Cicero, Stanford University.
Page 3: (*top left*) Andrew Brodhead, Stanford University;
(*bottom left*) Thomas Yim / © 2021 The Stanford Daily, Inc.
All rights reserved. Reprinted with permission.
Page 4: (*top*) Nikolas Liepins; (*bottom*) Jeff Singer/Redux.
Page 5: Michel N Co.

Book design by Daniel Lagin

Library of Congress Cataloging-in-Publication Data

Names: Baker, Theo (Journalist), author
Title: How to rule the world: an education in power at Stanford University / Theo Baker.
Description: New York: Penguin Press, 2026.
Identifiers: LCCN 2025038105 (print) | LCCN 2025038106 (ebook) |
ISBN 9780593832837 hardcover | ISBN 9780593832844 ebook
Subjects: LCSH: Stanford University—Administration—Corrupt practices |
Stanford University—Finance | Stanford University—Students—Attitudes |
Elite (Social sciences)—Education (Higher)—California—Stanford |
Student aspirations—California—Stanford | Business and education—California—
Stanford | Research and development partnership—California—Stanford |
Internet industry—California—Palo Alto | Tessier-Lavigne, Marc |
Baker, Theo (Journalist) | Stanford daily
Classification: LCC LD3030 .B35 2026 (print) | LCC LD3030 (ebook)
LC record available at https://lccn.loc.gov/2025038105
LC ebook record available at https://lccn.loc.gov/2025038106

Printed in the United States of America
2nd Printing

The authorized representative in the EU for product safety and compliance is
Penguin Random House Ireland, Morrison Chambers, 32 Nassau Street,
Dublin D02 YH68, Ireland, https://eu-contact.penguin.ie.

This is a work of nonfiction. Some names have been changed
to protect the privacy of the people involved.

For my parents, Peter and Susan,

and my late grandfathers, Ted and Steve

It is a well-known fact that those people who must *want* to rule people are, ipso facto, those least suited to do it.

—DOUGLAS ADAMS, *THE RESTAURANT AT THE END OF THE UNIVERSE*

I am not afraid of storms, for I am learning how to sail my ship.

—LOUISA MAY ALCOTT, *LITTLE WOMEN*

CONTENTS

YOUR STANFORD POCKET DICTIONARY xi

Prologue: Fear the Tree 1

1 Drafted to the War on Fun 15

2 The Impostor 35

3 Coupa Circuit 53

4 Binary Bomb 73

5 A Fucking Menace 99

6 Rule 119

7 Duck Syndrome 141

8 Harriet the Spy 155

9 [[NOT FOR DISTRIBUTION]] 173

10 The Good Paper 197

11 TreeHacks 215

12 **Solve for People** 229

13 **Free to Speak** 243

14 **No Room for Error** 257

15 **Money Is a Rush** 265

16 ***Finis Origine Pendet*** 279

Coda 295

ACKNOWLEDGMENTS 303

NOTES 309

YOUR STANFORD POCKET DICTIONARY

1. **10x engineer:** (n.) Better than you. A 10xer is a coder worth 10 "average" coders—although nowadays some influential Silicon Valley thinkers have argued (and paid) for the concept of 1000x engineers.
2. **Anti-signal:** (adj.) The tech-bro way of saying something looks bad.
3. **B2B:**

   (adj.) business-to-business, or a company that sells directly to other companies, not consumers. Often coupled with a software-as-a-service strategy, aka "B2B SaaS," and generally lucrative but dull.

   (n.) Bay to Breakers is a race across San Francisco that takes place each spring. Stanford students get up and get drunk at 5:00 a.m. while wearing absurd outfits, then take the train into the city together and participate in the race.
4. **Builders:** (n.) What you want to be. Generally refers to those at the forefront of innovation, creating for the sake of it. Also a title assumed by many pretenders.
5. **Coupa Circuit:** (n.) The intermeshed network of students, investors, scouts, and others who hang around all day at Coupa Café.
6. **CS107:** (n.) The computer science weeder course, known for its grueling final assignments, "Binary Bomb" and "Heap Allocator."
7. **Directionally correct:** (adj.) Pesky facts aside, you nailed it!
8. **Duck Syndrome:** (n.) When you look fine on the surface, but your legs are paddling like crazy just to keep afloat.
9. **Effective altruism:** (n.) EA was the most popular Silicon Valley philosophy when I arrived—basically just rebranded utilitarianism. After Sam Bankman-Fried's fall from grace, EA floundered.
10. **Eurotrash:** (n.) Stanford's traditional first party of the year. It was canceled.
11. **Fear the Tree:** (n.) A rallying cry Stanford students shout at sports events.

12. **Fizz:** (n.) An anonymous social media app started by Stanford students and only accessible by members of the community. Full of vitriol, rampant falsehood, and abuse; raised $41.5 million despite no apparent revenue.
13. **Friends and Family:** (n.) A Builders' society of sorts, where Stanford insiders congregate. Funded by VCs.
14. **Full Moon on the Quad:** (n.) A Stanford tradition where students go to Main Quad and all kiss each other under the full moon. Except now it's the bureaucratic version.
15. **Gift authorship:** (n.) The shady, albeit normalized, practice of researchers adding their names to papers they had little to do with. Generally done by those with seniority.
16. **Hangers-On:** (n.) Those bloodthirsty adults who are always on campus, always looking for teenagers they can exploit.
17. **High-agency:** (adj.) Greater than the rest, these Übermenschen have superseded the need for normal "rules" and inhibitions.
18. **Hoover Institution:** (n.) The influential conservative think tank housed at Stanford; home to iconic Hoover Tower, the tallest building on campus; led by former secretary of state Condoleezza Rice.
19. **Lean LaunchPad:** (n.) The most famous, most established startup class, teaching agile methodology.
20. **Marriage Pact:** (n.) The Stanford student matchmaking service that algorithmically pairs people once a year; has raised millions with no demonstrated ability to generate revenue.
21. **Nerd Nation:** (n.) Stanford's own self-description. They put it on our T-shirts.
22. **Ngmi:** (adj.) Not gonna make it, applied to those who don't have the hustle.
23. **No Filter:** (n.) An insider club bringing CEOs to have confidential conversations with Stanford students.
24. **Party Review Committee:** (n.) The PRC is the manifestation of Stanford's borderline authoritarian approach to student life.
25. **Pre-idea funding:** (n.) Who needs an idea to start a company these days? That's so passé! All you need is smart people and cash.
26. **Pre-revenue:** (adj.) You're making no money. But it's a good thing! Better to have no revenue but the *potential* for radical growth than a meager yet consistent profit.
27. **Pset:** (n.) Problem set. The basic unit of measurement for any STEM class at Stanford, usually assigned once a week, some requiring dozens of hours each.
28. **PubPeer:** (n.) The pseudonymous website where scientists scrutinize published research.

29. **Reality-distortion field:** (n.) The ability to redefine the world as you please through sheer will and insistence, facts be damned.
30. **Rollout:** (v.) To be rolled out is to be torn from your bed at an early hour as initiation to a competitive club.
31. **Rule:** (n.) How all insiders refer to How to Rule the World, the most secretive—and exclusive—hub for the Stanford inside Stanford.
32. **S.H.I.T.:** (n.) The Stanford Highly Incompetent Team was a group of car aficionados who built a race team in an underground garage with no budget.
33. **SLE:** (n.) The Structured Liberal Education, a first-year program whose students live together and study Great Books. Nerdy.
34. **Swe:** (adj.) Someone who has received a Software Engineering internship for the summer might say, "I'm swe."
35. **Technical:** (adj.) A judgment on your worth as a person.
36. **The Big Three:** (n.) *Science*, *Nature*, and *Cell*, the three journals that can make or break your career.
37. **The Plucked:** (n.) Stanford students who are found early and drafted to a parallel track with so much excess and access that is kept inaccessible to the hoi polloi.
38. **TreeHacks:** (n.) A hackathon, but also a gathering point for ambitious future entrepreneurs. Brilliant and saturated with money.
39. **The Turkey Drop:** (n.) When all those freshman long-distance relationships break up, usually around Thanksgiving.
40. **Unicorn:** (n.) A company that has achieved a valuation greater than $1 billion. Status symbol.
41. **Wantapreneur:** (adj.) Derogatory term describing those who want to be CEOs not because they want to innovate, but because they desire all the associated perks and status.
42. **War on Fun:** (n.) Stanford's bureaucratic crackdown on all facets of student experience. Not limited to parties.

HOW TO RULE THE WORLD

PROLOGUE

FEAR THE TREE

Everybody wants to rule the world.

—TEARS FOR FEARS

It was a secret. That's about the only thing I knew.

I was two months into freshman year at Stanford University, a coder quickly turning into an investigative journalist, and I'd arrived three minutes early to my tryout for the secret class, unsure what to expect.

The professor was nowhere to be found. "I'm here," I texted him, scanning faces around me to see if I'd missed someone. We were supposed to meet at Tresidder Memorial Union, the nondescript food court for visitors—the most public building at Stanford.

I had no idea who I was looking for. I mean, I knew his name, Justin, and that he ran a successful startup in Silicon Valley. I knew that he valued privacy above all else. And I knew that he was teaching a highly exclusive seminar for the winter quarter that required a cloak-and-dagger admissions process. But that was it. There was nothing about this class in the course catalog, nothing about it on the internet, and nothing that anyone would tell me—except that I definitely wanted to be in it.

My phone rang.

"Walk to your right, past the Panda Express, toward the tables," said the voice. "I'm in the corner."

Once I laid eyes on him, Justin stood out. He was tall and lanky, with shoulder-length hair and a full beard. His posture radiated confidence. He looked like a techno-Jesus. If Jesus were grilling teenagers in a food court, I guess.

Another kid was still sitting with Justin, and I recognized him from a recent dinner hosted by a venture capital investor, the kind of dinner that Stanford students—or at least a certain kind of Stanford student—get invited to all the time. The kid looked a little dejected, standing up and making way for me at the table without so much as a greeting. Justin motioned to the vacated chair and I sat.

"So, you know what the class is, right?" Justin asked.

"Um, sort of?" I answered hesitantly.

Justin glanced down at his leather-bound notebook, checking to see who'd referred me. To be worthy of an interview, you had to be tapped on the shoulder by someone already in the class; by virtue of my coding ability, two of Justin's chosen few had recommended me. Satisfied, Justin looked back up.

He summarized his aim succinctly. "There doesn't exist a substantial network of the most brilliant people at Stanford," Justin said. "By helping them find each other, the entire cohort is lifted up." His job was to figure out whether I belonged.

"Questions will be divided into two parts, your past and your future," he said. "I can tell everything I need to know about you in twenty minutes."

And, for what turned into half an hour, Justin quizzed me.

"What has been your highest emotional high?"

"What has been your lowest emotional low?"

"And what is the thread that ties them together?"

Justin sat ramrod straight, eyes burrowing into me. He didn't seem to blink. He told me that he was assessing me for my "scope of ambition, intelligence, and emotional quotient."

And, at the end, he let me ask some questions. There was only one thing I really wanted to know.

"What is the class actually about?" I asked. Left unsaid: What was the point of all of this? Why, exactly, had I just endured this interrogation?

"When I was at Stanford," Justin explained, "I learned that the only people who understood the world were the literal children of billionaires." Now he'd figured out those secrets for himself. "There are a number of simple but non-obvious frameworks that govern how the world works," he said. "By learning them, a huge amount of latent talent and potential in the most promising people can be unlocked."

And, if I got in, he would teach me.

CALIFORNIA WAS ONCE THE SITE OF THE GREAT GOLD RUSH THAT transformed America. "It was that population," wrote Mark Twain, "that gave to California a name for getting up astounding enterprises and rushing them through with a magnificent dash and daring and a recklessness of cost or consequences, which she bears unto this day."

He termed his own era of American excess the Gilded Age.

Yet the fortune generated by Silicon Valley in the past few decades has exceeded the value of all gold discovered during the first California boom two hundred times over, even adjusted for inflation, and concentrated the lucre in still fewer hands. Even the richest men of Twain's time would find Elon Musk's trillion-dollar pay package remarkable.

Once a bucolic region dominated by farmland and horse trails, this little stretch of Northern California now sets the agenda for the planet. That sounds like an exaggeration, but it's not. Every aspect of modern life is dependent on technology, and technology flows through here. The value of public companies based in the area is $14.3 trillion—greater than the GDPs of the United Kingdom, Germany, and India combined, with enough left over to cover the assets of every major bank in Africa. Private companies add at least another trillion.

Silicon Valley gave birth to the chips and computers and internet that we all rely on in the twenty-first century. Technology became king. As Bob Martin, an influential software pioneer, put it a decade ago, "*We* rule the world. The world doesn't know this yet." Martin explained that "other people believe that they rule the world," yet "we write the rules that go into the machines that execute everything that happens on this planet nowadays. No law can be enacted without software. No law can be enforced without software. No government can act without software. We rule the world."

Ten years later, the world may have taken notice. After all, the top tech CEOs in the world were the ones standing directly behind President Donald Trump at his inauguration while political leaders were shunted to the overflow room.

Today's tech tycoons are not dissimilar to the robber barons of Twain's time. Wealth inequality is by some metrics greater in Silicon Valley than in any other region in the world; just eight households in Santa Clara and San Mateo Counties hold more wealth than the entire bottom 50 percent of the population of these counties combined, more than half a million people. Together, the top 1 percent in Silicon Valley control forty-eight times more wealth than the bottom 50 percent.

Palantir, the data defense tech company cofounded by Stanford stars like Peter Thiel, is a Silicon Valley darling hoovering up many bright young engineers. Currently, its CEO, Alex Karp, makes more in a year than the *entire company* earns in gross revenue. This is possible because the company trades at well over five hundred times its earnings, thanks to Silicon Valley's unshakable belief in exponential future growth.

When the talented artificial intelligence researcher Ilya Sutskever started Safe Superintelligence, he launched with nine employees, a two-hundred-word placeholder statement, and zero articulation of a product, much less any revenue. The company was valued at $32 billion. Higher than the National Bank of Canada, the cosmetics giant Estée Lauder, and even the third-largest auto manufacturer in the world, Hyundai, which produces more than four million cars a year. SSI, meanwhile, has produced nothing.

Thinking Machines, another AI company, raised $2 billion at a $10 billion valuation in 2025, although the pitch to investors "offered no information about a product or financial plans," according to the *Financial Times*. Five months later, the startup was seeking more funding at a valuation of $50 billion or even $60 billion, Bloomberg reported.

Silicon Valley runs on the assumption of potential. It runs on the notion that heights are limitless and hurdles along the way will inevitably be smoothed by the exercise of brute will. It runs on the idea that the people in these startups will eventually produce untold riches.

So if this is a modern-day gold rush, the resource to mine is talent. And nowhere can you find more of it than Stanford University.

AT AGE SEVENTEEN, I, TOO, CAME WEST SEARCHING FOR GOLD. I WAS A true believer in the power of technology to effect change—I still am, I guess. But my relationship to this world has grown . . . complicated.

From the moment I set foot on Stanford's campus, I learned that teenagers like me were a commodity. We were to be protected and preserved, cosseted and buttered up, exploited, manipulated, funded, bribed, and cultivated. We were business.

A whole economy has sprung up around identifying the next great talent. Getting in on the ground floor of the next trillion-dollar startup makes your career, so adults hunt relentlessly for a meal ticket. They fetishize youth.

The perks lavished on a select few Stanford students are astonishing. I was just weeks into freshman year when I found myself at a party at a mansion in the hills, thrown by a student group that funneled cash from tech companies through a slush fund into the pockets of teenagers. I quickly discovered that there was a Stanford inside Stanford, an exclusive world of excess and access afforded to those identified as "high agency"—those special super-geniuses who will reshape the world in their image.

I also discovered a kind of rot.

What I loved about technology—the ability to create, the idea of doing something no one has ever done before, the engineering puzzle pieces that come together to make up our modern life—was often subordinated to naked ambition. Over the course of my freshman year, people I got to know in the tech world would admit to me to tax evasion and tax fraud, research misconduct, embezzlement and misappropriation of funds, securities fraud, insider trading, academic dishonesty, operating slush funds and shell companies, hacking, reckless endangerment, and abetting foreign dictators. The breadth and array of bad behavior was staggering. There was a culture, I discovered, that enabled and even embraced cut corners. And it went all the way to the top.

Right as I was gaining access to the Stanford inside Stanford, I found myself sucked into student journalism. It started small; I joined *The Stanford Daily* as a hobby. But not even a month into college, I stumbled across a story that would force me to commit. A story about the president of Stanford.

Marc Tessier-Lavigne was a world-renowned neuroscientist—and an extraordinarily wealthy former biotech executive—who'd been at the helm of the university since 2016 and maintained a sterling reputation. But when I began poking around, I found something darker: a slew of apparently fraudulent research studies bearing his name published across two decades.

Suddenly, the year I thought would be dominated by classes and coding marathons gave way to middle-of-the-night meetings with secret sources, anonymous letters showing up at my doorstep, stakeouts, attacks from powerful lawyers, and a frenzied chase to unearth the truth. What began with a student newspaper article about college parties led to my investigating a multinational corporation, a deal worth tens of billions, and the real story behind famous research that had purported to identify the cause of Alzheimer's disease.

All of this while watching in real time as my peers learned to commit the same kind of misconduct I was reporting on.

STANFORD, FOUNDED DURING THE GILDED AGE BY A ROBBER BARON who came west during the gold rush, was once a regional university, a magnet for wealthy Californians but no match for the academic rigor of the East Coast establishment. That's why they call it the Farm, in honor of Leland Stanford's horse farm, which once occupied this ground. That's why the mascot is a tree. And that's why Stanford's ethos was shaped around being an underdog.

All of that changed with the tech boom.

For the last few decades, Stanford has been an institution ascendant like no other, transforming into an international juggernaut with an admissions rate of 3.6 percent. Under the leadership of President John Hennessy from 2000 to 2016, more than seventy new buildings were erected, and Stanford became the top school in the country in fundraising, the first to surpass $1 billion a year.

Boosted by incredible resources and its symbiotic relationship with Silicon Valley, Stanford has made a strong claim in recent years to be the greatest university in the world. Almost every program aspires to be the best—the business school, the law school, the schools of medicine, humanities and sciences, and, of course, engineering. Stanford boasts the most influential in-house think tank of any university. It has won the Directors' Cup, given to the best overall collegiate athletics program in the NCAA, twenty-six of the thirty-two times it has been awarded. It has produced both the most ten-figure companies of any school and, in the most recent games, double the Olympic medals of the next-highest university.

By 2014, *The New York Times* declared that "Harvard Is the Stanford of the East." Yes, "riding a wave of interest in technology, Stanford University has become America's 'it' school, by measures that Harvard once dominated," with the upstart university unseating an institution synonymous with success from its founding in 1636. Since then, the gap has only widened. Harvard's yearly budget grew $2.2 billion between fiscal years 2013 and 2024; Stanford's grew $9.9 billion. Even if you remove the Stanford Hospital system, the university's annual revenue is nearly twice that of Harvard or Yale, despite educating about the same number of students. Stanford spends more in a year than Columbia has in its whole endowment. In fact, at $18.3 billion including the hospital system, Stanford's annual budget eclipses that of 116 countries. Nicaragua is a nation of nearly 7 million people, yet Stanford's expenses could cover the government's entire yearly budget—*times four.*

Stanford and Silicon Valley are intertwined in unique fashion. While the Ivy League has been a pipeline to Wall Street and Washington, half of Silicon Valley was literally built on Stanford land. They are codependent. The technology boom after World War II was born at the Stanford Research Park, where the microwave tube, ethernet, and the personal workstation were developed. William Shockley's attempts to commercialize a new transistor design at the park gave birth to the semiconductor boom that provided Silicon Valley its name (referencing the silicon needed to make computer chips). The early tech giant Sun Microsystems, which helped usher in the next wave of innovation, was named for "Stanford University Network," and the first website in the United States was created for the Stanford Linear Accelerator Center.

The Stanford Research Park has been home to the headquarters of Hewlett-Packard, Facebook, and Theranos. Nowadays, there are roughly 150 companies housed at the park, including Tesla, Google, and Lyft; the cumulative value of companies that currently maintain offices on Stanford land is north of $6 trillion. The venture capital firms, or VCs, are just up the hill, clustered along Sand Hill Road, ready to fund new startups from promising students, who then frequently set up shop nearby, hiring almost exclusively other Stanford students and kicking back some of the proceeds to the university. The whole system is integrated; Stanford even operates its own VC fund to seed students, bragging that companies it has incubated are "3X more likely to reach $100 million in valuation."

Stanford students worship the legend of Google emerging from a graduate student's garage, Instagram hatching from alumni network outreach, and DoorDash growing out of a class project by students who wanted food delivery to their dorm. A 2011 study found that Stanford alumni and faculty had founded forty thousand active companies; today that list includes giants like Anthropic, Capital One, Cisco, Electronic Arts, Expedia, LinkedIn, Netflix, Nike, OpenAI, Yahoo!, Zillow, and others. It also includes some you might not expect— Bain & Company, Charles Schwab, Trader Joe's, TSMC, Victoria's Secret, and more.

Last year, the Nvidia founder and Stanford alum Jensen Huang came back to campus to give a talk, after which he handed out five-thousand-dollar graphic cards with his autograph in gold ink. Students mobbed him, desperate for a signature, offering laptops, T-shirts, anything. And in his leather jacket, with his exhortation to work from dawn till dusk, seven days a week, fifty-two weeks a year, Jensen Huang was what passed for a rock star.

"There are a hundred and fifty people—and they're all men—who run the world," the billionaire Chamath Palihapitiya once told a Stanford audience. The students listened, enraptured; after all, the lecture was entitled "View from the Top." Palihapitiya continued, "Anyone who wants to go into politics? They're all puppets." Instead, to succeed is "to aggregate enough of the capital of the world to then reallocate it against your worldview."

And that's why so many people are desperate to go here. What is a Stanford degree worth? Well, at least $6.5 million to one family that paid its way in the door, the largest sum uncovered in the Varsity Blues admissions-cheating scandal.

THE TRUTH IS, STANFORD POSSESSES MANY ADMIRABLE QUALITIES. The professors are outstanding, the opportunities remarkable. Describing this place exhausts superlatives. But it's also fraught, an institution that relishes its image as an underdog long after it stopped being one.

Exactly a century before I arrived, Stanford president Ray Lyman Wilbur launched the First Million campaign—at the time, a daring act that marked the beginning of organized fundraising on campus. But he was already growing worried. He expressed "regret that students are often given too large an allowance of money, and some are given or loaned automobiles by their parents or others." He admonished, "There is no need to supply money for orchids for dance partners, or for taxi hire. The student who is not content to lead the simple, clean, industrious life expected on the Stanford campus should go elsewhere."

Life at Stanford today is not "simple, clean, industrious." In fact, an individual student with sufficiently promising ideas or tech now has no trouble raising seven figures on their own, as much as Wilbur sought for the entire institution.

Is that a good thing?

One of Stanford's mottoes, chanted at opponents during sporting events and printed on T-shirts, captures how I've come to see this place: "Fear the Tree!" Stanford is charming and full of character; after all, its icon is a tree. To be on the inside is exhilarating. But it is also a truly fearsome environment. Stanford seeks to compete on every field, and win. That phrase captures my own ambivalence. Is it a good thing to fear the tree? A bad thing? Is it a rallying cry or a confession?

DESPITE ITS RENOWN, FEW PEOPLE UNDERSTAND HOW STANFORD REALLY works. I've spent the last three years trying to figure it out. I've had more one-on-ones with billionaires than I've been on formal dates. I've encountered genius and misdeed at every stage, from wide-eyed freshman wannabes to accomplished masters of the universe. This book is my attempt to show you what I've found.

Accountability in Silicon Valley is a hard-fought thing. Power protects itself, secrets remain hidden in plain sight, and robust guardrails are lacking. This was certainly my experience in reporting on the president, whose research had escaped scrutiny for years. But it was also my experience in uncovering the underbelly of the student body.

The Stanford inside Stanford is nothing like the school that most of its students experience. In fact, its perks are purposefully kept hidden, its entry points—like the hush-hush class I interviewed to get into—disguised. The Stanford inside Stanford comprises the group of students who are expected to inherit the earth, those courted constantly by the rich and powerful because they might be the Next Big Thing. The same fifty people who show up at every single VC dinner, every single insider event.

To live in this world is jarring, like being swept along by a current; by the time you're conscious enough to look up you've been carried miles away from where you began. It is alluring, and dangerous. When teenagers are placed in an environment with great opportunity and scant due diligence, they learn that they can get away with things. First a little embellishment, then an outright lie. I watched people I met at the beginning of freshman year discover how to manipulate the world around them, raising money off false pretenses or siphoning funds for themselves.

Perhaps what is most surreal about experiencing this place is the bizarre farrago of normal, formative college experiences with utterly absurd context.

One time, I met another student at a dinner party in Menlo Park. He was bright, curious, and openly contrarian—and I enjoyed arguing with him. He offered me a ride back to campus. And, from behind the wheel of his Tesla, he began talking about drugs. "The whole reason I'm studying chemistry is because of LSD," he said. "Have you tried it?" I told him I had not. He continued to tell me about "ketamine, LSD, shrooms, ecstasy, cocaine." Only thirty minutes after we met, he offered, "If you want, I'll be your dealer." Yes, he said, "Just hit me up."

This was sort of odd, right? But also very college. Except I looked up the kid's website later: At age nineteen, he'd already raised nearly

$20 million for his software company, been named to the *Forbes* 30 Under 30 list, and had every prestigious validator of success. Even the drug dealers around here are cracked.

Recently, I was sitting in a small seminar on greed and the birth of capitalism. I noticed the kid next to me wasn't paying attention. He was on his laptop, tabbing back and forth between some sort of document and his text messages. Then I realized what he was doing.

While attending our history-of-capitalism course, my classmate was filling out the capitalization table for his new startup, determining what percentage of the company each investor and partner would get. The person he was texting was a top executive at one of the biggest companies in the world—his adviser. As the professor discussed avarice, I watched my classmate delete the percentage next to his own name and replace it with a higher number.

THIS BOOK IS TOLD THROUGH THE LENS OF MY FRESHMAN YEAR. IT WAS a weird one. I found myself torn between two worlds—that of a programmer glimpsing jaw-dropping wealth and that of a fledgling reporter revealing unsavory stories despite steep resistance. At one point, I returned a scientist's query about data falsification from the deck of a yacht. Later, I sent a tech company instructions about how to route large sums of cash while sitting in the newsroom of a daily student paper that could now afford to publish only once a week in print.

Throughout all this, I was trying to figure out just being a freshman—how to survive weeder classes, how to make friends, how to maintain a long-distance relationship, how to cope with grief, and how to live on my own across the country for the first time.

I was inspired to write this book in part by *One L*, Scott Turow's enduring account of his first year at Harvard Law School, which chronicled how pressure and privilege shaped students there in the 1970s. Like Turow, I've changed many of the names, especially of those under the age of twenty-five. That said, this is no roman à clef—there are no compound characters, no invented scenes, and no conversations that did not occur as described.

I have conducted more than 250 interviews with students, CEOs, VCs, Nobel laureates, scientific sleuths, professors, athletes, administrators, and more while reporting this book. My interview subjects have included three Stanford presidents (and the widow of a fourth), three Stanford provosts, and several trustees. I have also relied on extensive troves of documents, including financial filings, contemporaneous notes, images, blog posts, legal papers, internal memos, text messages, and slide decks. This book has been subject to rigorous editorial review, independent fact-checking, and legal vetting to present the most comprehensive portrait possible.

In the end, this is a book not about any one person, but about an institution that is profoundly influential—and deeply inaccessible. It is about a culture that embraces getting ahead at any cost, that lacks safeguards to fully address bad behavior, where geniuses are stockpiled, ready to reinvent the world but taught instead how to prioritize their self-interest.

This is a book about the kids being raised to rule the world, and what they're learning from those who already do.

As I finished my interview with Justin on that rainy day in November 2022, I discovered the true purpose of the secret class.

"The last thing I judge you on," Justin told me, "is who you identify." Justin was looking for "high-agency individuals" and said I could provide up to three names of other people I thought were exceptional—and that he would assess *me* based on how good they were.

It was a brilliant scheme.

Justin's class, it turned out, wasn't a real class in the sense of earning course credit, although there were lectures, discussions, and guest speakers, and it was held each week on Stanford's campus. It was more like a secret society, a Skull and Bones for the aspiring tech elite. It was a means to an end. Justin was networking with teenagers he expected to be useful in the future. Only he'd figured out how to flip the script and make them come to him.

Justin knew that a certain elite cohort of Stanford students wouldn't be able to resist the mystique he cultivated, the notion of this insider class no one would speak about, where only the very best of the best congregated to learn the secrets of the billionaires they aspired to become.

He called it "How to Rule the World."

CHAPTER 1

DRAFTED TO THE WAR ON FUN

Stanford is supposed to look perfect.

From the sweeping, manicured lawns of pristine chromatic green, to the palm trees and hulking glass auditoriums that frame historic archways, to the sparkling blue-water fountains, chlorinated so students can splash around beneath the California sun, it's all curated to leave an impression of wonder. Stanford is an oasis, a place where Rodin sculptures stand next to nuclear laboratories. It is gorgeous, expansive, and, most of all, imposing.

I arrived for my first day of college on a brisk September morning in 2022 full of nervous energy. I could recite the Stanford propaganda by heart. I'd watched all the videos, read the entire course catalog, and eagerly devoured research papers from a dozen different labs. Now I took it all in, the pine-and-eucalyptus-scented air, the seagulls perched atop terra-cotta-tiled roofs. My hand trembled slightly as I opened the door of my family's rental car. For some reason, the student orientation coordinators were wearing cow costumes as they jumped up and down to greet us.

Stanford had been my dream since I was seven, much to the surprise of everyone around me on the East Coast. I'd fallen in love with the notion that all this genius had been concentrated in one institution, coming together to reshape the world. "Buzzing with ideas and innovation, approaching questions with openness and curiosity, pursuing excellence in all we do—this is Stanford," the school's website claimed. *Things were happening out there.*

I wanted to be part of them.

It wasn't just the tech or the innovation. Stanford combined excellence with a quirky, freewheeling attitude that set it apart from its competitors. Students constructed makeshift boats to traverse Lake Lagunita and built motorized couches to get to class. Irreverence was said to be an integral part of the experience. When students graduated, they participated in the Wacky Walk. Instead of wearing staid black robes into commencement, graduates donned satirical costumes, teaming up to construct a Stanford-themed pirate ship, wearing cardboard representations of their favorite campus street signs, or dressing as Stanford "Cardinals," pairing the school's signature Cardinal Red with a play on Catholic iconography.

I loved the idea that Stanford, despite its competitive excellence, had somehow still retained the reputation of being laid-back, chill. The campus was designed to be isolated, offering a reprieve from the real world where students could go about the business of brilliance and have a good time doing so. Who wouldn't want to go to a perfect-looking place full of perfect-looking people, glowing beneath perennially blue skies?

This was the promise of Stanford: beauty, idiosyncrasy, perfection.

IT TOOK TWENTY MINUTES TO DRIVE FROM THE CAMPUS ENTRANCE TO my dorm. The snaking caravan of halting, overstuffed SUVs seemed endless. Nobody seemed to know how to use a roundabout. But it gave me a good chance to observe.

Students experienced every possible emotion all at once. Some cried and hugged their parents; some buzzed with enthusiasm; others were taciturn, almost in shock. I understood the feeling. Moving to a campus three thousand miles from home where I knew almost no one was intimidating. I was grateful for the opportunity, still pinching myself that this place would be my home. I didn't want to mess it up.

One of the first orders of business was to buy a bike, as walking from the door of my dorm to the edge of Palo Alto took an hour. On a campus of 8,180 acres, with an undergraduate population of just eight thousand, everything was spread out.

Soon I was situated on an overpriced hunter-green cruiser from the bike store, ready to take it for a spin. I biked past the class buildings that would be my lecture halls, noting that they all bore names like Gates (as in Bill) and Huang (as in Jensen), each containing tributes to inventions born at the Farm. A solar car built by students hung suspended from the ceiling in one engineering complex. Another building had a three-story atrium made completely of glass—every wall, even the roof.

At the edge of the engineering quad, two large buildings faced one another: Hewlett and Packard. They proudly marked the origin story of Stanford's greatness—brilliant students, William Hewlett and David Packard, who founded their company in a garage in 1938 with $538, creating what would ultimately become Silicon Valley. Now those of us who set foot inside their classrooms were expected to follow the Stanford example.

AT MY DORM, THINGS WERE LESS DAUNTING. ALONDRA, NAMED FOR the Spanish word for "lark," was three stories of reassuringly mundane drabness. Whereas the Stanford presented to the outside world was all glam, Alondra, a 1950s building with carpets overdue for a refresh, could've passed for practically any college dorm in America. There were shared bathrooms that would never again be so clean, common spaces with a piano and an oddly slanted pool table, and thin-walled rooms each containing a bookcase, a desk, a bed, and little else.

Because everyone lives on campus all four years—Palo Alto is ridiculously expensive—and because everything at Stanford is so damn far away, where you live has a dramatic effect on your life. Dorm culture can vary wildly. There are the co-ops, like Synergy, the nudist dorm; Enchanted Broccoli Forest, where weed reigns supreme; and Terra, where the judgy gays go. There are row houses, reserved mostly for social seniors, and apartment-style buildings, where nothing ever happens. But I was in a much stranger, much rarer environment: a haven of humanities.

For the next year, I would take a set of classes alongside the people I lived with, in addition to my regular coursework. The program I had signed up for was named the Structured Liberal Education, but everyone called it SLE (pronounced *slee*), and it was basically a Great Books course: a commitment to read at least a book a week throughout freshman year, from *Gilgamesh* and Sappho to Sartre and Arendt.

My plan for Stanford was to focus on computer science, but I'd decided to balance this out with SLE, intent on seeing many sides of campus. This was a more important choice than I realized at the time.

I learned quickly that Alondra was nicknamed "the Nerd Dorm" by other students—which said something at a university that openly called itself "Nerd Nation." (Yeah, really.) Living alongside me were the reigning American women's chess champion, the author of a calculus textbook (as she mentioned frequently), a Hong Kong heiress, a cerebral day trader who'd made hundreds of thousands of dollars in high school, and three world-class pianists. And also a son of undocumented immigrants and the lesbian daughter of a member of the right-wing Proud Boys who grew up in a trailer park.

Most intriguingly, the woman assigned to the room next door to mine had the same name as my long-distance girlfriend from high school, Lily Zhou. That seemed like a sign from the universe, though of what I hadn't a clue.

That night, I felt a surge of cautious optimism as I took in my barely furnished dorm room. The possibilities were endless.

ORIENTATION PROVED TO BE A STUDY IN CONTRASTS. I MET ONE KID whose parents had bought him a multimillion-dollar house just off campus, so he could have friends over or do his laundry when he needed a break from school. "You don't have a guest house?" another student asked me incredulously. She was seriously shocked. I was the one shocked when a different student asked me, "Why are all Jews so rich?" Over the next few weeks, some of my more sheltered classmates repeatedly asked how to operate those strange, mystical devices known as laundry machines. Several had to be guided through the process again and again before it finally clicked.

As for me, I arrived ready to let loose a bit. I'd never actually been to a party, at least not one hosted by young people. I mean, I was a nerd in high school. (Like, seriously, a complete loser. Even my Stanford admissions file pronounced, "He's an absolute nerd.") I'd gotten drunk a few times and once snuck off to the ancient forest just beyond school grounds to smoke weed with a friend, coughing up my lungs and giggling at the pitch-black solemnity of it all. But I'd never been to a bar or a club or "gone out."

The first Friday of freshman year was meant to be when people really, truly, finally celebrated the amazing thing it is to be a college student. For many Stanford overachievers—especially for this incoming Class of 2026 that had endured half of high school during the COVID pandemic—this was to be the first experience with freedom, an opportunity to say, "To hell with it all, let's have fun!"

But, alas, it wasn't to be.

Stanford's traditional first party of the year—"Eurotrash," hosted by the Kappa Sigma fraternity—was canceled by the university on short notice, with little explanation. No other events, parties or otherwise, took its place. Instead, on the first Friday of freshman year, I found myself with only homework to occupy me.

It's not like I really wanted to spend the night at a frat house anyway, but I did want to commemorate the occasion *somehow*. Coming to college was a big deal. I decided to go out and wander campus to see if there was something I'd missed. I found nothing. No concerts, no mixers, no parties, nothing to do. I encountered not another soul. It gave me the heebie-jeebies: Something about this place was *off*, like Disneyland after all the rides have closed and the park is emptied for the night.

It turned out that there was already a name for this. I'd just become an unwitting bystander to the War on Fun.

THE PHRASE HAD BEEN COINED A YEAR EARLIER BY STUDENTS FRUSTRATED that Stanford was exercising ever more control over their lives. The university had long before passed the threshold of employing more administrators than it enrolled undergraduates—and this showed. "There's no party like a Stanford party," someone joked to me after I arrived, "because a Stanford party was approved by a panel of administrators weeks ahead of time, has no alcohol, and gets shut down after twenty minutes."

They weren't exaggerating.

To host a social gathering, I would eventually learn, one needed to apply far in advance to the Party Review Committee, which only met once a week, on Tuesdays. The committee, a bureaucratic affront to spontaneity, comprised representatives from six university departments. (Titles included SUPER, OSE, SUDPS, RedEd, SUFMO, and FSL.) Few parties were approved, and even those that were could only last for a limited time, be hosted on certain days, and be open to specific people. A detailed proposal filling dozens of pages of requirements was required. And then there was the other essential component: the "Harm Reduction Plan."

Every social event, in Stanford's view, was a harm waiting to happen—the university's goal was to minimize the fallout. This framing, while perhaps understandable from a lawyer's perspective, had the effect of bludgeoning formative life experiences to death.

All decorations, even a few balloons, had to be approved ahead of time. Social media marketing and flyers were required to "align with the mission of the University." The all-powerful Party Review Committee even claimed jurisdiction over parties held *entirely off campus*. Yes, this War on Fun crossed sovereign borders.

Groups seeking to host off-campus events were required to provide not just the Harm Reduction Plan but a transportation plan for each guest, insurance details, the names of any vendors being used, and specific times of departure and return—at least two weeks in advance. Plus, Stanford warned, "off-campus parties may not be held at private residences. They must be held at venues with sufficient insurance, permits, and licenses."

All of this at a university with the motto "Die Luft der Freiheit weht." *Let the winds of freedom blow.*

Applying to run an event had become a full-time job. In fact, simply learning how to fill out the requisite forms and navigate the tangled institutional web required taking a specific registration-process course—with an exam you had to pass in order to apply to host a social event. Let me repeat that: You had to take a class. And pass an exam. To be able to apply to host a college party. "It's like getting audited by the IRS to get boba for people," one club leader confided in me.

Many organizations that had hosted events in the past were dying out, lacking the resources to mount a protracted campaign each time they wanted to gather. Dorm parties had been outlawed and prohibitions on alcohol were stringently enforced. Even graduate students, including those married with children, were allowed only certain mixed drinks up to a specific alcoholic percentage in the sanctity of their own apartments.

Fraternities were the last groups on campus with enough dedication to continue waging battle with the bureaucrats. But the administration was determined to break them, too. A few months before I arrived, every single fraternity had been placed on probation, each receiving a letter from a lawyer on the same day.

By the time I landed at Stanford, students were fuming, and it was impossible to escape discussion of the War on Fun. Every possible action a student could take was governed by regulation, detailed on one of Stanford's labyrinthine web pages. Officially, you weren't even allowed to make more than fifty-five decibels of noise past 10:00 p.m. The average conversation is seventy decibels.

Complaints about this stifling regulation had become impossible for the administration to ignore. "Stanford's long been known for its fun, irreverent, whimsical social scene," another official web page declared a few months before I arrived, "yet it just hasn't felt as vibrant as it could be." The university's solution was perfect in its bureaucratic logic: A Stanford Social Life Accelerator Task Force was convened to "undertake a broad based learning and engagement process with a diverse set of students, faculty, staff and alumni." This panel—couched in Silicon Valley's favorite noun, "acceleration"—was "charged by the Vice Provost for Student Affairs, the Associate Vice Provost for Campus Engagement, and the Associate Vice Provost for Inclusion, Belonging, and Integrative Learning" to figure out how on earth all the fun had disappeared.

It was like watching someone strangle themselves and then appointing a committee to investigate the cause of death.

Clearly, this was no longer the college of generations past. Equally obvious: This so-called war would make for a great first article in *The Stanford Daily*.

My grandfather would have loved that. Steve Glasser, a son of two social workers who found his calling in legal education, had died just two weeks before I started Stanford, and I was crushed. We'd shared an uncommonly close relationship—I was his only grandchild for ten years, and he absolutely doted on me. He taught me to sling a football, ride a bike, and cuss. I often stayed with him and my grandmother, sometimes for weeks at a time during summer. Gramps and I had bonded as the true night owls of our family; we stayed up chatting about our hopes and fears and lives. He was the first person I ever introduced to someone I was dating, the first person I traded family gossip with, and a man I admired deeply.

Gramps was the definition of fun. He told corny jokes by the dozen, adopted Yogi Berra as his philosopher of choice, and relished his own time in college. He would've taken endless amusement in Stanford's bureaucratic contortionism. Even while wracked with illness, he maintained a mischievous side. He used to tell me every time we passed the historic windmill near his home that he'd just seen it spinning before I arrived; before I realized that the windmill had been out of operation longer than I'd been alive.

I missed Gramps. And it was because of him that I decided to join the student newspaper.

There were two things my grandfather cared most about in the world, and the first was education. There was nothing more important to him than to learn, to be curious, to be open to the world. He read voraciously and had a genuine interest in everyone around him; to visit Gramps in the hospital was to learn that the new nurse had just started yesterday and her cousin was opening a café and she missed home in Georgia.

Gramps had moved heaven and earth to be at my high school graduation just a few months earlier. He'd been lying in the intensive care unit, at death's door, grappling with COVID, sepsis, and congestive heart failure, when he said, "I'm going to be there." Nobody believed him, but there he was, a month later, in a wheelchair yet beaming with pride. Soon he was back in the hospital, noticeably deteriorating. Still, he sported a Stanford T-shirt over his gown. He used to send me emails at 12:00 a.m. on my birthday each year—the last one I received ended, "You are a very fine young man in every respect, and I am so happy we spent so much time together while you were growing up." He'd been so excited to see me go to college; Gramps had started a college savings account for me when I was born. That he missed the moment by just weeks seemed cruel.

The second thing my grandfather liked to talk about more than anything was the time he spent working on his college paper. He would sit me on his knee and tell me tales of the campus newsroom. He believed that it had opened his mind, forced him to see more than he would've otherwise. Joining my own school newspaper would let me feel connected to his memory, even if it was just a small part of what I did.

JOURNALISM WAS THE ONLY CAREER PATH I'D EVER RULED OUT FOR MYself. My grandfather didn't actually end up as a journalist—he went to law school at his father's insistence—but both of my parents are reporters, who met in the newsroom of *The Washington Post*, and that was the life I'd been raised in: phone calls interrupting dinner, breaking news in the middle of the night, long conversations about politics. The idea that anyone stopped working on the weekend had not occurred to me until I was well into my school years.

I loved my parents dearly, but I'd been determined to find my own path. To some extent, that's why I'd been so drawn to computer science, a field they couldn't have cared less about. I was desperate to be my own person.

While I'd worked for the student paper in high school, I'd spent most of my time elsewhere; at Stanford, I expected reporting to be a similarly small proportion of my life. A way to honor Gramps, nothing long term.

NOBODY HAD REPORTED ON THE WAR ON FUN YET. THE SPRING BEFORE I arrived, a graduating senior had written a first-person essay for an alternative magazine taking the school to task, but the full extent of the crackdown was unclear. I felt that investigating could be useful.

The first step was to join *The Daily*. Unlike the rest of Stanford, the student newspaper had little red tape or organization. I simply showed up at the Daily House—an airy two-story, open-floor-plan newsroom owned by the student group that had been built with $4.5 million in donations a decade earlier but now sat mostly empty—asked to write, and went off reporting with no training or instruction. That suited me just fine. Unfortunately, I didn't actually know what I was doing.

I had a sort of intuitive sense of how to approach things—mostly just reach out to anyone who might have an interesting perspective. But I realized I knew nothing about how Stanford really worked. Who wielded power? Who was willing to give their thoughts? What titles mattered and which ones were ornamental? And, I soon added to my list of questions, why wouldn't anyone respond to me?

MY ATTEMPTS TO GATHER INFORMATION QUICKLY STALLED. DOZENS of emails to club leaders, administrators, frat bros, and safety advocates went unanswered. I was asking basically anyone I met if they knew anyone who had something interesting to say. Invariably, they would respond, "Yes! My friend actually had a crazy experience last year." To which I'd say, "Great, can you put us in touch?" and hear back, two days later, that the friend wasn't willing to talk. It was weird. There was this *fear*.

I reached out to a journalism lecturer, R. B. Brenner, for advice. R.B. was everybody's favorite teacher and served on *The Daily*'s advisory board. He was a short, always-smiling firecracker of a man, with infinite energy. He told me we should meet at Coupa Café for coffee.

Coupa was the main gathering point on campus. It was where all first meetings happened—for VCs, professors, and God knows who else. It inspired a strange amount of loyalty, too; proudly displayed was an image of seniors from the Class of 2018 dressed as Coupa Café cups at their graduation.

R.B. loved Stanford, he explained—he'd been teaching at the school since 2010, after a long career as a reporter and editor. Still, he told me, "very, very few students care much about journalism out here."

There was a small, excellent graduate program for journalists, but they kept to themselves. There was no undergraduate journalism major. "Many students don't read the news at all, and I can count the number of undergrads who want to be journalists on one hand," R.B. said.

He was right. Much later, when I was running a training for *The Daily*'s senior beat reporters, I asked the dozen or so in front of me to name their favorite article of any kind that they'd read in the last week. More than half said they hadn't read a single story in any outlet.

"*The Daily* can feel more like a social club," R.B. told me. Some people put in a lot of work and did amazing stuff, but the vast majority were disengaged. The new editor in chief, he told me, was a kid named Sam Catania who'd been elected after serving as chief technology officer. He was bright and energetic, R.B. said, but he didn't want to be a journalist and had never worked in a professional newsroom. After college, he was headed to a tech startup.

As far as I could tell, *The Daily* was a shell of its pre-COVID self, and the core team pretty small. Only a few writers covered timely stories. But reporting had been in decline even before the pandemic. In 2015, *Vanity Fair* described *The Stanford Daily* as "supine," saying there was "not much [journalism] left in the Bay Area." This was harsh but accurate.

Luckily, I didn't need anyone to give me urgency. What I did need was someone who would talk to me for this story. Stuck, I was going to have to resort to extreme measures. I was going to have to report from a frat party.

YES, THE FIRST PARTY I WENT TO IN COLLEGE WAS FOR THE PURPOSE of journalism.

It was called "White Lies," and everyone was asked to come with a confession written with Sharpie on their shirt in white lie form. I trooped out with a group from my dorm, sober and curious to see how the night would go.

A long queue awaited us, so thick with churning bodies that I couldn't see the front of the line. At one point, a fraternity brother leaned out a window and shouted: "Whoever can shotgun this beer in ten seconds gets in!" A young woman rose to the challenge and was soon whisked to the front.

Those of us without the desire to chug a warm beer tossed out of a window were not so lucky. But the benefit was plenty of time to people-watch. Some wore risqué outfits with overtly sexual messages. "I don't like anal" read one. Others were more reflective. "I don't want to date my situationship" read another. (Mine was among the stupidest. "I am decisive," I wrote, after spending thirty minutes deliberating over other options.)

At the top of the stairs was a table of frat boys wearing high-visibility vests—these were the so-called "sober monitors." Stanford required them. The frat boys checked IDs, admitting only Stanford students, and then allowed five or six people at a time through to face their final hurdle to entry. Two signs awaited entrants: A pledge to ask for and receive consent, which attendees were asked to read aloud. Then a second message for recitation: "I am on stolen land," it began, continuing in part, "I will commit to uplifting Indigenous and Black voices." This, I learned, was standard for Stanford parties.

Inside, the room was overfilled. Condensation crept up the windows as sweaty bodies pressed together in a seething mass. Aside from the beer for that one chugging girl, there was no alcohol. Outside in a courtyard, groups socialized in too-loud voices. Some smoked, others took care of friends who sat with dazed expressions on any flat surface. Stationed at regular intervals were more sober monitors in their bright neon-yellow vests, looking bored.

I approached the most put-together partygoers one by one, identifying myself as a reporter and asking to interview them about Stanford social life. In the party environment, thankfully, people were more willing to speak, giving me helpful anecdotes about the wilting social scene. I also got a few of the sober monitors to talk guardedly about the bureaucratic hurdles they faced.

Searching for my next interview subject, I ran right into my editors. They looked a little bashful. "It's the only place to go," said one. There was Mary, who'd been editor in chief the previous year and came back to be the news editor because no one else would do it, and Lucy, a chipper US National Team athlete. They were clearly inebriated and more exuberant than usual. We took a group photo and caught up for a bit. Then Lucy decided I was worthy of joining the exclusive Slack channel called "slay," where some of the most active *Daily* staffers exchanged banter, despite the fact that I still hadn't published an article. That meant the world to me. I belonged. Mary posted our photo to the slay channel, writing "little news reunion at sig ep <3."

I was still reporting when the lights came on and the music stopped. Although it was just 12:30 a.m., the fraternity had feigned an end to the party to clear out the freshmen. Those of us who weren't *in* with the frat—in other words, the unknowns, the people without access to the hidden drink supply, the newbies—left disappointed. I reunited with my editors and three of us ended up back at the Daily House chatting until 3:00 a.m. Lucy told us about a secret tryst she'd had with another staffer, we bonded over musical theater, and I learned about their time at Stanford. It was my first moment of true comfort in college.

LEADS I'D GOTTEN FROM PARTYGOERS PROVED FRUITFUL, AND THE president of a different fraternity—Sigma Nu—finally agreed to talk. So we met at Coupa Café and I got my first real testimonial.

Moritz Stephan was nothing like the frat bro caricature I had coming into college. He was deeply Germanic, an impressive software engineer, and couched every one of his sentences in terms of "liabilities."

Stanford frats, I would learn, were not like frats elsewhere. When one frat bro wanted to send explicit pics that would disappear, he made an app—and, by creating Snapchat, became the youngest self-made billionaire in the world. One of the frats had a secret penthouse in San Francisco that they used for parties. Another fraternity, as part of its hazing one year, singled out a pledge who was trying to quit smoking and bought him a nonstop plane ticket to Dubai with an immediate return flight, leaving him no time to leave the airport to smoke. Apparently, it worked.

Moritz was candid about the challenges facing his fraternity. With the new policies put in place by the administration, so few parties were being held that "when you do host them, there's just way too many people. Last year, there were a couple of parties where six hundred to eight hundred freshmen and sophomores were trying to storm into our house, breaking through windows, physically and verbally assaulting members doing door security. And we just had to call the police on ourselves to get everything cleared out."

He wanted to achieve an "inclusive" environment, but with the risks as high as they were and the process as onerous as it had become, "we have to be hypercautious now." Indeed, "we have to control the risk and control the liability."

More like the CEO of his frat than its president, Moritz was focused on the business, the logistics, the safety. I had no doubt that he could drink as well as anyone else, yet he certainly gave every impression of responsibility. He talked about the crackdown last spring that had basically eliminated drinking on campus. "I mean, I'm of age, I just went to San Francisco with my friends," Moritz said, "and the number of freshmen that I saw—girls by themselves, trying to get into crappy bars in bad areas with fake IDs—was just scary. I think it's just a matter of time until something happens."

It turned out that safety advocates—nondrinkers, medical workers, and even Stanford's own on-the-ground administrators—were just as furious over the War on Fun as the frat bros.

Recent decisions to crack down on open drinking had led students to drink hard liquor in secret, taking a number of shots in quick succession because they knew that their resident assistants were required to report them if they were caught and that the scant few parties that cleared the bureaucratic approval process would serve no alcohol.

I collected stories about young women passed out in bushes, about faculty mentors so frustrated that they actively told resident assistants to ignore the school's policies, about severe alcohol abuse by students who spiraled alone in their rooms. I talked to first responders who disclosed an increasing rate of "transports," or hospitalizations, due to alcohol poisoning.

As an employee of the office of alcohol policy eventually told me, the university's policies were "hopelessly out of touch with reality." They were, he said, "absolute shit." Attempts to curtail dangerous drinking had instead increased it. Indeed, when the Eurotrash party had been canceled, students with nowhere else to go had thrown a "nomad" party, wandering around campus and climbing light poles. Rules aimed at reducing fire safety risk ironically caused far more of it, because so few parties were approved that rooms would be stuffed way over their limits. The War on Fun was downright dangerous.

This was all part of a broader sanitization, a rewriting of Stanford's own mythology. Legendary themed dorms, like the French House, which used to host popular wine and cheese nights, or Haus Mitt, once known for its Oktoberfest celebration, were renamed with numbers. It was not enough for the houses to curtail alcohol; even their personalities were being stripped.

AS STANFORD WAS BECOMING MORE POWERFUL, IT WAS BECOMING INcreasingly corporate, less like a vibrant hub for teenage exploration and more like a business—a thriving one at that.

At the beginning of the year, Stanford's president, Marc Tessier-Lavigne, had unveiled the Doerr School of Sustainability with a billion-dollar donation from the venture capitalist John Doerr and his wife, Ann. It was the university's first new school since the School of Humanities and Sciences was opened in 1948.

Tessier-Lavigne had had big shoes to fill in taking over from John

Hennessy six years earlier. Hennessy has a legitimate claim to being the most transformative leader in higher education in the twenty-first century. His tenure saw the university's reputation skyrocket. Named "the godfather of Silicon Valley" by Marc Andreessen, Hennessy was a celebrated computer scientist. Walter Isaacson wrote the introduction to Hennessy's memoir, saying that the "trait of wide-ranging curiosity is one that distinguishes the truly creative leaders of our time as well, including Steve Jobs, Bill Gates, Jeff Bezos, and John Hennessy." Hennessy's peers were tech leaders, which made sense, because it was his coziness with Silicon Valley that had ensured Stanford's growth. After stepping down, he became the chair of the board of Alphabet, Google's parent company.

Tessier-Lavigne had assumed the presidency as a pioneering neuroscientist and former biotech executive. He'd led Rockefeller University in New York before being appointed by Stanford and was considered a singular talent. The first in his Canadian family to go to college, he later earned a Rhodes Scholarship and went on to academic acclaim. His experience in industry was also a plus, and many hoped that Tessier-Lavigne would do for the life sciences what Hennessy had done for computer science.

The president was known on campus as MTL. I didn't know anything about him, but the founding of the Doerr School seemed like an impressive feat. From what little exposure I had, MTL appeared hyper-logical, cautious, and controlled—a good avatar, then, for the life the university had in mind for its students. The president's first step upon arriving at Stanford had not been to articulate a grand vision but to begin a three-year "Long-Range Planning" process. Nobody could really tell me what they'd come up with.

It was definitely a contrast from the previous reign. Hennessy had written in his memoir that "frequently parents would ask why we didn't ban alcohol in all campus dorms and police the ban vigorously." He "responded that such an approach would create undesired effects: students would drive off campus to consume alcohol, which was clearly more dangerous, or they would drink covertly, increasing the risk that a highly intoxicated student might not get help."

Lo and behold, that's exactly what had happened after Hennessy left.

Who knew how much MTL had to do with any of this? He seemed focused on ensuring the university's status as a world-class juggernaut. And to that end, perhaps the War on Fun was the price inherent in becoming an institution so clearly in the public eye, with a reputation to protect. The reimbursement processes that required a dozen sign-offs, the research approval procedure that lasted months, the faculty appointment files and data-use agreements that took hours and hours to assemble, the student clubs constantly interacting with lawyers—perhaps it was simply the inevitable result of growth, of becoming such a sprawling, complex institution. Whatever the exact cause, something of the alchemy that had made Stanford special was seeping out, committee by committee.

WHEN I WENT TO STANFORD'S COMMUNICATIONS TEAM FOR COMMENT on my War on Fun investigation, the school enacted its own Harm Reduction Plan.

I'd encountered fear throughout my reporting process from sources who worried about blowback from the administration. The president of Sig Ep—the "White Lies" frat—had agreed to an interview to try to clean up whatever unauthorized quotes his subordinates had given me during the party, but stood up and walked out after I told him he couldn't read the piece in advance. Several club leaders and resident assistants had asked me not to use their names, lest they be disciplined or lose their positions or funding. Ultimately, more than fifty people had declined to comment.

I'd thought the reaction overblown, honestly.

But, after I sent my list of questions to the university and they learned that I'd convinced employees of their office of alcohol policy to speak with me, my perspective changed. The director of the office sent an email to a group of employees "we are guessing" had leaked to me. "If you are approached by *The Daily* about your work . . . or anything related to what we do," the director wrote, "it needs to get cleared by me first." He told them that they'd agreed to a policy governing their interactions with the media, and that someone had violated it by speaking to me. But I was provided their contracts and training materials and could find no such policy—and when I asked the director if he could provide this agreement, he refused.

Stanford declined to answer specific questions, but provided a statement acknowledging a drop from 158 parties that had been officially registered during the first few weeks of the fall quarter in 2019 to just 45 parties during the same time period in 2022. They pledged to earmark more funds for row houses to throw events. And, with the university's perspective now obtained, I finally had everything ready to assemble my piece.

I reassured the sources I'd guaranteed anonymity that I would protect their identities, and Sam, my editor, backed me up. He backed me up, too, when the Sig Ep fraternity president called *The Daily* furious that I wrote about him walking out of our interview.

My first-ever piece for *The Stanford Daily* was published just before midnight on October 24, 2022, exactly one month and four days after I moved in, quickly becoming *The Daily*'s most read article of the year. It was accompanied by a photograph of the Stanford Tree mascot waving a "Stanford Hates Fun" banner two days prior.

Later that week, the mascot was suspended for his protest.

CHAPTER 2

THE IMPOSTOR

"No one will respect you if you aren't technical."

That was the simple truth that governed all of Silicon Valley, Logan told me. "You have to have the right qualifications for anyone to take you seriously." To refer to someone as "technical" or "nontechnical" was to summarize their entire character—their entire value.

It was my first weekend at Stanford, and my friend Logan was taking me out for coffee in Woodside, where many of the richest Valley dwellers reside. It was a quiet, leafy town, just twenty minutes from campus yet remarkably rural. Logan bought me a drink, then navigated us to a table outside to talk.

It was, in a word, surreal.

Sitting in front of us was a brand-new, bright red $750,000 Ferrari with the vanity plate FALIURE. Around the corner in a twenty-minute-parking zone sat an unattended low-slung sports car that attracted little notice; as a lifelong car nerd, I recognized it as a 1950s Porsche 550 Spyder, an extremely rare collector's item worth between $4 million and $5 million. The 550 had been Porsche's first race car, with only ninety ever produced—one of which infamously carried James Dean to a fiery death. In any other town in America, I would've assumed this was a fake. Then again, as Logan pointed out, we were sitting next to Buck's, an unassuming diner where billions of dollars in Silicon Valley deals had been made. Just around the corner lived a dozen billionaires who could buy a historic Porsche for the equivalent of pocket change; why shouldn't they pop down to the shops in a 550?

Real or fake, the point was that I couldn't tell. The rules of reality that governed everywhere else didn't apply here.

LOGAN WAS TRYING TO GET ME SITUATED. HE'D NOW BEEN AT STANford three years and was the only other undergraduate I knew here from back home in Washington, DC. Graciously, he agreed to tell me some of what he'd learned.

"There are some people around here nobody dares to fuck with," he said, trying to explain how power became concentrated in Silicon Valley. "When you have a Basquiat in your bathroom, what's anyone going to do about it?" (Indeed, one student I later met claimed to have seen this bathroom Basquiat at a particular billionaire's dinner party.)

Stanford could be a path to the heights of the tech world. Kids here, Logan told me, were doing it all. Take the social media site that everyone at the university was using now, Fizz. It was anonymous and allowed only users with a verified @stanford.edu email address to join. The students who founded it had raised $41.5 million, despite not showing ads, not charging users, and promising never to sell user data.

Or look at how people got dates. The Stanford Marriage Pact, which claimed to algorithmically match students based on their responses to a survey, got $5 million from venture capitalists. (Again, despite no ads, no subscription fees, and a pledge to never sell data.)

"But you have to break in fast," said Logan. At Stanford, freshmen made their names as technical prodigies within weeks. "They want to find people as early as possible," Logan said of the investors, scouts, and other Hangers-On who mooched off students, and "you have to stand out."

I REALLY WANTED TO STAND OUT. I MEAN, I WANTED TO BE SPECIAL. I wanted to be validated and *doing things*, the way Logan told me the top engineers were.

People were now paying attention to my War on Fun story—it was referenced on the front page of *The Wall Street Journal*, and Stanford responded to my reporting by posting an online fact sheet that began "Does Stanford hate fun? No, of course not!"

But I wanted to play the game of Stanford as Logan had described it and prove that I had what it took. Journalism wasn't going to do that. I had to be technical.

From a young age, I loved coding, having discovered that software programs could turn thoughts into action. I designed my first website at age seven and sloppily disassembled a computer for the first time at age ten. I spent free time building little tools and games, solving stupid problems in my life. Eventually, in high school, I moved on to more complex tasks—building a simple gradient descent AI model from scratch and using natural language processing to study whether the tweets of congressional Republicans had become more semantically similar to QAnon content over time. (They had! By 120 percent between 2019 and 2021!)

I was intoxicated by courses I had taken on cryptography, open-source development, and, especially, machine learning. I devoured the latest AI research, struck by the excitement of a world-changing field in which people were making huge leaps forward.

I vividly recall the release of OpenAI's seminal Codex paper in 2021, documenting an AI coding tool that produced near-human output. I was sixteen, at a Pitbull concert with some high school friends. We'd snuck in Fireball in fake tampons to drink at the moment he sang the song "Fireball," an up-tempo party tune named after that horrid cinnamon-flavored whiskey. Then I got a notification on my phone—the Codex paper, the one I'd been awaiting for months, was out. I pulled up the research site ArXiv immediately, ignoring the music blasting so loud that it vibrated through my teeth, and read through the dense seventy-two-page report.

Technology was so exciting to me that it began to occupy my thoughts at all hours. It even caused me to fall in love.

At the beginning of senior year of high school, I was serving as co-president of the computer science club when I met an impressive junior who wanted to join the board. Her name was Lily Zhou. Lily and I got to talking about programming and soon realized we shared a passion for the same niche interests. We bonded over computer science research and neuroscience blogs we both read for fun. Soon, the club stopped mattering at all, because, in every possible way, Lily outclassed me. She was far smarter, far more experienced, a much better coder, and had already worked in a lab. That first conversation lasted hours, bouncing wildly from model interpretability to Oliver Sacks to Ada Lovelace, typography, and connectome mapping, ending only when we were kicked out of the library at closing time. I was besotted.

It was, I'm aware, an incredibly nerdy love story, but I'd never met someone like Lily. She was not only brilliant but also gorgeous, kind, and funny. Soon we were a couple.

Now I was at Stanford, and she was a senior in high school. We'd stayed together, despite the distance, and I hoped that she would join me at Stanford the next year. For the first time in my life, I was now surrounded by other people who worshipped at the altar of tech. The secret code that Lily and I had shared was instead the common vernacular. Coding was no longer something most people around me ignored. It dominated.

EVERYONE AT STANFORD TALKED ABOUT BEING A "10X ENGINEER," referring to the notion that a very small subset of programmers were leaps and bounds more talented than the rest and could perform the work of ten normies. A 10x engineer was the lone hero rewriting an entire codebase overnight or swooping in to conjure a perfect solution to a vexing problem nobody else could understand.

That . . . wasn't me.

Some people I was encountering at Stanford were the kind of prodigies you read about in books. They'd worked on projects in middle school that dwarfed anything I'd ever attempted. They'd started studying multivariate calculus before I finished geometry. They casually mentioned their experiments aboard the International Space Station or the recruiters from Google who were already trying to hire them.

A sophomore named Nick, in particular, struck me as otherworldly. He was just *better* than everyone else. A fucking genius. (And, somehow, remarkably humble.) At sixteen, when I was sitting in my room dreaming about cool AI research, Nick was already doing it. As a sophomore in high school he'd been a coauthor on one of the most important papers published in the field.

I truly loved programming, but I just didn't have that touch of brilliance. I knew my strengths—I was enthusiastic, a quick study, a hard worker—yet I also knew my ceiling. I had the tools to be competent, not to excel; I would never be the *best* coder, the 10xer. So, I had to find another angle.

I TOOK LOGAN'S ADVICE TO "BREAK IN FAST." I CONVINCED THE STANford Internet Observatory, an innovative initiative studying internet technologies, to hire me as a research assistant, building on work I'd done to document disinformation flows in high school. I reached out to professors I wanted to meet—a neuroscientist, a historian, and a tech ethicist whose books I'd read, as well as a historian of ancient Greek art whose class seemed interesting. To my amazement, they all responded to my cold outreach and agreed to meet with me, humoring an overeager freshman.

The most important decision I made in my quest to hit the ground running sprouted from a conversation with Nick, the fucking genius. I learned that he'd skipped the intro sequence of computer science classes to jump right to CS107, known as Stanford's weeder class. Like Organic Chemistry for premeds, CS107, more than anything else, filters out the true computer science majors from the wannabes. It's a brutal course, delving into extremely low-level coding that scarcely resembles the programming most coders do on a daily basis. It requires you to painstakingly shift around the literal bits and bytes that modern computer programming languages handle for you. This is akin to writers learning how to make their own paper, pen, and ink, only quite a bit more complex. Many students drop computer science entirely after CS107. But Nick had sailed through it in his first quarter at Stanford, and I was determined to copy him.

I told Logan my plan. "I strongly advise against it," he responded. "I actually enjoyed 107, but I don't know anyone who came out of it 'okay' in a conventional sense." The last two assignments were legendarily difficult. "People bond over it as a defining moment of their Stanford CS careers," Logan said. "I don't think I was alone in thinking it was overhyped until I did it and witnessed 107 office hours during those weeks. Lots of shameless public tears."

I'd never heard him complain about a class being difficult before. But my desperate need to take on a challenge and prove myself won out. People at Stanford who didn't grind their way to success were "ngmi"—not gonna make it. I wanted to make it.

I texted Logan, "welp, yay masochism," and obtained permission from the instructor to skip the prerequisites. I was one of about half a dozen freshmen in the class of three hundred. And I was incredibly anxious.

THE DIRTY TRUTH IS THAT NOBODY COMES TO STANFORD FEELING LIKE they belong. I mean, how could you? Stanford's admission rate has plunged to an almost unbelievable 3.6 percent, down from nearly twice that a decade before, quadruple that two decades prior, and nearly seven times that in 1994. Getting in today is a statistical fluke, a crapshoot. Many more-than-qualified applicants are denied entry. And even those who get in don't feel they stack up around so many superstars.

Plus there's the cost. The sticker price to attend Stanford is now higher than ninety-five thousand dollars a year. Even with generous financial aid—72 percent of undergraduates receive some kind of assistance from the school—it's still a tough pill to swallow, one that can place huge burdens on families. Students understandably feel the need to justify the investment being made in their futures.

Impostor syndrome is rampant, especially among freshmen. Valedictorians go from the best of the best to just another straight-A kid in a place stuffed full of them. Basically everyone feels the clawing insecurity I did. To get into Stanford is to be told you are extraordinary—among the high achievers and the strivers, it is treated as a value judgment on your worth as a person. Do you "deserve" to get in? people ask.

Nobody deserves to get into Stanford. The wealth, the opportunity, the concentrated resources—it's impossible to say anyone at seventeen or eighteen is worthy of that. Because people frame acceptance as something you "earn," they tie up far too much of their self-worth in a deeply flawed admissions process. In reality, getting into Stanford isn't a "reward for all your hard work." It's an opportunity, a bit of very good luck. No one is entitled to admission; it is a chance that must be seized, not the goal in and of itself.

I went to a pressure-cooker high school where the college acceptance process pushed people to outrageous lengths. Last year, on Ivy Day, when most prestigious colleges release their admissions decisions, a senior at my high school took his own life. Another kid apparently tried later that week.

Some students who get into schools like Stanford develop God complexes. Others dwell on evidence of their inadequacy. Some balance superiority and inferiority at the same time. Many simply have no idea how to evaluate themselves. Conditioning people to think that the most brilliant, the most worthy, the most ambitious students in the world go to Stanford is at once understandable and deeply harmful—to those who get rejected, and to those who are handed more opportunity than they can possibly know what to do with at a young age.

Schools like Stanford are aware of the issue. I asked John Hennessy about this once, knowing that the admissions rate had been cut in half during his reign as president. "Stanford and other schools like it preach inclusivity, but at the same time they're inculcating exclusivity. Is it a healthy thing for an institution to admit three percent of the people who want to come to it?" I asked him. "No, I don't think it's particularly healthy. The process has become so selective," he said, trailing off as he searched for the right answer. But of course there wasn't an easy answer—expanding undergraduate class size, as Hennessy had done, might help, but obviously the problem was systemic.

Everyone at Stanford arrived desperate to find their place. So what did it take to fit in?

I DISCOVERED THE ANSWER ONE LATE OCTOBER NIGHT AS I WAS SEARCHing for my own place at Stanford. I was sitting in the Daily House less than a week after my War on Fun story, and this was my first production night as a writer. The print paper published only once a week and was produced every Thursday; my story, though it had been published online a few days before, would lead the front page. So I showed up to see it all get put together, even though I had a CS107 problem set to tackle.

CS107 was already grinding me down. I'd turned in the first problem set—"pset" in Stanford lingo—feeling triumphant that I'd gotten my code to pass all of the tests and work flawlessly. Then the grade had come back: 83 percent. Although all my solutions were correct, I'd committed several style errors, not familiar with the Stanford-assignment conventions that everyone else had already learned. I felt white-hot shame and vented to Lily in a text: "I really don't want a bad grade in CS this is going to live on my shoulders." I felt like a fraud.

"bae," she wrote back, "an 83 doesn't mean you'll get a bad grade for the entire class."

"I mean if things only get harder from here . . ."

Now I still had to finish the second CS107 pset, and even though I'd spent hours on it the previous night, the deadline was fast approaching. I should've hunkered down in the library, but I forged a compromise with myself, deciding to go to *The Daily*'s production night and just work on my code there.

Instead, around 10:00 p.m., the tip came in: A man had just been removed from Crothers Hall, a large freshman dorm known for its shabbiness. Apparently, he'd been pretending to be a student, living there since the beginning of the year.

Sam, my editor, called out, "Can anyone go down to Crothers and write about this?"

I knew I had CS107, I knew I couldn't really afford to delay . . . but I mean, come on, it was an impostor! And he'd been caught in Crothers Hall, no less—easily the most derided dorm on campus. I volunteered, as did two junior editors, and soon we were biking toward the story, my pset forgotten.

RESIDENTS OF CROTHERS HAD JUST BEEN INFORMED ABOUT THE REmoval via Slack. As we made our way inside the dingy dorm, chatter bounced off the walls; machine-gun-quick voices shared stories about the man they'd lived alongside without knowing who he really was.

His name was William Curry. Raised in an affluent suburb of Birmingham, Alabama, Curry was, by all accounts, a smooth talker with a flashy smile and a toned physique. He was a recent high school graduate, and had, for the past three weeks, ingratiated himself with the Crothers community. Those I spoke to were eager to tell me about their experiences with the impostor. He was funny, gregarious, solicitous, they said. He told them he was a sophomore who'd been placed in temporary housing in the Crothers basement because his dorm room had flooded, and no one had any reason to doubt this story. In fact, some residents began to fear that this could happen to them, too, that maybe their own rooms would flood and they'd suffer the same fate.

Curry had been such an unobtrusive presence that the primary emotion expressed was shock—not anger, not fear, but shock. Because he'd fit in so well.

"He was fucking normal as shit," said Alisha, a freshman whose adrenaline was clearly pumping as she gesticulated wildly. He'd baked brownies late at night with the residents and developed running jokes. At times he asked questions about classes and the difficulty of specific psets.

By coincidence, one of the true residents of Crothers Hall had attended the same Alabama high school that Curry had. At first, the student, Graham, was suspicious to see Curry in the dorm—Curry wasn't really known in high school as Stanford material. But seeing him here, living in the same place, the doubts had faded. "We took a picture together and sent it back home to, like, clear the confusion, settle the rumor," Graham recalled.

And that was pretty much the extent of the concern, right up until this moment, when the truth had been revealed. "He was such a nice guy, he seemed harmless," said one student. Even now, many residents didn't seem too bothered that an impostor had been in their midst. Said another freshman: "This guy didn't do anything harmful to anyone, I mean, damaged some property but didn't do anything harmful to an actual human."

As to why he did it, nobody had a clue.

BACK AT THE DAILY HOUSE, THE TWO OTHER REPORTERS QUICKLY added their interviews to a document while I went online to seek more information. I found Will Curry's four-hundred-meter track times—

several seconds off the Stanford pace—and an Instagram where he identified himself as "stanford 25'" (with the apostrophe in the wrong place) and a recipient of a Coca-Cola scholarship. I quickly confirmed that he had not in fact received the selective award. Then I added the internet details along with my own interviews and wrote through the piece to combine everything.

As Cassidy, one of the other writers, went to sleep—she had a disciplined schedule, which Sam mocked her for gently by writing "Cassidy is the War on Fun" on our newsroom quote board—I handed the story to Sam and Mary. This time, the editing process was lightning fast.

At 2:14 a.m., we published. And I went back to work on CS107.

THE REACTION TO THIS STORY WAS INTERESTING. QUICKLY, EVERYONE AT Stanford was talking about it, and some beyond the community were, too.

Some parallels were drawn between Will Curry and Steve Jobs, the visionary Apple CEO who'd lived at Reed College for several months as a seventeen-year-old, staying in dorms even though he was not a student. Jobs, like Curry, had attended classes, made friends, and embraced the college lifestyle, all while not actually being enrolled. Jobs, of course, went on to incredible success, and credited Reed—where he would later give a convocation address—with sparking his love of sleek design. A calligraphy class he "took" gave him the inspiration for the design of the Mac, Jobs confessed during his 2005 Stanford commencement speech, since viewed over 120 million times.

If being an impostor had gone so well for Jobs, pretending to be a Stanford student couldn't be all that bad, could it? After all, not only had Jobs done the same thing, but he'd paid tribute to his time as a college interloper on the Stanford stage, in what *Wired* two decades later called "the greatest commencement speech ever." And in some ways, was this not the epitome of the unfettered, devil-may-care culture Stanford sought to embody? Wasn't Curry, in taking the initiative, exactly the kind of person who deserved a Stanford education?

Some people made this argument. Okay, so Jobs had at least been accepted to Reed before he hung around the dorms, while Curry had not gotten into Stanford. Why not just officially admit him? Students seemed to embrace the impostor. At a hackathon that weekend, one team created a virtual reality game called The Will Curry Experience, dramatizing—and celebrating—his deception. The game won a prize.

Meanwhile, it was a throwaway line in our story that, to my surprise, generated controversy. Buried in the piece was the acknowledgment that resident assistants, too, had thought Curry was a student and let him in. The RAs, though, were hypersensitive about being blamed and directed their ire at *The Daily*. Before the article was published in the wee hours of the night, they'd gone to the freshmen we'd interviewed and told them to retract their quotes, scaring them about the ramifications of speaking to the press. Sam again backed us up, explaining that they were free to add additional comments if they desired, but that once you've said something in an interview, you can't take it back. Soon there was a minor Fizz campaign attacking my cowriters and me, accusing us of "turning campus against the Crothers RAs." "Know your place," said one commenter. "Fuck journalists. Cancer on society," another wrote.

TO BE FAIR, I STILL DIDN'T REALLY KNOW MY PLACE. BUT THERE WAS one lesson that I'd been implicitly taught that would prove instrumental. It wasn't something I'd been told, just a sense I'd absorbed over time, that the secret to all journalism was a simple rule: <u>Always follow up</u>.

You never get the story right the first time. Or rather, you never get all of it. Information isn't accessible yet, or you don't know the right questions to ask, or something new happens that alters the importance of what you do know.

After our initial Curry article, we heard rumors that the impostor had actually shown up before, implying there was more to the story. My cowriters had homework to do, so they bowed out. But I was determined to get to the bottom of it, CS107 be damned. I'd found a thread, and now I had to see what happened when I pulled it.

Over the course of the next few days, I talked with a dozen additional witnesses—classmates, people who'd lived alongside the impostor, a former girlfriend, and even his high school principal. The portrait they painted was far darker than initial impressions. And this story began not a month earlier, but nearly three years prior, when the impostor first began to plot his stay.

Will Curry, it turned out, was a con man. A serial manipulator. Lies flowed from his mouth as easily as spent breath, building upon one another to erect a tower of elaborate deception. Curry lied to students, his girlfriend, casinos, friends, police officers, teachers, coaches, his own family, and me without once betraying a hint of guilt. He constructed an alternate reality, then forced those around him to inhabit it.

Curry's intrusion in Crothers was not his first. In fact, as I discovered, he'd begun laying the groundwork for his scheme back in 2019, spreading the lie that he'd been recruited to Stanford. By 2021, he was living on campus full-time, staying in at least half a dozen dorms over the course of the next year.

Each time, he concocted a new story. To some, he represented himself as a neuroscience student, to others a track star (sporting a lifted Stanford Athletics backpack), and to still others a transfer student from Duke, explaining why he popped up out of nowhere.

He'd lived longest in a small dorm called Murray, where he became so embedded in the community that the resident assistants included him in a game of Assassin, basically a campus-wide water-gun fight, with each of the dorm's residents assigned a target. Curry's assassin told me that she'd nailed him in the chest with a blast of water, to which he'd responded, "No you didn't!" and run away with a notable wet patch on his shirt.

While Curry was living in Murray, he was also maintaining a romantic relationship with a Stanford student, telling her the Duke transfer story and pretending that he owned an apartment off campus where he lived. Instead, Curry had devised various ways of breaking into Stanford buildings. He climbed through the window of one dorm, jimmied the lock on another. Not every intrusion was so daring—oftentimes Curry just walked in behind someone else. But at other times, it appeared to students he was using what must have been a stolen ID to scan in.

Curry was first discovered as an impostor in late fall 2021, after he broke into a student's dorm room. He told sheriff's deputies who responded that he was a homeless man trying to escape from the cold. They removed him from campus and instructed him not to return; less than a week later he was back. A few months later, Curry was again removed after he broke into a different student's room while she was away for the weekend. She'd returned to find the strange man sleeping in her bed. Again, deputies told him to stay away and again he returned in less than a week—this time moving into a dorm only one hundred feet from the one from which he'd just been ejected.

And this revealed the most galling part of the story. Although Stanford had known of Curry's presence on campus since 2021, no notice had ever been issued. No warning had ever been given. And, though he was repeatedly removed, each time they received the call, deputies seemed unaware of his previous intrusions, accepting Curry's explanations and merely telling him to stay away. He had never been arrested, and no criminal charges had ever been brought.

Resident assistants had asked Stanford for complete lists of those who were supposed to be living in the building. The school had denied those requests on "privacy" grounds. Thus dorm leaders had no reason to doubt Curry's story, despite its inconsistencies.

AFTER CURRY AND HIS GIRLFRIEND BROKE UP, THE IMPOSTOR BEGAN to harass her, sending threatening messages and spying on her. He'd observed her inputting her iCloud password and logged into her account, tracking her movements and reading her private messages. When he discovered, months later, that she was going on a date with another man, Curry began to spam her phone with texts and calls in the middle of the night. "Put whatever guy your [*sic*] with on the phone or I won't stop," he wrote. "Your choice." Four minutes later, "I'll Kill You."

The woman was freaked. She reported to the university's Department of Public Safety that she was being harassed, producing some of the threatening messages. In response, university safety officials said there was little they could do. Stanford is required by federal law to send messages to the community about safety threats; the woman asked if Stanford would send one about Curry. "No," she was told, "we don't want to scare people too much." Back on campus in the fall, Curry's ex-girlfriend saw the impostor entering Crothers Hall. She called the police to report it, told them that he was intruding again and exactly where to find him. The Department of Public Safety never pursued it.

Instead, it was one fatal error, weeks later, that did Curry in. Living in the depressing basement of Crothers, where he'd broken into an unused suite, Curry had decided to spruce up his abode. Late at night, he made his way to the dorm's common room and took the TV for himself, snipping the security wire and absconding with the flatscreen. That was a mistake. When one resident later caught a glimpse of the TV in Curry's room and reported it to an RA, the impostor was found out and, once again, removed. As with the prior incidents, the RAs and deputies were unaware that Curry had intruded before.

MY INVESTIGATION INTO THE IMPOSTOR WAS RELEASED ON HALLOWeen, a day of assumed identities. This time, the story penetrated far beyond the Stanford community.

Soon Curry's face, and the images of his Tinder account I'd tracked down, were everywhere, plastered across national news. *The Washington Post*, the Associated Press, the *San Francisco Chronicle*, CBS, CNN, and other outlets picked up the story, writing a set of nearly identical pieces that ended each paragraph with the phrase "*The Daily* reported." Yet the one institution that should've addressed the Curry story didn't.

My investigation relied on an extensive documentary trail and testimony from those who had known Curry in the most intimate settings. I chronicled the trail of damage he'd left in his wake, including the ex-girlfriend and the students whose rooms he invaded. I wrote about another woman who was living in temporary housing in Crothers after having been harassed in her former dorm. The only other resident of the basement, she'd been trapped inside her room, terrified, as Curry tried to break down her door. "I ended up moving back into the same building as the person who was harassing me, because I just didn't feel safe at Crothers anymore," she said. And, in the face of this con man's actions, I showed how Stanford had repeatedly failed to protect its students.

The university stonewalled me for days, ignoring all requests for comment. In fact, when I reached out directly to a deputy who'd removed Curry in 2021, I got an angry message from the spokesman for the Department of Public Safety, demanding I address questions to him alone. But I'd already sent him questions—and he continued to ignore them.

It took a full week after Curry was removed, and a huge amount of national media attention, for the school to say a word, clearly having decided they could no longer just ride it out and hope the story disappeared. Stanford admitted to "gaps" in its protocols and promised "an immediate review," in a statement provided to other news outlets but conspicuously not to *The Daily*. University officials pledged they would make it impossible for something like this to happen again. And they all but exonerated themselves by citing "the unique aspects of this case and Mr. Curry's persistence and ability to ingratiate himself with our student community."

Curry had, in fact, figured out how to fit in on the Stanford campus—something so many people who'd actually gotten in struggled to do.

Like Curry, Stanford students would lie to get ahead. The majority of computer science majors who signed up for the Marriage Pact said they would "rather cheat on a test than fail." People casually embezzled dorm funds for dinners or goodies. They pretended to have COVID to get free DoorDash credits. And Fizz would often buzz with anonymous misinformation, treated as fact.

In one instance, hundreds of comments over the course of a week or two said that a freshman had been arrested for stealing tens of thousands of dollars' worth of valuables. The origin of the rumor? A spat between two roommates over whose clothes were on what side of the room. The Fizz comments slowly amped up the accusations, competing with one another for attention, until the girl who was their target was left isolated, kicked out of clubs that feared "the controversy," and judged across campus for a crime she hadn't committed.

A lot of people believed a conspiracy theory that the housing system was broken because many students were "faking disabilities" to get better rooms. When asked for evidence to support this, the originator of the rumor said they could "vibe-corroborate it" based on the fact that people looked healthy but got disability housing.

The company behind Fizz was known to make dubious claims, too—like telling *TechCrunch* it was used by "95% of Stanford undergrads," even though the app was only available to those with an iPhone. The same week I wrote about Will Curry, I learned that Fizz contained a security vulnerability in its codebase exposing private user data to anyone who clicked on an unprotected database. Fellow students had pointed this out to the founders of Fizz, who, instead of thanking them for being good Samaritans, threatened to sue and, in a letter penned by an attorney, "press felony charges."

TWO DAYS AFTER MY INVESTIGATION WAS PUBLISHED, *GOOD MORNING America* sent a correspondent to the Daily House to interview me and Cassidy, one of my coauthors on the first story, for a spot on the impostor. I skipped a CS107 lecture to do the hit.

My editor Sam had run a local TV show of sorts in high school—helping to expose, as his coup de grâce, that school buses routinely rolled through stop signs rather than halting fully—so he showed up to coach us. He assigned Niko, the star *Daily* photographer, to go around campus and shoot B-roll for the big shots. He also brought two *Daily* T-shirts for us to wear on air. "But," Sam told me, "you can't keep it." I could borrow the shirt for *Good Morning America*, but I wouldn't have earned it until my tenth article.

CHAPTER 3

COUPA CIRCUIT

At first, the thundering bangs didn't rouse me. Then I heard the music. At full volume. I tumbled out of bed, confused and disoriented—it was 5:00 a.m., less than three hours after my Will Curry piece had been published, not even an hour and a half since I'd gone to sleep. I opened the door and was greeted by a small group of students who surged toward me and cheered, slapping me on the back and congratulating me.

I'd just received my invitation to the big leagues.

This was, in Stanford parlance, a rollout—the announcement that I'd been accepted into a club. Of course, a simple email would've sufficed, but clubs at Stanford have a tradition of dragging their newest recruits out of bed heinously early in the morning and introducing shell-shocked inductees to one another in pajamas. My club was TreeHacks. And it was one of those secret power centers I'd been encouraged to seek out.

TreeHacks was modest in its ostensible mission: It was a hackathon. By the traditional definition, a hackathon is a competition where nerds like me get thrown together in a room and don't sleep for two days and come out of it with a new product or machine or program, with basically no restriction on what you can or can't create. Normally, these are pretty low-key affairs, born out of the legendary tinkering sessions at the dawn of the tech era. The energy is high and the stakes low; the point is not really what you build, it's that you've engaged in the exercise of building.

TreeHacks was the oldest and most established hackathon at Stanford, and I'd known I wanted to join it since freshman year of high school, when I first heard about it. I was told that it was a hallmark of the university, where all the smartest kids congregated to put their heads together and generate innovation. Now I was going to be on the team running it.

In my freshman year, 1,700 college students from around the world would converge on Stanford to compete for hundreds of thousands of dollars in prizes, supported by hundreds of mentors, judges, and sponsors. What set TreeHacks apart was not just its scale but its vision. The hackathon placed far more emphasis than other hackathons on everything hackers did when they *weren't* working on their projects. TreeHacks weekend comprised dozens of workshops and fun side quests, as well as famous speakers and giveaways, all of which had to be planned by its organizing team of Stanford students. Oh, and we had to raise all the money. Not just to pay for prizes and hardware, but for the free flights, food, and accommodation provided to student contestants. No other college hackathon paid for all of its participants to come, or came close to the breadth of TreeHacks.

Yet, despite all that, the event itself was just a sideshow. Because the true mission of TreeHacks, I came to understand, was to serve as a funnel for talent, to identify promising entrepreneurs as soon as they arrived on campus and smooth their way into the Silicon Valley whirlpool.

See, there was a difference between those who "did" TreeHacks—the competitors, to whom the event was just a weekend—and those who were "in" TreeHacks. The organizers, seeing behind the scenes.

TreeHacks had a reputation as a "high-signal cluster" on campus. The organizing team was purposefully small—about twenty "saplings" each year, culled from hundreds of applications by overqualified Stanford students. Each year after the event, it would turn over to a new crowd, with the leadership elected from last year's class and everyone else departing to make way for the next sapling batch. And the process yielded as saplings some of the smartest, most driven people I'd ever met.

The TreeHacks team was catnip for investors. They believed that each organizer had the potential to create a great new company. People who were selected to run TreeHacks were supposed to be the kinds of pure Builder types upon whose backs Silicon Valley flourished. Thus they got fast-tracked to the top.

That part wasn't advertised. In fact, the tight-knit, uber-ambitious group tried to make sure that the people who got in were actually interested in the mission of TreeHacks rather than the immense personal rewards it could bring. It was expected, and was explicitly outlined to me on numerous occasions, that the secrets of TreeHacks were to be closely held. And there were, of course, more than a few secrets.

I'D WALKED INTO MY INTERVIEW WITH THE CODIRECTORS TWO WEEKS earlier. It was the most afraid I'd been on campus. I had looked up my interrogators beforehand—their résumés were superhuman. Sara had started and run half a dozen hackathons, worked at seemingly every major tech company, and projected hyper-competence. She was able to break down any problem into actionable chunks—and then, somehow, work her way through them all at once.

Then there was Vedant. "Vedant is going places," I heard a dozen times. Vedant was a talented coder and a smooth talker. He'd founded countless ventures already. In high school, an organization he created delivered more than 2 million meals to people in need. Another project got around predatory phone provider charges by allowing people to access the internet without a costly cellular service plan. It reminded me of the blue-box hacking Steve Jobs and Steve Wozniak did in their early years, getting around long-distance phone charges by tricking the telephone networks. For Jobs and Wozniak, this early hacking became a legendary part of their origin stories. I couldn't help but wonder whether the same would be true of Vedant.

I walked into my interview just after that of a kid I knew who had cofounded several companies, even appearing on *Good Morning America* to promote one. I'd never founded a successful company or done any work with any real impact. Plus, I'd missed my first interview entirely.

Like many students, I was suffering from frosh flu and dozed off by accident, exhausted by yet another sleepless night. The interview was scheduled for 9:00 p.m. I woke up at 11:00 p.m. I was mortified. I figured my chances were less than zero. Still, I managed to snag another interview slot—making it, thankfully, on time.

"TreeHacks is super super startup-y this year apparently," Logan had texted me. "I would come with a general sense of ideas which are interesting to you / startups which you might want to work on." I came up with a half dozen concrete pitches for the hackathon and tried to quell my nerves.

Luckily, I liked Vedant and Sara. They were engaging and thoughtful. They'd come with questions for me, while taking notes on laptops. But, quickly, the prepared lists went out the window and it turned into a conversation. They seemed shocked that I was taking CS107 freshman fall. "Are you insane?" asked Sara. For my part, I was struck by their drive. They spoke of TreeHacks not as a college club, but as an endeavor demanding absolute commitment.

For whatever reason, the chemistry clicked. I didn't expect to get in. But I was exhilarated, nonetheless.

VEDANT WAS THE FIRST PERSON TO GREET ME AT MY ROLLOUT, CLAD head to toe in a giraffe onesie. He was all smiles. I threw on jeans, still disoriented, and we fled my dorm before anyone could complain about the noise.

Parth, the tall, fine-featured social chair of the club, was still blasting my rollout song from his shoulder-mounted speaker. Like baseball players stepping up to the plate, each TreeHacks applicant had selected a record to be played in case they were admitted to the club. At the time, I hadn't thought hard about it, choosing the first song queued on my Spotify: The Neighbourhood's "R.I.P. 2 My Youth." It was, in retrospect, a bit on the nose.

I was one of the first few saplings picked up on my side of campus, so I joined the gang as we broke into various dorms and found our targets. The sun slowly rose as we gathered the last of the group, finally piling into rented Zipcars to go out for a team breakfast. I squeezed into the trunk of a mini-SUV, listening in as everyone excitedly introduced themselves.

Over a pile of pancakes in downtown Menlo Park, I got my first picture of the full ensemble. We were seated at a single, extended table, noisy and, apart from one glamorous woman—a designer, unsurprisingly—all deeply disheveled. The group divided naturally into clusters of three or four, all of whom had their own conversations going. Most of it was fairly standard fare—upcoming midterms, projects people were working on. But there was also an energy. A hum.

TreeHacks was run like a startup, with a flat structure. By turning over each year, it forced innovation and ownership. Each year's saplings were given the reins and told to make the event their own. People discussed new themes, new sponsors, new events. We proposed having an Intel nighttime drone show and using industrial laser projectors on the side of the engineering complex. The possibilities seemed endless.

To my embarrassment, I had to leave breakfast halfway through after receiving a call from a source on the Will Curry story. I knew better than to leave it to voicemail—news doesn't wait for anyone's schedule. But by the time I finished my interview in the parking lot, everyone was standing up to leave.

The breakfast had been a welcome, our codirectors said, but we would get to know one another for real just a week later when it came time for the fall retreat. "It's one of the highlights of the year, so *make sure you come*," Sara instructed. "Trust me, we have some fun stuff planned."

Then I was back on campus, as if I'd never left.

AT STANFORD, A FRIEND WITH A STARTUP ONCE REFLECTED, "YOU GET plucked." One moment you're just a student going about life; the next second, everything has changed. Because once you know that the Stanford inside Stanford exists—and once you get offered a seat at the table—you can never go back.

There's an inner cohort of those identified to be the potential next innovators. They all show up at the same VC dinners, text the same billionaires for advice, attend the same app launch parties.

Every schmuck with a Python shell and an ego comes to the Farm believing they're going to be the next great entrepreneur. But there are two mistaken assumptions that underpin that belief: (1) Simply wanting to be a great entrepreneur makes you one, and (2) opportunities are equitably distributed. Neither is true. Instead, the insider world of Stanford is populated by the connectors and the personalities. Its gates are guarded assiduously because its value depends on exclusivity. And to get in, you have to find yourself "plucked" by the right group—or you have to go through someone like Ivan.

IVAN CAN'T TELL YOU EXACTLY WHAT HE DOES. HE WORKS A LITTLE with this company, a little with that one; he got called in to run a product launch in New York last week, right now he's sourcing a European castle for the summer, oh, and he's hosting a party next week to introduce some investors to promising students—you should totally come! Ivan is a twenty-year-old fixer.

He spends each day, usually from 7:00 a.m. until well after dark, drinking coffee. Or more accurately, buying people coffee. His office is a little metal table at the Coupa Café, where one goes to see and be seen. From the second he sits down until the minute he packs up, people troop in to meet him one by one, like a series of patient farm animals waiting for their chance to feed at the trough.

Our meeting was set for 11:45 a.m.

Ivan had reached out to me a few weeks earlier, not long after I joined TreeHacks, describing himself as an investor "focused in on the undergrad ecosystem of Stanford." He said we had mutual friends who had spoken highly of me, and that he "would love to meet and chat" because he was "very curious with how you do some of your current sourcing."

I asked who our mutual contacts were and he named two Stanford students I'd met but hardly considered friends—and, he admitted, he wasn't really friends with them, either, "more work colleagues." Still, I was intrigued. I agreed to have coffee.

When I arrived, Ivan, smiling brightly, was clasping hands with a circle of guys I didn't recognize. As I walked over, they scattered like a flock of birds. Now it was just us. Ivan trained his eyes on me. I was taken aback by their intensity and color, a shade of shockingly brilliant blue. Then Ivan flashed a smile and greeted me with a hug. He was disarmingly familiar, and invited me to sit.

"I want you to teach me how to interview people," Ivan said. Not for journalism, he quickly added, but because he said his job was to be discerning, to know who was going to make it and who wasn't. "My job is to root out the wantapreneurs," he said. The pretenders. Those who talked the talk and purported to be the Next Big Thing, but didn't have the hustle or vision or ruthlessness to hack it. "I've met thousands of engineers," said Ivan, "and I think only six have what it takes."

Ivan was a member of what I came to think of as the Coupa Circuit, the group of near-permanent residents of that café who made deals and had "coffee chats" and performed entrepreneurship each day. Talent scouting was a big thing at Stanford, with venture capital firms such as Sequoia, Lightspeed, Pear, CRV, Founders Fund, Accel, Social

Capital, and Spark Capital paying to identify the best of the best young. But scouting opportunities were opaque. You had to be known to the right people to qualify for a schmoozing session, and basically every introduction happened at Coupa under Ivan's watchful eye.

Little by little, he told me his backstory.

"My parents didn't always grow up with enough," Ivan said. They were immigrants who'd worked their way up to the middle class. He wanted better. "I don't want my kids to ever have to think about money the way I had to," he said. "I want to make money."

Ivan had been recruited to play D1 sports at Stanford but faced a devastating spinal injury after just a month. "It was shattering," he told me. "I kind of expected people to help me, but no one did," he went on. So he channeled the energy and discipline he'd developed as a world-class athlete into a new task: becoming rich.

As he told me this, I looked Ivan up and down. He was still built like an athlete—those perfect biceps and trim physique couldn't have come by chance. He had sandy hair and an endearing birthmark on his left ear, which, combined with the startling blue eyes and the quick smile, meant Ivan was quite the looker. He betrayed no indication of having gone through the physical ordeal he'd endured. He was polished, confident, and laser-focused on his goals.

"I've always been very transparent with you," Ivan once told me about a year later. "I'm very commercially minded." He continued, "I don't really care about curing cancer or working on climate change or doing any of that enough to spend the next ten to twenty years of my life working on it." Instead, "the number one thing I want to do is work with these super young founders and sit on cool boards." So he had to find the right ones. And that's why he'd sought me out—because maybe I could help him find people of use.

I guess I've spoiled the ending by telling you that we kept in touch. Well, we did. In fact, that was one of Ivan's great strengths, maintaining relationships over time. Who knows how someone can be useful down the line? This in turn made Ivan very useful in his nebulous role running "special projects" for two billionaires. So we kept talking. This would not be the case for many of the others trying to get something out of me at the time.

A LOT OF RANDOM PEOPLE, LIKE IVAN, WERE REACHING OUT TO ME IN the wake of my first few articles in *The Daily*. Sometimes they had news tips, a few of which turned into articles. Sometimes they espoused crazy conspiracy theories, which I ignored. Mostly, they didn't have very much to say at all.

I was getting emails and phone calls all the time; letters addressed to me from prisons even started showing up at the Daily House. Other people wrote to me from different continents asking me to look into their cases, something I was obviously powerless to do.

Then the Stanford Department of Public Safety called me for help. I picked up the phone and discovered a sheriff's deputy on the other end asking how to find Will Curry and if I knew people he talked to. I politely explained that anything I could share publicly had been posted to *The Daily*'s website. Besides, I didn't know where Curry was. Although he, too, started talking to me after my initial articles.

At first, Curry solely wanted to engage over the harassment element of the story. He denied it adamantly. He threatened to sue me for "liable," as he put it in one message, if I printed the story. Since I was in possession of documentary evidence, I published the article anyway.

After the investigation came out, Curry began to respond more extensively. He agreed to an interview and promptly admitted to the intrusions. He acknowledged that he'd been lying about being a student for years, even to his own family. It all seemed like a joke to him. "Most people I've talked to don't think it's that big of an issue," he said.

As we continued messaging back and forth, Curry became friendlier. We had extended conversations about his home life—his mother had died years before; his brother was, supposedly, living in the United Arab Emirates; his father was distant, selling the family home. Curry admitted to things he absolutely should not have. He provided photographic evidence of himself committing various minor crimes, thinking I'd find them cool. He even invited me—several times—to go gambling with him in a casino, even though we were both underage.

Steve Jobs was described by admirers as creating a reality-distortion field, possessing the ability to "convince himself, and others around him, to believe almost anything with a mix of charm, charisma, bravado, hyperbole, marketing, appeasement and persistence." Curry seemed to think he had this, too. He called me expecting that, once I listened to him, I would quit my reporting. His charm had worked so many times when questions arose that he was sure he could talk his way out of this.

Curry wanted to be my friend, or at least make me think I was his friend. "I'll be in town this weekend, wanna grab coffee or something?" he asked unprompted some time after the story about him was first published. When he invited me to a poker game and I tentatively agreed to meet up, he said, "this is all just recreational right, u ain't tryin abt another article 💀." I told him that would depend on whether he said anything newsworthy. "Aight I'll try to steer away from those topics," he said, and kept talking to me anyway.

Curry was cocky and, despite his odd candor about some things, continued to lie brazenly. He was also incapable of understanding how others might see him. At one point, while arguing that few people had been disturbed by his presence, Curry told me, "If it wasn't for how much I personally respect privacy, I would give you the names of people I know who I consider friends and who also consider me a friend." I asked whether he thought living under false pretenses in a Stanford dorm was an invasion of privacy, and he didn't respond.

CURRY'S BRAVADO WOULD'VE MADE HIM RIGHT AT HOME IN THE COUPA Circuit. Everyone there was a good talker and self-possessed. And, unlike Ivan, many weren't particularly honest about their motivations.

Like Curry, they didn't understand that their words could constitute confessions.

Julian was the second member of the circuit I got to know well. He saw himself as a savior of the downtrodden—and by that he meant the billionaires. Truly, he couldn't understand why they got such a bad rap. They were heroes, value creators, pioneers. While he wasn't one yet himself, Julian assumed he would be someday. So it was his mission to defend them.

We were in a small philosophy class together and he opened up our first discussion by taking furious offense at Plato's contention that "guardians," or rulers, should not be allowed to own private property. "*Nonsense!*" cried Julian. "What makes a city great is great management," he said, "and amassing great wealth is proof you're capable of it." Perhaps great wealth should actually be the requirement to rule, he suggested.

Julian disliked the notion that becoming a billionaire should be viewed as a negative. "Today, we don't even think about desire for profit as greed," he said. "We take it for granted that one would want to grow their wealth," which "ultimately benefits others." Sure, some might argue that "greed is bad," Julian said, "but if we don't use the word 'greed,' if we use the framing of profit for positive-sum accumulation and distribution of wealth," well . . .

At Stanford, Julian was a convener. Like Ivan, he set up camp at Coupa Café most days and saw a steady drumbeat of people cycle through. He liked introducing people and loved exercising social influence. Didn't you hear about the dinner he just cohosted with a billionaire CEO? He even had his own new invite-only group. The Lake Lagunita Yacht Club, he called it, hearkening back to the days when Stanford's long-dried-out campus lake actually contained water. (For environmental reasons, the university no longer kept it filled.) Julian chose sepia-toned design language that was meant to evoke a sense of class, as was the launch party, where he served Aperol and champagne.

But really, the point of the Lake Lagunita Yacht Club was to signal who was in and who wasn't.

The day after he got merchandise for his new club, Julian told me, "I showed up to Coupa and there were six people wearing the hats." He was proud of how in-demand it was. In fact, "I had to revoke merch from some people I promised it to," he said, since too many wanted it. After all, the yacht club for the lake with no water was a strictly exclusive group.

IN CLASS, JULIAN WAS A BIT OF A MENACE. ONE TIME AFTER SKIPPING a discussion, he showed up at the next session and admitted that he'd gone swimming instead. "I apologize for my absence, but I think what I was doing was a service since I gave other people the opportunity to speak who might not usually," he said. Later he told everyone, "Not to flex, but I have been the biggest value add to this class." Yes, he said this out loud.

Outside class, Julian was every bit as brash, though much more interesting. He was genuinely savvy and had good instincts for useful tech. His CV was full of startups, work for Big Tech firms, and other relevant experience, though, like Ivan, his real résumé was his Rolodex. Julian knew everybody—or at least everybody who mattered.

Sitting at Coupa one afternoon, Julian explained to me that the secret to success was not waiting for anyone to give permission. "You can just do things," he said, repeating Silicon Valley's favorite mantra. He would reach out to anyone, propose anything, build whatever he desired. Julian was self-empowered.

Whenever he encountered a problem in his daily life, Julian didn't accept it as intractable but figured out a solution. If there was an app letting him down, he'd spend a weekend re-creating it from scratch with the features he needed. When he found Stanford's social scene wanting, he created a club to bring people together. Even when he realized that living in a communal space wasn't much to his liking, he'd engineered a fix—now he lived in a house with three bedrooms all to himself, having made friends with the owner, a Silicon Valley super-designer. This was Julian's strength. While you or I might whine about living in a dorm with radioactive carpets and vaguely urine-smelling, hair-ridden showers, we accept it because we're told there are no alternatives. Julian created alternatives.

But there was a key difference between him and Ivan.

One day, shortly before the launch of the Lake Lagunita Yacht Club, I was passing through Coupa on my way to an interview. I spied Julian and said hello. He pulled me into a dap-up, the kind of full-body, chest-to-chest greeting that the dude bros invoke, and held out his phone. "I'm buying a space suit!" he said. It was for a party. We got to chatting and turned back to philosophy, the subject of our class. I realized I'd never asked him before, so I queried Julian: "Is there a moral philosophy you find most attractive?"

And Julian, the billionaire-wannabe who considered a wealth tax "the single most dangerous proposal in politics," looked me square in the eyes and said, "In many ways, I'm a Buddhist."

THAT KIND OF SUMMED UP THE STANFORD INSIDE STANFORD.

Sure, Silicon Valley talked a big game about changing the world and embracing merit. But most of the time, that wasn't how it worked.

Because so many people *desired* the glorious life of the entrepreneur, the real access points to Silicon Valley power were obscured. Stanford had two big entrepreneurship clubs—the Affiliated Stanford Entrepreneurial Students, or ASES, and the Business Association of Stanford Entrepreneurial Students, or BASES—and membership was considered by many to be an "anti-signal." Identifying yourself as the kind of person who wanted to be an entrepreneur did not make investors more likely to fund you.

Even technical talent didn't count for all that much. It's true, many people belonging to the Stanford inside Stanford were impressive, but so were many who were cut out, left floundering to look for opportunities without guidance. Among a certain crowd, reputation mattered more than skill. Were you a known entity? Had you been identified and scooped up and recruited to join a "high-signal" cluster?

The Plucked congregated in plain sight but remained hidden. Passing through the Coupa Café would give no sense of what was really happening around you. Insiders found one another in clubs like Friends and Family, a student-run Builders society that hosted hacking sessions every week and gave out ten-thousand-dollar "micro-grants"; programs like the Pear Garage, Floodgate Reactor, or Interact Fellowship that offered ultimate access; and classes like ME410, innocuously titled Introductory Foresight and Technological Innovation, or the Mayfield Fellows Program, a twelve-student-a-year initiative to launch Stanford students on the path toward "high growth technology ventures" through "rigorous entrepreneurial leadership education." None of these was technically secret. Anyone could apply on their websites. But you had to know they existed, what they meant, and who could get you in.

For my part, I was only just beginning to skim the surface. Three days after my Curry investigation was published, I received an invitation to interview for that secret class called How to Rule the World, referred by two of the Plucked. Justin, the self-fashioned professor, arranged to meet me in a few weeks. Meanwhile, TreeHacks gave me my first glimpse of how the Stanford inside Stanford really rolled.

ABOUT TWENTY MINUTES INTO THE CAR RIDE, WE BEGAN SLIDING into each other, elbows meeting groins and faces colliding with shoulders. It was a week after rollouts, and we were on our way to the TreeHacks fall retreat. Clearly, we'd taken a wrong turn. We seemed to be in the middle of nowhere, on a winding, narrow path leading up and up and up. My cell phone had no service, which was a problem because I was still trying to connect remotely to Stanford's servers and work on my CS107 homework. It was even more of a problem when the Uber driver asked, "Are you sure this is the right way?" and none of us could answer.

Then, at a distance, we spotted it: a multimillion-dollar mansion nestled in the hills, completely isolated. Thirty acres and a wraparound view, all ours.

It was just about sunset when we arrived. The panoramic windows showcased rolling, densely forested hills without another human being in sight. Inside was equally impressive, with a cavernous, two-story great room, a spacious kitchen, bedrooms that would accommodate the entire crew, and even a game room with Ping-Pong and pool. In other words, the perfect setup for a party. Especially with the towering pile of alcohol on the table.

I was still coding for CS107. I tried to hunker down in one of the bedrooms and focus, ignoring the soaking tub that was larger than the bed in my dorm. I'd knocked down every error except for a nasty little bug on the last test case contained in the assignment's "sanity-check" (a series of tests to check the functionality of your code before you submit it). The noise from downstairs, however, proved too alluring. At the urging of other saplings who kept walking in on me, I submitted what I had and gave in to the night's revelry.

There were probably about thirty or forty people downstairs. There were fresh-faced saplings and club officers presiding like proud older siblings, reminiscing about their own experiences with TreeHacks. And then there were some unfamiliar faces. Alumni.

The TreeHacks community was tight-knit. It wasn't a cult, exactly, but the group inspired real devotion. This was the ninth iteration of TreeHacks, and every codirector from the last decade remained engaged. Although most had graduated and started companies, steered VC firms, and done God knows what else, alumni still trekked to the secluded retreat on a Friday night. To meet us.

There were large trays of catered food and seating areas set up around the house for people to gab in small groups. I eagerly loaded up a plate with stir-fry noodles, already sick of dining hall meals. And, as I turned to find somewhere to sit, Vedant, the codirector who had been one of my interviewers, came up behind me and grabbed me by the shoulder.

"Ready to get lit?" he asked.

I laughed and gave him a side hug. His enthusiasm was so genuine that I couldn't help but be taken in by it.

"Let's go!" I responded.

It was, in fact, the first party I'd been to with alcohol—my first real party of any kind at Stanford. Vedant told me he was going to take a shot with every sapling and invited me to join him in the first one. If ever there was a way to forget the horrors of my CS107 assignment, the unholy collection of drinks sitting in the corner would do it. The club officers had brought a whole trunk's worth of alcohol—four types of vodka, seltzers of different varieties, beer, rum, whiskey, and basically every other kind of memory-killer. When I'd asked what to expect of the fall retreat beforehand, I was told to expect "heavy intoxication." Clearly, the codirectors were ready to make that happen.

Vedant and I took a shot from an industrial-size bottle of Tito's. And the party began to take off.

Vedant, Parth, and I, along with Jackson, a ripped Nebraskan startup founder, set up a game of beer pong in the game room. I'd never played beer pong. I sucked. Soon there was a whole crowd gathered to watch. I tried desperately to keep up; I couldn't, but it was still fun.

The partying, the shots, the beer pong—it felt like college was supposed to. Yet it was all a little bit off. Vedant and Parth were wearing TreeHacks-branded corporate Patagonias as we bonded in a sprawling luxury pad the student group had financed with corporate cash. The networking, too, was real. Alumni weren't just showing up to get drunk; they were eager to meet the team, to take charge of the most promising saplings and guide them through the strange new world they'd just entered. And as much as the party itself was unhinged, the people were not—even drunk, conversations focused on math Olympiads, research grants, and successful company exits.

After Vedant finished kicking my ass in beer pong, the codirectors gathered everyone in the game room and stood on the stairs. "Welcome to retreat!" said Sara, the other codirector. "And welcome to TreeHacks!"

"We're so excited about this incredible cohort," Vedant continued. "And we set up a little surprise for you."

The surprise was a poker tournament. No buy-in, no investment—everyone could play. And whoever won would get a thousand dollars. Because why the hell not? What club doesn't run poker nights in mansions where they give away free money to freshmen?

After the cheers and claps subsided, Vedant—already a little tipsy—called out again loudly. "ALSO everybody, Theo Baker is here! Theo is absolutely killing it at *The Daily*," he said, and went on a little spiel about my articles. I blushed bright red. I, too, was tipsy and had no idea how to process the compliment in a room of intimidating people. I wondered if it was a kind of warning—there's a journalist in our midst, or something. But when I approached Vedant afterward, he seemed sincerely proud.

THE POKER TOURNAMENT WAS SET TO BEGIN SOON, SO I GOT ANOTHER drink and chatted with Sara, who, as befitted her well-put-together personality, was sober and polished.

"How do you even afford all of this?" I wondered aloud to her.

"Eh," she said, shrugging her shoulders. "TreeHacks kind of has a black hole budget. Things just disappear into it."

She didn't elaborate further.

Then Sara was dragged away to finalize the poker tables and I found myself talking to a senior named George, who'd been standing to the side with a cracked-open beer and seasoned smile, enjoying the chaos around him. He was a FOTH—Friend of the House—welcome at any shindig even though it was the freshmen and sophomores who organized each year's TreeHacks event. George recognized me from my journalism and sought me out.

"This is huge stuff! Everybody is talking about it," George said.

I laughed and said thanks, but hey, *this*, TreeHacks, tech—that was what I really wanted to focus on.

"No, but seriously," he said, "my girlfriend and I talk about you all the time. She graduated last year, but she's getting to your articles within minutes and sending them to me."

Then he asked casually, "Do you have something else in the works?"

I smiled, a hot flush rising to my cheeks. It was a mundane question, one I should've been used to. Certainly one I should've anticipated upon meeting someone new. But as it happened, I'd just been looking at something earlier that day.

"Yeah," I confided as I thought about the secret I was keeping. "There's something a lot bigger."

"No way," he said. "Is it about the administration?"

"I can't tell you," I replied. "I have to be really careful with this one."

And with that, I made my excuses.

THE NEXT MORNING, OVER A BREAKFAST SPREAD AT THE DINING TABLE, rays of gentle sunlight flowing through the panoramic windows, I sat down to eat with a sapling named Riya, who introduced herself to me.

"I know, we chatted for like a half hour last night!" I responded with bewilderment.

"Bruh, that's so embarrassing," she said, having forgotten.

So we reintroduced ourselves.

It struck me that the goal of the rollout and the goal of the retreat were one and the same—to force us to be comfortable around one another, even in vulnerable situations, before we got to work. In that sense, it was a success. We had so little time before the hackathon that we couldn't afford poor communication. Also, well, TreeHacks had a black hole budget and money to burn.

We sat quietly as we headed in our Uber Black back to campus, driving past idyllic homes with Porsches and Teslas out front. And I remember all of a sudden being overcome with a sense of unease. Was this my life now? What even was this?

"Does anyone else feel a little weird about everything?" I asked aloud.

"What do you mean?" asked Jessica, another sapling.

"I don't know, just, like, the amount of money and everything. Doesn't it all feel a bit excessive?"

"I guess," Jessica said, noncommittally.

I let it sit for a few seconds before trying again. It was hard to articulate my queasiness, since I'd been just as much a participant as anyone else, but as we passed by the outside world in the sound-deadened chamber of our Escalade, I couldn't help but think it all strange.

"I mean, it seems like a big waste of money, right?" I asked. "Like, it's fun, but imagine what that money could do for, like, a food bank."

No one responded, and the comment hung in the air, unacknowledged.

CHAPTER 4

BINARY BOMB

The tip was oblique, delivered by a friend.

I'd spent the previous night, Halloween, working on a story that was published, as always, in the early hours of the morning. Then the message appeared in my inbox. "Hi Theo, I know you probably are getting a lot of tips," Jacob wrote. He was a recent alum who'd reached out initially after my War on Fun article, and we'd texted back and forth since then about Stanford gossip. Now, Jacob had come across a blog post from a few years prior. It "contains an interesting tidbit on MTL that might be worth investigating," he wrote.

I clicked on the link, which steered me to a site called PubPeer, an online forum where scientists dissect and discuss published studies. I plugged in Marc Tessier-Lavigne's name and began to scroll through the page. My brow furrowed. There were comments going back to 2015, noting miscellaneous "irregularities" in specific experimental results. "This highly cited *Science* paper is riddled with problematic blot images," an anonymous commenter had written about a paper published in an elite journal that listed Tessier-Lavigne as one of two authors. The anonymous observer had attached figures overlaid with arrows and highlighted boxes showing areas of different images in the study that appeared to have been duplicated and spliced together.

I wasn't exactly sure what I was looking at. But one thing caught my attention: Two images from a different 1999 study, one purporting to show a protein at zero hours of growth and the other labeled as showing one hour of progress, were the exact same image. The only difference was that the second had been shifted upward, giving the appearance of growth. I could see it with my own eyes; the panels were clearly identical. That couldn't be right, could it?

Of course, a scientist of Tessier-Lavigne's stature wouldn't be so stupid as to photoshop experimental results, I thought. Besides, all these concerns had been floating around online for at least seven years. Surely someone would've looked into it if there really was something there, right? I mean, he was the president of Stanford. The papers that people were commenting on had all been published before he got the job; these critiques must have come up during a vetting process. All the studies were still online and often cited; none had been corrected or retracted. Whatever people were seeing was probably nothing.

But it couldn't hurt to check.

I'D ALWAYS LOVED THE BRAIN. IN FACT, I'D WRITTEN MY COLLEGE ADmissions essay in part about cognitive science research. For a week in my junior year of high school I'd trooped around with a dog-eared copy of a Princeton professor's 1976 treatise, *The Origin of Consciousness in the Breakdown of the Bicameral Mind*, stuffed in my backpack as I worked my way through the dense tome. (Until I met my girlfriend Lily, I had no one to talk about it with.)

Still, when I consumed information about the brain, it was almost invariably filtered through another source. I read books, not research studies. And I'd never been in a lab, much less conducted any experiments. So when it came to assessing Marc Tessier-Lavigne's research, I was unsure how to proceed.

I knew only one established scientist who worked in a field adjacent to MTL—a man named Karsten I'd encountered years prior—and I decided to ask his opinion. I figured Karsten might give me a gut check both on the relevance of the accusations and on Tessier-Lavigne himself.

I sent a link to what I'd come across. He called me right away.

"Don't do this," he said sharply. "Marc Tessier-Lavigne is unassailable, and you do not want to go after him."

I was taken aback by his tone, which was harsher than I'd ever heard him.

"Marc is a legend," Karsten said. "Whatever this is, you do *not* want to get involved."

"Got it," I responded. "Definitely not trying to imply anything and obviously just trying to get a sense of things from someone who knows a lot better."

And it was true—I had no particular investment, nor did I really understand the words and pictures in front of me. I asked Karsten about the specific papers on PubPeer. I wanted to know whether, even ruling out misconduct or misdeed, there was something interesting about it.

"Yeah, I mean, I haven't actually gone through the stuff you sent," Karsten responded, "but I know Marc and I just know that he's not the kind of person you want to accuse of anything."

I WANTED TO KNOW MORE. THERE WAS AT LEAST SOME DUPLICATION in the images—I could see that. But I didn't know how much or how important it was.

I tracked down contact information for a handful of investigators who specialized in research fraud and image alteration and reached out, hoping someone would respond. Then I pretty much forgot about it. I was working on a separate story about increased security presence on campus.

Plus, I had CS107 to worry about. Always.

IT WAS ETHICS WEEK IN CS107, AND WE WERE LEARNING ABOUT SOMEthing called Therac-25. Jerry Cain, our professor, had brought homemade scones for the few people who still bothered to show up to the lecture in person—most of us watched online later, zipping through the tape at double speed. It was the great irony of the course's brutality that it was taught by such a kind man, a laid-back, graying professor who told good-natured jokes about his husband and brought his dog Doris to class. He was known to everyone by his first name and sent out a weekly newsletter to us "jolly CS107 assemblers" that recapped class content and also details of his personal life—new restaurants visited, recipes attempted, and dog-focused excursions.* While Jerry's teaching style was not for everyone, I found him compelling. And nobody could deny his proficiency. Jerry had been responsible for creating the Like button at Facebook.

Jerry seemed particularly enthusiastic about this week's content, which began, unusually for him, with a history lesson.

Produced in 1982, Therac-25 was a radiation therapy machine—a "cancer zapper." It was a revolutionary product. Unlike its predecessors, Therac-25 was computer controlled, faster to set up and therefore able to be used on far more patients in a day. It was an example of how programming could shake up industries and even save lives. But there was a catch, Jerry told us. A buffer overflow.

A buffer overflow is the result of a program attempting to write, or save, a greater quantity of data than the memory it has been allocated. Say I have requested space for six characters, and I try to save a word that is seven letters long. Unless guarded against, this will cause a buffer

*A sample snippet from Jerry's CS107 email newsletter: "The Doris stroll was fun as always, but it was particularly entertaining this time. We crossed paths with some mounted policemen at Dolores Park, and it became clear she thought the horses were just some ultralarge dog breed she'd never encountered. She. Was. Smitten."

overflow. Although it sounds minor, buffer overflows are dangerous. They can result in lost data, malfunctioning programs, and access to off-limits parts of a computer—access that hackers can exploit to steal data or gain control over their victim's product. In the case of Therac-25, the result was even worse.

Failures in the Therac-25 code resulted in four deaths and two permanent injuries after patients were given massive overdoses of radiation. But the human failure was the most galling. Instead of addressing the issue, the manufacturer of Therac-25 insisted for years that its machine was incapable of producing a radiation overdose and kept its machines in service. Even after the FDA labeled the machine "defective," the manufacturer declared the issues resolved by a hardware patch and Therac-25 returned to treating patients. Still, they missed an overflow. Another massive radiation overdose occurred.

It was a sobering story that underscored the best practices Jerry was trying to teach. The code hadn't been independently reviewed, nor had the combination of hardware and software been tested before the machine was deployed in a hospital. Arrogance, a rush to produce a product, and unwillingness to address problems had deadly effects.

We later discussed Jerry's lecture in our section, the lab led by a teaching assistant each week. Each section was about twenty or so students. My TA asked us to raise our hands "if you care about ethics and stuff like this." I put mine up and looked around. Not a single other arm was in the air. People didn't even care enough to pretend ethics mattered to them.

A DAY AFTER MY SECTION, THE CRYPTO EXCHANGE FTX COLLAPSED. ITS eccentric young founder, Sam Bankman-Fried, known universally as SBF, had been a hero of Silicon Valley. But the whole crypto empire was built, essentially, on a pyramid scheme. SBF had funneled customer funds into his investment firm, Alameda Research, enriching himself through the misappropriation of more than $65 billion. While concealing the fraud at the heart of his company, SBF cultivated a reputation as a wunderkind looking to change the world.

SBF's image was built on the illusion of morality. He claimed to be the foremost advocate for effective altruism, a trendy ends-justify-the-means philosophy that required him to make as much money as possible in order to give it away. Effective altruism was the most popular ethical system in the Valley. The concept had been mostly foreign to me as an East Coaster; luckily, I'd had a primer on my first day of class from a charismatic lecturer named Rob Reich.

Reich had given the inaugural lecture for our Structured Liberal Education program in the Socratic format, asking questions and challenging the responses that students gave. "If you were on your way to a job interview," Reich began, "and you saw a baby drowning in Lake Lag"—Stanford's Lake Lagunita, shortened, always, to Lag—"would you jump in to save the baby even if it meant missing the interview?" Everyone nodded. "Obviously," said one student. "What if you were wearing a nice suit? And you knew it would be ruined?" Reich asked. Of course you would save the baby. So, if you'd be willing to sacrifice hundreds of dollars to save the life of a child in front of you, why aren't you willing to spend that money to save a child on the other side of the world? Why not donate most of what you earn? Why not pay to distribute mosquito nets, the most cost-effective way of preventing countless malaria deaths?

Effective altruism made intuitive sense. How could you argue against it? Of course, the reality—just as with utilitarianism, the centuries-old moral system that EA effectively rebranded as new—often ends up being much less neat. It reduces the world to a simple series of calculations that, inevitably, can quickly become skewed. It allows people in Silicon Valley to tell themselves that they are behaving ethically when, in reality, they are merely applying gloss to familiar exploitative tactics.

Bankman-Fried was Silicon Valley's favorite kind of mythical figure—a Philosopher Con Man. He enjoyed the adulation of the media and the markets alike, all the while living in a sprawling Bahamas penthouse and raking in the dough. It was every Stanford student's dream: a young founder who made it big while focused on changing the world. But SBF's evangelism, he admitted in text messages with a reporter, was "mostly a front." In Silicon Valley, he wrote, there were only "winners and losers," fighting a "dumb game" to "say all the right shibboleths so everyone likes us."

Effective altruism was fashionable when I arrived at Stanford. Posters appeared around campus advertising events and grants connected with its adherents. My favorite one, framed in two messages: "AAAAAAAHH the world is so messed up what should we do!?!?!?" read the first text bubble. "The Effective Altruism Fellowship," a second bubble responded, with a QR code attached.

SBF grew up on Stanford's campus. His parents were respected professors at the law school who taught, among other things, legal ethics. When SBF was arrested, a handful of Stanford professors bailed him out. SBF had attended MIT, but his connections at Stanford had helped him secure funding and the Silicon Valley ecosystem helped build the company. His partner, Caroline Ellison—coconspirator, ex-lover, and the head of Alameda Research—was a Stanford alum.

After he was arrested in the Bahamas and extradited to the United States, SBF returned to Stanford on house arrest in his childhood home, just a block from the president's mansion, where MTL resided. Irony, for those who cared to see it, was everywhere. I learned that SBF had been invited to speak to a Stanford technology ethics course just prior to his company's collapse, an obligation he could no longer meet, since he was locked away about a stone's throw from the lecture hall where he would've held forth.

On campus, he was a focus of great interest. There were SBF-themed parties, and students regularly made pilgrimages to sneak a look at his place of confinement. For some, SBF's story was a cautionary tale of avarice and overambition, but others told me that they still wanted to be like him, just without the fall from grace.

I think they missed the point. Then again, some startup people at Stanford listened to the soundtrack of *The Social Network*—a story about bad behavior by irresponsible teens vested with too much power—for inspiration while they coded. They wanted to be like the characters. One angel investor even hosted a private screening of the movie to inspire the teens he was funding. A business-focused friend had recently told me that he was taking an ethics class focused on fraudsters. "We were all there to figure out how they got caught," he said.

SBF wasn't the only Stanford scandal in the news. Only a few months earlier, Elizabeth Holmes had been sentenced to prison for defrauding investors with her scam blood-test startup, Theranos, which she pioneered as a Stanford student and made into the next buzzworthy thing through the help of Stanford connections. Her earliest investor was Tim Draper, a Stanford alum and creator of "Stanford—The Game," who continued to call her a "visionary" well after she was indicted and her house of cards fell apart. Draper admitted that he'd never even visited the company he invested in.

Another Stanford alum, Do Kwon, had witnessed his undoing over multibillion-dollar fraud just a few months before Holmes's sentencing. Three nations soon pursued criminal charges for his role in creating the cryptocurrencies Luna and TerraUSD, which, in collapsing, caused hundreds of billions of dollars of losses in the wider crypto market. Two other Stanford alums, Adam Bowen and James Monsees, entrepreneurs who met and developed their company at the university, were also in the midst of dramatic unraveling. Their uber-successful Stanford startup Juul, once valued at $38 billion, stood accused of aggressively targeting teenagers with nicotine products and helping to get a whole new generation hooked on addictive substances. Bowen and Monsees had been flying high, raising a $12.8 billion investment in 2018, then reportedly spending nearly all of the cash on employee bonuses and shareholder dividends. Their company, like many other Stanford exports, had claimed that it would change the world for the better, helping to wean smokers off cigarettes. Instead, Juul marketed its products toward adolescents, misrepresenting them as safe, and allegedly fired those who raised concerns. In June 2022, the FDA pulled its products from the market; the company was later forced to pay billions in damages. (The FDA reversed course and approved Juul products in July 2025, but the company remains a shell of its once-dominant self.)

That all of these cases were ongoing at the same time was striking to me. But I had no way of understanding to what extent they were related to one another or to Stanford, if at all. I still hadn't quite learned how it all worked.

I SHOWED UP EARLY FOR OUR FIRST OFFICIAL TREEHACKS TEAM MEETing. I never show up early to things, but I wanted to prove that I was taking this seriously.

I was on the sponsorship team, the team that would rake in all the dough. Preparations were well underway for this year's event, Vedant told us, and he'd already raised hundreds of thousands of dollars. But he'd done it almost entirely on his own. Now it was our turn to come up with companies to target for money.

"We're going to raise three hundred thousand dollars more in the next two months," he said. Not "we want to," not "we have to," just "we will."

Vedant began to quiz us on companies and sectors we would target. For once, I felt ahead of the curve. I'd spent an hour or two preparing for the meeting and pointed to specific companies and potential sponsors to consider. The validation I got when Vedant said, "Good stuff," was huge.

Vedant also showed us the ropes. "Warm intros always work best," he told us. "If you know someone at a company, or you know a VC that funded a company, try to leverage that to make it inside."

The sponsorship packet was sleek and formulated to match the event's design scheme. Much of the pitch to companies centered on the ability to reach the remarkable talent pool of students at TreeHacks.

Since we were selling access, it was important that we actually had a valuable collection of competitors. The tech team built a portal ensuring that each application submitted—more than fifty-five hundred in our year—would be read by at least three TreeHacks members. The three scores would then be weighted and algorithmically adjusted.

Each of us would read at least three hundred applications, comprising a series of written answers, résumés, and submitted projects. We would then check boxes that applied to the applicant—for example, "won a prize at a major hackathon," "worked at a reputable tech company," "completed a *super cool* personal project," etc.—and assign them scores in "technical experience," "passion," and "how strong of a fit for TreeHacks?" We gave a rating from one to four. But there was also a big red button. At the discretion of each team member, there was the option to assign someone a 999, reserved for people who were "OUTTA DIS WRLD VERY RARE!"

TreeHacks prided itself on diversity, attracting students from four continents and at all skill levels. It maintained an even gender split in its participants—rare in the hackathon world—and worked hard to spot people who would most benefit from the opportunity to participate.

The result was a list of attendees worth paying to meet. Vedant walked us through the sponsorship tiers we were selling, explaining benefits at each level. A Cedar sponsorship, beginning at twenty-two thousand dollars, would allow a sponsor to make an onstage demonstration at the opening ceremony in front of all 1,700 hackers. An Oak sponsorship bought access to our custom MeetMe platform for connecting hackers with sponsors after the event.

"A lot of sponsors also do in-kind gifts," Vedant mentioned. "One year, we got Disney to sponsor us, and we still use all the lightsabers they gave us to run our lightsaber fight."

I asked what we had to do for all that money. Vedant said the answer was basically just to keep the sponsors happy. "Respond to them at all hours, try to work with them, make sure they have a good time at the event. The more they come back year after year, the better."

We weren't actually governed by real contracts. The money, for the most part, would simply be forked over and we could do with it as we chose. "They trust us," Vedant said, "and many of them want to get on our good side."

Vedant created a group chat to keep everyone on the sponsorship team in touch. He called it "big billy ballers," with a dollar sign emoji at the end. Then, as we were dispersing, Vedant asked me to hang back. "Listen, I can tell you're taking this seriously, and obviously you're going to be my right-hand man in this," Vedant said. "If you keep it up, you'll definitely be codirector next year."

I was startled. To be a TreeHacks codirector puts you in a very rarefied category. It gives you a place at every table. This was what I'd come to Stanford for, and the chance had just opened up in front of me.

Too bad I was about to blow it.

ELISABETH BIK IS A SUPERSTAR IN HER FIELD, A DUTCH MICROBIOLOGIST who quit her lab to become a full-time science sleuth, an investigator who, by the time we met, had already reviewed more than one hundred thousand research papers for signs of misconduct. *Nature*, the science journal, referred to her as the "super-spotter of duplicated images." *The New Yorker* called her "Biology's Image Detective." She was, in other words, the woman I needed to talk to.

I reached out to Bik via Twitter and was surprised to receive a response right away. I sent her a longer email, forwarding the concerns I'd seen about Marc Tessier-Lavigne's research papers on PubPeer. At that point, I'd already used a forensic analysis software tool to look into some of the allegedly manipulated blots and was confident that some experimental results appeared more similar to one another than they should have, but I still couldn't really say what that meant. "I'm not savvy enough in this field to understand all of the critiques leveled and how much weight they carry," I wrote to Bik, "and it would be great to be able to express what is or isn't there in language our readers would understand."

The email that she sent in reply would change everything.

Bik analyzed nine papers upon my request, all of which named Tessier-Lavigne as a coauthor. These papers had to do with some of MTL's famous research on neurodevelopment and how our brains stitch themselves together. Four of them, she said, had no real issues. But the other five—well, she had some questions.

"I have marked in red the image problems that raise serious concerns here," she wrote, proceeding to break down the figures in question. She identified "gel bands [that had] been reused," "sets of duplicated panels," "potentially altered photos with a mirrored band," and a battery of other issues.

Over Zoom later that day, Bik explained. As she made sure to stress in the email, some of the PubPeer concerns revolved around what she called "beautification"—essentially minor photoshopping to clean up the edges of figures. Several of these papers had been published right when Photoshop was first gaining popularity, before conventions had been fully established. Beautification was bad practice, but not fraud.

Yet there were other, more significant discrepancies. "This one is pretty serious," she said, pointing at a figure from a 2008 paper published by the European Molecular Biology Organization in *The EMBO Journal*. "It looks like there was some photoshopping to remove some of the bands and replace them with something else."

According to Bik, there are three types of duplications in scientific publishing. Type I refers to simple, identical duplications, one-for-one copies. Type II duplications are those in which two images are shifted or rotated. And Type III involves the duplication of specific sections within the same image. The first category can often be explained by sloppiness or honest error. The second category, less frequently so. And the third category of duplication is most likely caused by intentional alteration. In some of the papers Tessier-Lavigne coauthored, there appeared to be a level of alteration that, in Bik's view, "suggests an intent to mislead."

But how serious was this? And what did it say about Tessier-Lavigne?

Bik's tone was analytic and scientific, and she went to great lengths to be specific with her allegations. Several of the papers, including the 2008 *EMBO Journal* one, did not include Tessier-Lavigne as a senior author, instead featuring him as a middle author with less authority. Speaking about a 2003 study in which Tessier-Lavigne was a middle author, Bik made sure to emphasize this difference. "I don't think that is really a paper where I think he had any direct oversight of the experiments," she said.

On others, though, Tessier-Lavigne was the senior or corresponding author. And on some of those papers, there appeared to be Type III alterations. "It's something that looks at least very sloppy," Bik told me, adding that she hoped Tessier-Lavigne would respond to the issues seriously. Some of the discrepancies appeared to have been done "on purpose," and "if that was done intentionally, that would be falsification," she offered. "But it's hard to prove." In biological sciences, conclusively determining misconduct is extremely difficult. Some of the studies extended back to 1999 and were so old that their original data were likely long gone.

"The denominator is important," Bik told me. If a clear pattern emerges from a specific research group, it says something about their practices. It wasn't clear yet what Tessier-Lavigne's role in all of this had been—it could very well have been nothing given the multiple authors on each paper. But the issues were serious enough that she was sure they should be addressed.

After about an hour, Bik and I got off the call and I sank into my chair.

"Well, what the fuck happens now?" I asked nobody in particular.

THE BIK CALL SET ME OFF FULL-TIME DIGGING INTO TESSIER-LAVIGNE'S work. I reached out to other misconduct investigators to see whether they corroborated Bik's analysis. And I began to immerse myself in the science.

I stayed up until 5:00 a.m. that night reading scientific literature and trying to understand what image alteration meant. In biology, unlike other disciplines, I learned, images are of vital importance. The figures in a study are not illustration, they are evidence, directly confirming or disproving the theories advanced in a paper. And, since something like 90 percent of all studies published are positive results, confirming a hypothesis, there is a clear incentive toward getting the "right" answer.

The Tessier-Lavigne studies had been read tens of thousands of times and been published in highly acclaimed journals including *Science*, *Nature*, and *Cell*—the big three, the most selective publications in the world. The influence of these publications is enormous, and the pressure to be published in their pages immense. It can easily mean the difference between a postdoctoral researcher finding a full-time job or getting pushed out of the field.

The study that had first caught my eye—the 2001 *Science* publication with only two authors, Tessier-Lavigne and a member of his lab—had been cited by subsequent research papers and review articles more than seven hundred times, a towering sum placing it in the ninety-eighth percentile for its field.

By Bik's estimation, that paper included figures that had been clearly altered. "The photoshopping was done intentionally, there's no way around it," she'd told me. The paper appeared to contain three panels altered around the edges, whole-panel duplications in three other figures, an incorrect panel blank in another figure, and, most seriously, the manipulation of several portions of a central experiment, perhaps as a way to avoid showing different results. If Bik was right, this paper, one of Tessier-Lavigne's most cited works, was seriously problematic.

And none of this squared with Tessier-Lavigne's public image.

In the coming days, I took to reading every single thing I could about Tessier-Lavigne. Every article, every profile, every speech. He was so . . . spotless. I could not find a negative word about him anywhere. A *Nature Medicine* profile quoted a fellow scientific powerhouse describing him as "essentially . . . perfect." A friend pegged him as someone "for whom things always seemed to go just right." A Nobel laureate gushed, "Marc could lead the country."

As a cub researcher, Tessier-Lavigne created an entirely new field in the 1990s, discovering netrins, the proteins responsible for axon guidance. This was vital research. MTL had illuminated something fundamental about how our brains develop, unraveling a mystery that had stumped others. Tessier-Lavigne then went from a lab at the University of California, San Francisco, to one at Stanford, where he worked for just two years before being hired by Genentech, the biotech giant, where he ultimately came to supervise fourteen hundred scientists as the company's chief scientific officer. In 2011, he became the president of Rockefeller University in New York and then, in 2016, the head of Stanford.

As I teetered toward sleep each night that first week, I tried to reconcile the image of a man so revered with the picture of those little duplicated blots that had become seared into my brain.

THE POSTS ON PUBPEER RAISING QUESTIONS ABOUT MTL HAD BEGUN IN 2015, right when Tessier-Lavigne was being considered for the Stanford presidency. Had this come up in the university's due diligence? Had the board of trustees considered it unimportant? Or, more interesting, had the trustees missed it entirely?

As I explored further, I learned that image manipulation had been frequently ignored—by institutions that failed to dig into credible accusations, by scientists slow to correct the record, and by journals that viewed misconduct as tarring their image. Peer review was not designed to catch falsification in figures, and issues raised post-publication usually went nowhere.

Bik and several colleagues had conducted a landmark study showing that nearly 4 percent of published studies include "problematic figures," with at least half of those showing signs of "deliberate manipulation." Yet just 0.04 percent of published studies were retracted.

In recent years, Bik and other integrity crusaders—like the teams behind PubPeer or *Retraction Watch*, a blog dedicated to tracking retractions and misconduct—had brought more attention to the issue of falsification. Online analyses often focused on an experiment type called a Western blot, a widely used technique to detect specific proteins in a sample. Many Western blots were falsified, and sleuths like Bik had grown adept at identifying those manipulations. Still, they often had trouble getting their concerns heard.

Bik had actually identified some concerns about a Tessier-Lavigne paper on PubPeer years before our interview—something neither of us realized until we began speaking. She also hadn't realized that Tessier-Lavigne became president. "What is he, like, dean or something?" she asked me during our interview.

In the case of the papers I'd asked Bik to review, MTL was the only common author linking them all. Whether he knew about the alterations I could not say yet, but this had evidently happened several times under his supervision and never been corrected, which to me was a story worth pursuing.

PubPeer notifies authors of concerns raised about their papers. Had Tessier-Lavigne seen the posts in 2015 and disregarded them? Had he known about the discrepancies for seven years and done nothing?

As I sought sources, I was careful not to do anything that would give away that I was working on the story. The first step was to corroborate Bik's account and establish plainly that there was some sort of problem, which needed to be done discreetly. And I was continually reminded how touchy the issue was.

I ran into a friend, Jim, about a week after my interview with Bik.

A senior Stanford official, Jim had been an important counselor and a trusted confidant to me. I told him what I was working on and he blanched. "If you do this, you have to be extremely careful," Jim said. "They will go after you." I asked him to say more, but he waved me off, just as Karsten, the scientist, had. "I can't. I work with Marc every day. I can't be involved in this at all."

I reached two other forensic image analysts who agreed to go through the Tessier-Lavigne papers as Bik had. Both independently confirmed her assessment.

I spoke to as many experts as I could to understand the process of preparing experiments for publication and how something like this could happen. Each emphasized that the alterations I showed them weren't normal. One neurobiologist, a leader in his field, remarked, "If I saw these sorts of things from someone in my lab, I would fire them on the spot. Wouldn't try to correct. Wouldn't try to have a conversation. Would just fire." The thing was, no matter how confident they were, most of the other scientists did not want to be named. They were scared, they told me, of what would happen if they made an enemy of such a powerful man.

I was told, repeatedly, that I was taking on a story that could be very uncomfortable. "This is very, very risky for you personally," one scientific peer of Tessier-Lavigne's cautioned. "They're likely to pursue you aggressively."

By now, I did not have any question that the story was worth investigating. I naïvely assumed, though, that I could do it all and give up nothing. That the story would simply be one aspect of my Stanford experience. Instead, I found myself increasingly making compromises in other parts of my life to hunt down more details.

"BINARY BOMB" IS THE MOST ICONIC CS107 ASSIGNMENT—AND VERY possibly the most iconic assignment at Stanford. Here's how it was introduced in 2017:

> Those nefarious Cal students have broken into our myth machines and planted some mysterious executables we are calling "binary bombs." These programs are believed to be armed and dangerous. Without the original source, we don't have much to go on, but we have observed that the programs seem to operate in a sequence of levels. Each level challenges the user to enter a string. If the user enters the correct string, it defuses the level and the program proceeds on. But given the wrong input, the bomb explodes by printing an earth-shattering KABOOM! and terminating. To deactivate the entire bomb, one needs to successfully defuse each of its levels.

By my year, the assignment had technically been renamed (the rumor was that a Stanford student had been working on their code at an airport when the "bomb" language got them taken aside by security and interrogated). Everyone still called it Binary Bomb, though.

The goal of the assignment is to defuse a series of "bombs" by tracing through the binary code of an ATM and a secure bank vault to identify secret passwords. Binary is literally the set of 0 and 1 instructions sent to a computer. It doesn't look like code, and it doesn't give you much to work with. The whole thing is a puzzle, a chase to track down clues and find the secrets contained within the information you're handed. In theory, it seemed cool. In practice, I was miserable. All the work on my article had left me with just two days to complete the assignment.

I realized how bad it would be the second I downloaded the files. "Lily I'm so so so so scared for binary bomb," I texted my girlfriend. "It's due on Friday. And I haven't started. And people are already crying." I texted someone in the class, admitting that I was just getting going. "If you run out of tissues I have extra 😭," she responded.

I pulled an all-nighter. Then another. It was so complicated. I'd cruised through the first level and even gotten through the second level without much trouble, once I'd identified the central hurdle. But the third level, the most important and difficult, broke me.

I WAS FRUSTRATED WITH MYSELF. EVERYTHING HAD BEGUN TO FALL by the wayside as the MTL story consumed me. My parents expected me home for Thanksgiving. I'd scarcely spoken to them in ages because every time I came up for air, I'd forgotten about the three-hour time difference and they were already asleep. As I was working on Binary Bomb, sweaty and on the verge of a panic attack, my parents called. I let the phone ring. "Hey bud, tried calling. Hope all is well," my dad texted. I couldn't explain that I was struggling with a mess of my own creation.

I'd become a terrible friend, too. My friend Sergio had a finalist interview for a Rhodes Scholarship. I'd promised to do a mock interview session to prep him. I forgot to show up.

Lily also noticed me growing distant, and I felt my heart breaking a little. She'd supported me through so much. For a while, it had seemed like the two of us were taking on the world together. We'd cosplayed adults, playing house for a week that summer while her parents were out of town. We danced around the living room; I listened to her play piano, her hands flying around the keyboard; and she sat on the kitchen stool, watching me slice onions and garlic for dinner. At one point, we went into the city and found a couch at the Boston Public Library. I picked out a book and we decided to read it there and then. For a couple of hours, we sat side by side, peering at the same pages, flipping through from start to finish. It sounds silly, but I was in love with how quickly she read, how I was never the one waiting at the end of a page. Now, though, she was waiting for me to resurface.

Binary Bomb had a final, no-extension deadline. But I couldn't make it. Desperate, I emailed Jerry, the professor. I couldn't tell him about the MTL story that was consuming me, so I explained that my grandfather had passed away at the beginning of the quarter—and that my other grandfather, my Pappouzi, with whom I was also close, had rapidly deteriorated in his Alzheimer's and been placed into hospice care, his lungs riddled with cancer. This had taken more of a toll on me than I'd cared to admit, and writing the email left me sobbing.

Just months prior, both of my grandfathers had been at my high school graduation, waving from the crowd and telling me how proud they were of me. They were friends themselves, and, while very different personalities, shared a propensity for the sort of great guffaw that could fill any room. I felt the sudden absence of that laughter profoundly.

Jerry, class act that he was, granted me extra time. It made me cry all over again. But it was a good cry, in a way, finally allowing myself to acknowledge that I had genuinely been struggling with my emotions.

I redoubled my efforts on Binary Bomb. I worked throughout the six-hour flight home for Thanksgiving. (The assignment rebranding had worked—I was not bothered once as I stared intently at my laptop, nor, as far as I can tell, ever considered a terrorist threat.) Even upon arrival in DC, I hardly greeted my parents before darting upstairs to my room in the attic, barricading myself until I could come out victorious. And, in the wee hours, the solution finally revealed itself.

The third level, the secure vault, had a vulnerability I could exploit. Its password reader would stop scanning the input at the first non-number character; however, it didn't protect against a buffer overflow, the Therac-25 design flaw. I crafted an exploit to rewrite the vault passcode. It worked. I assigned myself fictional millions from the compromised "vault" and submitted my responses, just in time for Thanksgiving.

As much as I struggled with Binary Bomb, I also enjoyed it. I loved the chase. The intricate puzzle, the challenge of fitting all the pieces together until everything finally made sense. Until I understood.

DESPITE THE MISSING GRANDFATHERS AT THE THANKSGIVING TABLE, we had a good time. For a few days, I shut out Stanford. I cooked up a storm and allowed myself to sleep, fully, for the first time in a long while.

My parents were surprised by my transformation. College, I guess, had already changed me more than I'd expected. They noticed the hole in my ear from a first-week-of-school dare to get it pierced. Foolishly, I'd thought the skin would heal over. My grandmother teased me about my long hair and scraggly five-o'clock shadow. Most of all, though, my family seemed surprised at the journalistic obsession that I still refused to call an obsession.

I'd never wanted to do journalism precisely because my parents already had. There wasn't much room to make my own reputation when they'd already figured the field out—and my parents were pros. They met breaking the Monica Lewinsky story together, before heading off to cover Vladimir Putin's rise to power in Russia and the wars in Afghanistan and Iraq, and now wrote about Donald Trump's Washington.

I had great admiration for them, and for journalism, which I viewed as a public good undertaken at great sacrifice. I loved hearing my parents' stories. Yet that was their thing, not mine. Both of them had known from a young age they were destined to be reporters; I was the opposite.

Still, it was true that I found myself increasingly intoxicated with the rush of a story. I loved that I would begin the process bewildered and confused, knowing nothing, and that, through force of will, I would eventually fit the pieces together. I loved that it was *hard*. And I loved, more than anything, that my work would directly determine whether information became known.

As I was explaining this to my parents the day after Thanksgiving, I brought up the story I was working on about Marc Tessier-Lavigne. I was eager to show them what I'd uncovered. I pulled out printouts of the scientific figures in question and laid them out on our dining room table, trying to show how parts had been spliced and moved around. To my dismay, they didn't get it. My dad, especially, was unconvinced. "This guy is a world-renowned scientist," he said, "and you're a seventeen-year-old kid." I tried to explain that the concerns I was relaying came from experts in the field and told them more about my efforts to find sources. "Just be careful," my dad said. "Maybe you could investigate a professor instead of the college president to start?" I reassured him that I would spend another month or two on everything before I published, and we left it at that.

THAT NIGHT, WHILE WE ATE DINNER, I DISCOVERED THAT ONE OF THE journals had responded to concerns on PubPeer the week before, writing, "*The EMBO Journal* is aware of these issues and is looking into this." Suddenly, this was a breaking story. A major scientific journal was investigating the concerns. As I explained the news at the dinner table, my parents agreed that I had a story after all and encouraged me to get a move on to avoid getting scooped. Even though Tessier-Lavigne was a middle author on the specific paper in question, it presented me with the opportunity to report everything else I'd been working on.

I called Sam, the *Daily* editor. "Holy shit," he said. "We need to get going. How quickly can you write this?"

"I'm flying back to Stanford tomorrow," I responded. "I'll have something by the time I get off the plane."

This was too sensitive a story to leave up to *The Daily*'s regular process. We alerted our lawyers at Davis Wright Tremaine, a top First Amendment law firm on the West Coast, which did pro bono work from time to time for *The Daily*, and we looped in the two journalism advisers on *The Daily*'s board, R. B. Brenner, the Stanford lecturer who had been so supportive already, and Tracy Jan, a Stanford alum who served as the deputy health and science editor at *The Washington Post*. R.B. recused himself, since he worked for the university, but Tracy stepped up. "I wish you'd have told me about this sooner," she said. Nevertheless, she would be there for us. "Give me a draft and I'll edit it."

WHILE I'D SPENT THE PLANE RIDE HOME CODING, THE PLANE RIDE back was reserved for journalism, frantically assembling the story. By the time I landed, I had a two-thousand-word draft detailing the accusations of research manipulation connected to the president of Stanford that had been levied for years and never reported.

In an effort to make the story as bulletproof as possible—knowing that student journalists have to earn their credibility from scratch—I limited my story to only its strongest elements, holding back information that I didn't have enough on to report yet. Now we had to go to Tessier-Lavigne for a response. I readied questions about each individual allegation and sent them to Sam and Tracy. I also drafted questions for the scientific journals that we would name in the piece and went back to my sources to get better information about what the European journal's statement meant. My questions had been approved by the editors by the time I arrived at my dorm, and I sent them off.

Given how reluctant the university had been to engage with me in the past, I figured the response would be minimal. But we had to be prepared. Michele, the graphics editor, was tasked with whipping up an illustration based on figures from the paper, and editors coalesced around my copy, debating how the story should begin. Structuring the piece was tough—the other papers, the ones on which MTL was senior author, were obviously the more important ones. But the fact that a journal was investigating a paper on which the president of Stanford was a named author was the most indisputable fact. This story wasn't just coming from us; the suspicions had been validated as serious by the very journal that published the paper.

I hustled over to the Daily House. Tracy was a thorough editor, and her help made me feel much more comfortable with publishing. The lawyers adjusted language to ensure we were on safe legal ground.

The piece was nearly done when I received an email from a Stanford spokesperson, Dee Mostofi, that responded at length to the questions I'd asked Tessier-Lavigne. My jaw dropped. I'd sent the queries just five hours earlier, and the response was nearly seven hundred words. It also included a defense against allegations about a paper that I hadn't even raised. I couldn't help but suspect that Tessier-Lavigne had been preparing for a while for someone to ask these questions.

In the statement, Mostofi revealed that Tessier-Lavigne had known about problems in two *Science* papers and a *Cell* paper since 2015, when the PubPeer allegations were first raised. He said that he'd reached out to alert the journal editors that very day, noting that the *Cell* editorial team deemed it a nonissue and that he'd "submitted corrections to the other two papers to *Science* but they were not published." That immediately struck me as odd. They were not published? Really?

There was no doubt in my mind that the university's response had been written by MTL himself. There was too much technical information, assembled too quickly, for it to have come from the communications team. Plus, the writing and style were unlike any of the statements that had come from them before. But Mostofi insisted that the response be attributed to Stanford, as though the school itself was defending MTL.

The most important part of the statement was the claim, repeated several times, that the issues "do not affect the data, results, or interpretation of the papers." I ran it past the scientific investigators who had reviewed Tessier-Lavigne's papers for me. Elisabeth Bik wrote back, "I do not agree with the statement that these issues have no bearing on the data or the results." She continued, "I hope that Dr. Tessier-Lavigne will not brush off these concerns as irrelevant. There appear to be a lot of visible errors in these papers, and some duplications are suggestive [of] an intention to mislead. Dismissing these as not affecting the data is not very reassuring. The reader might wonder how many non-visible errors might be present in other parts of the data." Ouch.

With the university statement issued, it was go time. I told one of my advisers that we'd received a response from Tessier-Lavigne. "Well," he wrote, "the gates are open and the horses are on the track."

I RACED TO INCORPORATE TESSIER-LAVIGNE'S DEFENSE INTO THE PIECE. I wanted to make sure that he had his say and that the story was as thorough, fair, and evenhanded as it could be. Sam and I decided to design interactive graphics elements to show the exact figures discussed, allowing readers to view the original image and an annotated version that pointed out where alterations might have occurred. It was particularly useful for cases that were more difficult to see with the naked eye. For example, in one image a blot had been copied, reversed, and stretched, making it hard to recognize from the original.

Then the lawyers reviewed my finished copy. Eric Stahl, a partner at Davis Wright Tremaine, had dropped everything on a Monday night to assist. He was incredibly good-natured and, rather than being upset at the late-night phone call, seemed to enjoy being a part of the breaking news. At one point, Eric and I found ourselves on opposite sides about whether to include a specific quote; I pleaded my case and he relented. "Have you ever considered being a lawyer?" he said with a laugh. By the time we were finished, it was past midnight, and Eric gave us the all-clear before heading off to bed.

Alone in the Daily House, Sam and I fretted over the final details, reading through the piece again and again. It was just the two of us in the end, which was fitting—we were the two whose futures would be entangled with it, my name on the piece and his on the masthead. It was only my tenth article, the one that would finally earn me a *Stanford Daily* T-shirt and key card access to the building. At 2:08 a.m., Sam clicked the Publish button and I took a video. "I hope I don't get kicked out," I laughed, only mostly joking.

The next morning, all hell broke loose. A bomb of my own had been set off.

CHAPTER 5

A FUCKING MENACE

The email notifications began mounting before I woke up, a torrent of constant pings. Twitter had spread the story far and wide. "Oh snap," "WTF," "Damnnnnn," and other expressions of astonishment flew back and forth. My favorite came from a Brit: "If I woke up tomorrow with my head sewn to the carpet, I wouldn't be more surprised than I am right now."

I'd known the investigation had potential, but I hadn't expected the extent of the reaction. The combination of Marc Tessier-Lavigne's Boy Scout reputation and *The Daily*'s status as a student newspaper made the story seem all the more to have come out of left field. The reporting seemed to pass muster: The sourcing was rigorous and the allegations were real, although left open to interpretation.

Campus was abuzz. A quick glance at Fizz showed me that all top twelve posts on the app were about the story, as were dozens more. I spotted a meme with Tessier-Lavigne's face superimposed over the Green Goblin's quote from Spider-Man, "You know, I'm something of a scientist myself." A poll posted on the site asked, "Did he do it?" and a number of comments were made about me. Tammer, a *Daily* editor, sent me one with a few hundred upvotes: "Decades from now, today will be seen as a pivotal moment in the collapse of the big charade that represents our institutions. This is Theo Baker's Watergate moment and he is an astounding journalist." I laughed at the ridiculousness of it, but I was privately more flattered than I should've been.

Within hours, other news outlets were after the story, publishing pieces that echoed what I'd written. I noticed a line in the *San Francisco Chronicle*: "University officials did not respond to multiple requests for comment from the *Chronicle* Tuesday." This intrigued me. Clearly there was some internal deliberation by Stanford over what the response should be, perhaps a recalibration even. Otherwise, why wouldn't they simply have sent the *Chronicle* the same statement they sent me?

I reached out directly again to Tessier-Lavigne requesting an interview. I wanted to walk through the specific images with him, to get more context. To hear him explain things in his own words would be a million times more revealing than any canned half-response email. My mail tracking software showed that he opened the email soon after—and kept reopening it. It was forwarded and, over the course of the next few hours, viewed twenty-three times. I didn't get a response.

A few hours later, though, the *Chronicle* finally did. And I was entirely unprepared for what it contained:

> The university will assess the allegations presented in the Stanford Daily, consistent with its normal rigorous approach by which allegations of research misconduct are reviewed and investigated. In the case of the papers in question that list President Tessier-Lavigne as an author, the process will be overseen by the board of trustees.

HOLY SHIT.

I sent the news to a Slack channel with my editors. "This is fucking craaazy," wrote Lucy. Only around twelve hours after I'd left, I rushed back to the Daily House to report the latest development. Of every possible response from the university, this was the one that I'd least expected.

It's not that I hadn't considered an investigation possible. But for it to have been announced within hours? And for the board of trustees to have initiated it? With my previous investigations, Stanford would ignore the issue, then downplay it, then, after outside pressure reached a certain peak, say it would be addressed. We'd skipped a couple of steps this time.

Of course, not everything had changed. Stanford's communications team—even though it said explicitly that its comments were in response to "allegations presented in the Stanford Daily"—had issued the statement to other news outlets, keeping *The Daily* in the dark. The communications team kept ignoring us, before eventually forwarding the statement they'd sent to everyone else.

Oh, well. I didn't need Stanford's flacks to give me a scoop. I'd let Elisabeth Bik know the night before that the university had brought up the 1999 *Cell* paper unprompted. I hadn't included it in my initial article because her concerns over the paper weren't serious, and I didn't want to conflate the issues in the 1999 paper—which seemed unintentional—with the potentially more serious issues in the *Science* papers.

But Bik had taken another look at the *Cell* paper and found something she'd initially missed. "This is a very big one," she wrote me. "Parts of different blots appear to have been copied and rearranged." And even more important: "These are not irrelevant, buffed up areas, but areas representing experiments." This was a third paper on which Tessier-Lavigne was a senior author that seemed to have serious issues. It was an influential study, cited 950 times. And I'd be able to publish the concerns before anyone else. Since I hadn't included the *Cell* paper in my first article, nobody else even knew to pay attention to it.

WHAT DID THE BOARD KNOW? COULD THE FACT THAT THE TRUSTEES acted so quickly suggest prior knowledge? I had no idea. In fact, I knew nothing about the board.

It was 1:00 a.m., just twenty-three hours after the initial scoop, when we published our story about the investigation of Tessier-Lavigne. But I was still working. Combing through the website for the board of trustees, I began to compile dossiers. Of the thirty-three members, there was not a single academic, nonprofit head, or university leader aside from Tessier-Lavigne. They were, by and large, extremely prominent, extremely successful businesspeople. Many of them were billionaires, including Jerry Yang, the board chair and a cofounder of Yahoo!; Clara Wu Tsai, the co-owner of an NBA team, a WNBA team, a professional lacrosse team, and the Barclays Center with her husband, a cofounder of Alibaba; Jim Coulter, cofounder of the private equity giant TPG; José Feliciano, cofounder and managing partner of his own investment firm, which, among other assets, controls the Chelsea Football Club; and several others. No wonder Stanford was becoming increasingly corporatized.

They were an intimidating force. And, unfortunately, hard to get to.

Over the next few days, I would manage to reach a few trustees, but they all brushed me off. One complimented my reporting, another hung up before I could finish telling him my name. I hadn't expected much, of course. Businesspeople with billions in their pockets know how to stick to the company line. (Usually.) But I thought that reaching out as early as possible would show that I was serious about this reporting, and down the line it might help convince someone to talk.

At the moment, though, I was running a fever. "My head feels like it's being split open with an axe," I texted Lucy. She didn't respond. Past five in the morning, I finally turned in, eyes exhausted from uninterrupted computer glare in a room lit only by contraband multicolor LED strips.

I WAS UP BY 10:00 A.M. I'D PLANNED TO GET TO WORK ON MY CS107 final assignment—the dreaded Heap Allocator. It was known as a brutal test for even the most determined coder, a herculean challenge that pushed many to, or past, their limits. Some people found it simple, if time-consuming. They're freaks. Most of the class had started working on Heap Allocator two weeks before, and they were still pulling all-nighters. I had three days. And, making things worse, I only vaguely understood what I was supposed to be doing.

But I hadn't even finished reading the requirements when I got an email that derailed my plans.

"Theo, hope you're enjoying your time in the spotlight," wrote Holden Thorp, the editor in chief of *Science*. Yeesh. I didn't know how to take that, but given Thorp's comments on Twitter, where he expressed annoyance with the short window of time we'd given him to respond (approximately seven hours), it didn't seem friendly. Still, he confirmed that Tessier-Lavigne had reached out to *Science* in 2015, four years before Thorp arrived at the journal, to issue corrections to his papers—and Thorp added a mea culpa saying that "an error on our part" had prevented the publication of the errata. What kind of error wasn't specified, but he wrote on behalf of *Science*: "We regret this error, apologize to the scientific community, and will be sharing our next steps as they relate to these two papers as soon as possible."

It was an incredible, and baffling, admission. How could they have failed to publish corrections they had in hand? And had Tessier-Lavigne simply let the issue go when they weren't published?

I knew I had to write a story about this. I felt a twinge of guilt as I closed the Emacs shell on my computer, casting aside CS107 yet again. But it had to be done.

My editors didn't get the significance at first. "alright lmk when you can draft up a change," Sam texted. He wanted to slot it into the investigation story that had been published the day before. But I resisted, saying "this is a big enough development to deserve its own headline." It helped validate Tessier-Lavigne and added credibility to the argument that he'd acted as he should have. Plus, featuring it would show that we weren't out for blood—we weren't trying to "get" MTL, all we wanted to do was cover the story wherever it led. *Science*'s statement promised next steps, which, coupled with the board's investigation, ensured that this story wouldn't go away anytime soon.

Within three hours, we had a piece on our homepage.

SCIENCE'S COMMENT, AS IT TURNED OUT, WAS FAR FROM THE MOST life-changing event that took place on November 30, 2022. Hours later, OpenAI released ChatGPT, and AI broke into the mainstream.

I was impressed from the first time I used it, texting Sam astonished reactions to different outputs. Still, I had no idea how important it would be. ChatGPT triggered a boom that increased the value of the top six Big Tech companies by $8 trillion within two years. Soon, everyone at Stanford would be pivoting to AI. Crypto had fallen out of favor because of SBF; now, less than a month leader, a new feeding frenzy began.

But my attention was largely directed elsewhere.

The next day two more MTL papers emerged with signs of manipulation. Once again, Elisabeth Bik was my most fearless source. Commenting on one study, she told me, "I would testify in court that, in my professional opinion, it is digitally altered."

I checked her analysis with other experts and, once it was corroborated, went to Tessier-Lavigne and the university. They kept quiet, but others were opening up. Holden Thorp, the *Science* editor, agreed to give me an interview after some badgering and praised Elisabeth Bik, while dropping the tidbit that Tessier-Lavigne had not followed up once with *Science* since submitting the corrections in 2015. I also tracked down a scientist in Tessier-Lavigne's field who told me that concerns had first been relayed to him about some of these papers in the early 2000s. If so, could Tessier-Lavigne really not have known until semipublic allegations surfaced in 2015, as he claimed?

The board issued its first official statement on the matter through a letter from Jerry Yang, the chair. "I am appointing a Special Committee of the Board to examine the facts underlying the allegations, to assess the significance of any findings, and to make recommendations to the full board," Yang wrote, adding that he would serve on the committee alongside Carol Lam, a former US attorney for the Southern District of California; Jeffrey Stone, a former chair of blue-chip law firm McDermott Will & Emery; Jim Coulter, the cofounder and executive chair of TPG; and Felix Baker, a cofounder of Baker Brothers Advisors.

Yang didn't end his statement there, though. "I also want to note," Yang wrote, "that since President Tessier-Lavigne's appointment in 2016, he has effectively led the university with integrity and honor." I knew immediately that wouldn't go over well. Announcing an investigation into scientific integrity by praising the integrity of the investigation's subject sounded an awful lot like prejudging the outcome.

The sleuths were certainly skeptical. "I can tell you right now," Nancy Olivieri, a well-known whistleblower, told me. "I recognize the pattern because it happens all the time. They're going to have an internal, non-expert, conflicted, confidential investigation, and then guess what?" Nothing.

WHEN I STARTED LOOKING INTO THE BOARD MEMBERS NAMED TO THE investigating committee, I noticed that Felix Baker appeared to be the only person on the committee with any kind of scientific background, having received a PhD in immunology from Stanford, and that his investment firm, which he founded with his brother, was particularly secretive. It didn't have a website, and as Bloomberg noted, "information about its founders and performance is hard to come by." Especially because "the brothers assiduously avoid the press." Great.

I began scrolling through the investment firm's filings at the Securities and Exchange Commission. Sitting in the library, as a couple of students not so subtly made out in the stacks a few rows over, I discovered that Baker Brothers Advisors maintained an $18 million investment in Denali Therapeutics, the company that Tessier-Lavigne had cofounded in 2015, remained on the board of, and in which he was deeply financially involved. Why on earth would the board put Baker on the committee with such an obvious financial tie to the subject of the investigation? Had he divulged this and been allowed to serve anyway? Or were they all so interconnected they didn't even bother to consider conflicts of interest? Did they think nearly $20 million was too paltry a sum to matter? For an investigation less than a week old and already plagued by doubters, this wasn't a good look.

I emailed Stanford's communications office about Baker's investment. As usual, they didn't respond. Then, the next day, a message landed in my inbox from an unknown sender: Aidan Ryan, a crisis communications executive at Edelman, one of the most powerful public relations firms in the world. Stanford's board had hired Edelman to take over communications about the investigation, Ryan told me, and he would be my liaison.

Immediately, I could see that Ryan took a very different approach to his job than Stanford's in-house team. "Feel free to email me anytime and we'll do our best to get you what we can," he wrote. Unlike the Stanford team, which often ignored my emails and which had never once agreed to an interview or even a phone conversation, Ryan understood that the best way to have your perspective represented in a piece is to engage the writer. He offered me an embargo on the release of the committee's next statement, whenever that would come.

An embargo is an agreement in which a source gives information in advance to a reporter who promises not to publish until a specified time. This gives reporters extra time to prepare their stories instead of having to react instantly upon receiving a statement. It often works out better for the institution issuing the statement, too, since reporters are likely to be more accurate and write better stories when they aren't rushing to meet a deadline.

Ryan's email also informed me that "the Board and its Special Committee wanted to make sure you knew that—to avoid any question of potential conflicts—Dr. Felix Baker has requested that the committee proceed without him as a member." Jesus, okay, I thought. Here was exactly the reason not to let up on the gas.

I asked Ryan some natural follow-up questions. When did Baker step off? Were questions of potential conflicts of interest raised before the committee was appointed? Would he be replaced? While Ryan at least gave me the courtesy of replying, he didn't answer any of my queries.

Meanwhile, another alleged manipulation, this time in a 2003 *Nature* paper for which Tessier-Lavigne was a coauthor, had been uncovered by another sleuth, who emailed me with the finding. The analysts I'd been working with had missed it, but, once alerted to the offending panel, were adamant: "This one is very significant," said one. Bryon Hughson, the researcher who'd identified the image, explained that his analysis "indicates that not only were two separate blots copied and pasted within the same published image, but that the positioning and brightness/contrast of these blots were modified so as to conceal the fact they are copies. This indicates an intent to deceive readers."

As I typed up my article, I heard back from Richard Smith, a respected former editor in chief of the British Medical Association's *BMJ* journal I'd asked to comment on the investigation. He responded to my questions, then added a comment that stunned me:

"It would be wise of the president to step aside while the investigation is underway."

At this point, I'd given up on heap allocator, my CS107 assignment. I ended up writing seven articles that week about the widening scandal. I couldn't stop. I was obsessed.

Soon, it wasn't just Smith publicly urging Tessier-Lavigne to step aside. One senior Stanford Linear Accelerator Center scientist, David Chassin, confessed that "this story is evolving in ways that make me question my decision to come to Stanford and SLAC to conduct my research in the first place." He continued, "Had the research been conducted at SLAC I imagine we would already be processing MTL's paperwork for dismissal for cause. . . . The credibility of the entire institution is at stake and it should be painfully obvious to all that his personal privilege is subordinated to that of the organization he leads." Others at Stanford agreed. "There's too much at stake," a senior administrator told me, although they did not want to be named. "It would strengthen the perceived credibility of the investigation" if MTL stepped down, a celebrated Stanford scientist added.

Still, there was little direct evidence to tie Tessier-Lavigne to wrongdoing. I couldn't really imagine him falsifying the data himself—and nobody of any consequence had accused him of that. The questions were instead about his oversight of the researchers who worked for him in his labs—and how he responded once questions were initially raised years ago. As the saying goes, "It's not the crime, it's the cover-up." Was there a cover-up?

Aidan Ryan dipped into my inbox again a few days later to announce that the board had hired the powerhouse law firm Kirkland & Ellis to conduct its review. Kirkland is the largest law firm in the world by revenue and maintains a somewhat ruthless reputation; it also has some undeniably excellent lawyers, and the one Stanford picked, Mark Filip, came highly recommended. Filip, who had served as a clerk to Supreme Court Justice Antonin Scalia, was a former federal judge and deputy attorney general during George W. Bush's presidency.

Filip maintained a generally positive reputation, as far as I could tell upon quick inspection. Nevertheless, a look at his résumé left me with questions. At the Justice Department, Filip had reversed previous policy to rein in prosecutors going after white-collar crime (his new rules were known in the legal field as the "Filip Factors"). After leaving the Justice Department for private practice, Filip represented BP in litigation over its disastrous Deepwater Horizon spill, which killed eleven people and released 134 million gallons of oil into the Gulf of Mexico. He represented Goldman Sachs after it was charged for its role in laundering billions of stolen dollars in Malaysia (called "the world's biggest financial scandal" in *The Guardian*). He represented JPMorgan Chase after it was sued for market manipulation. And he orchestrated a deal for Boeing after crashes of its 737 Maxes, allowing senior management to get off the hook entirely. (*New York* magazine's headline: BOEING SETTLED 737 MAX CASE FOR ALMOST NOTHING.)

Filip was clearly talented at protecting his clients' interests. What interests would he be protecting in this case? Was Filip's job to get Stanford off the hook as much as possible? Or would he really dig in and report his findings?

When I next spoke with Aidan Ryan, he told me the board would not commit to releasing Filip's findings. In fact, Ryan made clear that Filip had no timeline, no prescribed budget, and no precise mandate.

TESSIER-LAVIGNE WASN'T GOING TO WAIT FOR THE RESULTS OF THE investigation to assert his innocence. He wanted to defend himself, although he didn't want to face public questions from me or anyone else. "MTL felt it was beneath him," one person who spoke with him at the time would later tell me. In the days after my first article about his research, several advisers had urged him to sit down for an interview. He refused. Instead, he began to plead his case directly in the court of public opinion.

Tessier-Lavigne created a web page on his official lab website to address the allegations. Rather than responding to me directly, he would use this site to rebut and deny. And, to ensure he was heard, he would deliver his missives directly to the faculty from the official Stanford presidential email account. As a scientist "dedicated to the rigorous pursuit of the truth," Tessier-Lavigne wrote, he wanted light to "be shed in full on these matters." Over the next eight months, I would ask dozens of questions of Tessier-Lavigne; never did the president directly respond. Instead, he tried to control the narrative, ultimately publishing more than 10,500 words in responses to my articles on his Stanford .edu website.

I was surprised by this strategy initially, as were some academic observers. I was surprised, too, that it took him so long to persuade people to come forward to defend him on the record. It was nearly a month before an op-ed submitted by fellow Stanford scientists would "urge caution in rushing to judgment," reminding the community that Tessier-Lavigne was, after all, a giant in his field. The op-ed was published on the opinion side of *The Stanford Daily* (approved by Sam) and signed by seven authors who described themselves as "Stanford faculty members who conduct biological and biomedical research." They didn't mention any personal connection to Tessier-Lavigne.

But I later learned the letter had been orchestrated by Susan McConnell; she and her husband, Richard Scheller, were among Tessier-Lavigne's closest friends. McConnell had drafted Tessier-Lavigne to Stanford in the first place two decades earlier, when he started a lab and co-taught a course with her. Two years later, Scheller had been the one to recruit Tessier-Lavigne away from Stanford to Genentech, where he served as chief research officer. McConnell and Scheller lived a block from Tessier-Lavigne and his wife, Mary Hynes, and they frequently socialized. After my first article came out, they began to coordinate a strategy. Scheller worked behind the scenes while McConnell shopped around an early draft of an op-ed that was far more strongly worded in Tessier-Lavigne's defense than the version that ultimately came out, which focused more narrowly on urging due process before judgment.

Most of the signatories were in Tessier-Lavigne's tight scientific orbit—not exactly independent observers.

The quarter ended and I went on vacation, but my work didn't stop. There was too much news.

On December 15, *Science* and *Cell* placed Editorial Expressions of Concern on several Tessier-Lavigne papers. These warnings officially notified readers that the validity of data was under question, and undercut MTL's defense that any inadvertent errors had not affected the overall integrity of the papers.

The joint notices had been spearheaded by Holden Thorp, the *Science* editor who'd pushed other journals to mark the papers, too. This was to Thorp's immense credit. Journals have historically been reluctant to confront misconduct allegations and bear significant responsibility in allowing fraudulent research to pollute the scientific record. *Science* had failed to address the issues in two of Tessier-Lavigne's papers in 2015, and Thorp was determined at least to notify the public that concerns existed, while deferring to the Stanford investigation to determine next steps.

In an interview, Thorp told me "retraction is absolutely on the table," the first official acknowledgment of the severity of the allegations.

As the story widened, my obsession was cemented. Thorp's first email to me had torn me from CS107, and I'd never looked back. I didn't even attempt Heap Allocator. It was the first time in my life I'd done such a thing—and my grade in the class, on track for an A, came in at only a B-minus, the lowest I'd ever received. This was what I'd come to Stanford expecting to be my primary focus, and yet I couldn't bring myself to care. My first term completed, reporting for the paper now felt more important.

HOLIDAY SEASON WOULD BE TOUGH. I'D ALWAYS SPENT CHRISTMAS AT the redbrick New Jersey suburban house where my mom grew up. But this year it was only a few months since my grandfather had died, and no one was prepared to do that again. Instead, we planned a trip as far away as we could reasonably stomach, keeping to the sun-soaked West Coast. Nana and I played tennis every day, recalling my long matches with Gramps until just six months before he died.

One morning, stopping for a water break during an intense back-and-forth with a better player, I received a note revealing that a $29.2 million payment had just been made by a Stanford professor to fulfill a judgment in a civil fraud suit. Sure that other publications had received the same information, and feeling the same competitive rush all journalists feel to break the news first, I darted off the court and began typing a story based on court documents right away. Soon, I sent my editors a brief breaking-news item, a placeholder that could go up while I worked on the full story. Sam published it right away, scooping the news. Within hours, a complete piece was on the web. My parents sat on the beach, soaking in the sea breeze; I locked myself in the hotel room, seeking more information. I liked chasing a story. And this one turned out to be very interesting.

PERHAPS THE GREATEST, IF NOT FULLY APPRECIATED, KEY TO STANford's ascension has been its approach to intellectual property. Stanford encourages entrepreneurial activity by its faculty and students, then rakes in revenue from their discoveries, deliberately cultivating the no-borders relationship with Silicon Valley that has led to its unique rise.

And the man who prompted this approach was a professor named Stan Cohen.

Cohen was a Big Fucking Deal. He'd been the first geneticist to transplant genes from one living organism to another, before arguably jump-starting Stanford's entire modern research enterprise. Together with a scientist named Herb Boyer, Cohen had invented recombinant DNA technology, the first tool that allowed scientists to edit, transfer, and study genes on a wide scale. This was revolutionary. Stanford filed for a patent in 1974, and in 1976, Boyer cofounded a company to take advantage of the tool and develop drugs. He called it Genentech.

Genentech is widely regarded as the world's first biotechnology company. Boyer and others—including Richard Scheller, the MTL friend who left graduate school after just two months to become employee number five—managed to upend scientific wisdom, and utilized the patent they'd licensed from Stanford to create artificial insulin for the first time. It was a spectacular success, giving rise to an entire industry—and, through Cohen, transforming Stanford.

Stanford's leadership crafted a novel licensing strategy to profit from Cohen's research while still allowing it to proliferate widely. At the time, other universities typically avoided patenting research, especially basic research like the recombinant DNA discovery. Stanford's new approach was deeply controversial; now researchers cite its novel patent structure as the "gold standard." In the seventeen years the patent was active, Stanford garnered hundreds of millions of dollars from Cohen's invention. By 1997, the final year the patent was active, it accounted for 62 percent of Stanford's total patent income. The money, and the new strategy that radically expanded the way universities could profit from discoveries made by their faculty, allowed Stanford to substantially expand its research wing.

Over the decades, Cohen continued to serve on Stanford's faculty, conducting research and reigning as one of its preeminent figures. In 2016, he told investors about another major discovery: He knew how to treat Huntington's disease. In fact, he was founding a company that, in internal documents, declared its aim "to develop a cure, not a therapy." Cohen said he would be able to start a clinical trial in less than a year. This was, to say the least, incredible. Huntington's is a fatal neurodegenerative disease with no known cure, characterized by brutal, unrelenting decline in motor and cognitive abilities. A cure would be worth billions. In 2024, Novartis paid nearly $3 billion for a drug that provided only modest improvement.

Cohen told investors that his research had found the gene that caused the degeneration suffered by the victims of Huntington's, and he'd identified a compound he called HD106 that would pass the blood-brain barrier and attack the offending gene. Even better, he said, HD106 had already been approved by the FDA in the 1970s for treating a different condition. This meant Cohen could skip the costly, yearslong process that would normally precede a clinical trial. Developing a drug is notoriously difficult; the preclinical toxicology and animal studies required before running a clinical trial for a drug candidate typically take years and millions of dollars. Cohen didn't need all those tests, he told investors, because he had an assay that would prove the efficacy of the drug target and allow them to speed-run the process.

It was bullshit. HD106 was not a cure for Huntington's. Nor would there be a clinical trial in 2017. Nor would there be a clinical trial ever. In fact, while Cohen had touted the drug's approval by the FDA in securing financing from Moshe Alafi and his son Chris, who invested $20 million, the Stanford superstar had neglected to mention that the FDA had withdrawn its approval in 1976 after the drug caused loss of limbs and death. The drug was placed permanently on the FDA's "DO NOT COMPOUND" list.

The resulting four-year lawsuit was a painful slog. Cohen, a "world-renowned pioneer," as his lawyers described him, hadn't defrauded just any investors: The Alafis were close friends of his. Moshe Alafi and Cohen had spent years supporting each other, even visiting each other in the hospital. They lived nearby and often observed the Yom Kippur holiday together. But when Cohen went into business with the Alafis' cash, things got ugly. The lawsuit was a personal tragedy as much as a tale of deceit.

Cohen, it came out during the lawsuit, had been cheating on his wife as she lay dying of cancer, and appointed his paramour to a lucrative position at his new company while also employing her in his Stanford lab. He hadn't disclosed his relationship with the woman to either his company or Stanford. In fact, he took measures to conceal it, and the hundreds of thousands of dollars he siphoned from the company to pay her. At every step when concerns were raised, Cohen had obfuscated. He'd had the first CEO of the company fired and attempted to run the company himself while still operating his Stanford lab. When a board member raised concerns about the company having no CEO, no chief scientist, no chief medical officer, and few other experienced scientists to aid with the drug development, Cohen fired him. And when Cohen eventually admitted that the HD106 target would never go anywhere, he proposed to dissolve the company and pocket the remaining $13 million of the investment.

The Alafis sued and eventually won, with Cohen found liable for "a species of actual fraud . . . and deceit" by a California judge. It had been a trying battle, and Cohen had fought tooth and nail. At one point—over the key question of what Cohen had disclosed and what he had omitted—Cohen gave false testimony, claiming that he had informed Chris Alafi of the FDA ban while soliciting the investment. Under further questioning, he admitted this was untrue. Cohen "was not credible regarding his conversations with [the Alafis] prior to the initial investment," the judge wrote.

While the judge did not conclude that Cohen had intentionally misled the Alafis, she did find him responsible for "negligent misrepresentation" and imposed a judgment totaling $29 million, which, when I caught wind of the story in late December 2022, had just been paid out.

Despite Cohen's fame and achievement, the story had never been reported—a common occurrence at Stanford and in Silicon Valley for misconduct allegations. I went to the university for comment on whether Cohen would face any repercussions. The communications team responded that "the university was not aware of this lawsuit and was never a party to it" and refused to answer questions.

Their claim, like Cohen's during the trial, was untrue.

Stanford had, indeed, been aware of the lawsuit. It owned the intellectual property at issue, had been subpoenaed in the case, fought the subpoena, and ultimately provided numerous documents and several witnesses. Why the communications team hadn't bothered to check on that before responding was beyond me. Perhaps Stanford wasn't used to being fact-checked.

Cohen faced no known consequences from the university for his role in the fraudulent company, even though it originated from research done in Stanford labs. Cohen had not only behaved unethically in his business venture, according to the court judgment, he'd admitted to potential violations of the university's rules on sexual and romantic relationships and involvement with external companies. But the university, so quick to trumpet the great advances that occur on its grounds, seemed far more hesitant to address the misconduct of its faculty.

When I confronted the spokespeople about their false statement, they admitted it was wrong and apologized. But when I asked whether Cohen would face any punishment or whether they condemned his conduct, then and on several subsequent occasions over the next year, there was nothing but silence.

THE DAY AFTER CHRISTMAS, COHEN'S HIGH-POWERED CORPORATE ATTORNEYS sent a threatening letter to Sam and me accusing us of "defamation" and "character assassination" for publishing an article about the case. Thankfully, they had no ground to stand on, and *The Daily*'s lawyers politely told them to back down.

I was still a couple of weeks short of my eighteenth birthday, and it was the first time I'd received a legal threat. But it didn't shake me from my increasing journalistic compulsion.

On Christmas Day, my parents had found me awake earlier than usual, pacing and muttering like a madman. "How do I get inside Genentech? How do I get inside Genentech?"

An anonymous letter had shown up at my door just before I left for break, hinting at an incident of apparent research misconduct at the company, an incident that Tessier-Lavigne had supposedly been instrumental in keeping quiet. If I could prove it, this might be the biggest break yet in the whole MTL saga, tying him more directly than previously known to alleged scientific wrongdoing.

My parents were sympathetic, but they dragged me back to the family, where my shrieking little cousins were eagerly tearing through wrapping paper, delighted by each new present. My family prodded me to open one of my own and I picked a small package—socks—before unwrapping another.

It was a custom-made T-shirt that my parents had ordered. On it was emblazoned a quote from a family friend, himself an experienced investigative journalist, who texted them with delight upon seeing my MTL reporting: "Theo Baker is a fucking menace!"

Yes, I thought, and I wasn't ready to let up anytime soon.

CHAPTER 6

RULE

"We're here to kidnap you," Derek said as he rolled down the window of his Tesla. I laughed and Derek flung open the door. "Come on, let's give you the tour!"

Derek was a classic Silicon Valley success story, a man who achieved what so many Stanford students dream of: He was a Unicorn founder. In Silicon Valley parlance, a Unicorn is a startup that reaches a valuation of $1 billion or more. Founding one means instant cachet (especially if, like Derek, you've dropped out of college). Despite the overwhelming number of startups that are pitched and funded every day, vanishingly few reach that height: One Stanford study found that the probability of a company growing from seed funding to Unicorn status was just 0.5 percent.* Now, Derek was going to show me how the world he'd conquered really worked.

I didn't know Derek well. This was our first meal together, to be held at one of Silicon Valley's iconic locations, the Rosewood Hotel, where the starting price for a night's stay is four figures. The Rosewood, which

*Meanwhile, another Stanford study found that 17 percent of *all* Unicorns in the US were founded by Stanford alumni or faculty.

markets itself as "the modern clubhouse for Silicon Valley," is a go-to spot for meetings and the tech world's wining and dining, in part because it sits directly on Sand Hill Road, the headquarters for many of the most powerful venture capital firms, on land owned by Stanford. Derek had proposed the Rosewood as a necessary experience for me to have, and planned to show me Sand Hill afterward.

Why he was doing all of this was a bit of a mystery to me, at least at first. Derek had reached out via cold email just a few months into my freshman year, asking if we could meet. While ostensibly his job was running a company, he told me, "my secret job is working with interesting people." He was a scout, constantly on the lookout for anyone of use. An adult version of Ivan, the Coupa Circuit fixer.

I took Derek in during the short drive to the Rosewood. He was in his late thirties, tall and self-assured, with a pronounced Adam's apple that journeyed up and down every time he began a sentence. He was funny and solicitous, never talking down to me. He wanted to know what I thought of Stanford and its people.

To my surprise, Derek had added two guests to our meeting: Matthew, a state senator, and Gideon, Derek's nine-month-old son, who sat contentedly in a high chair at our table. Both were bald; both kept mostly quiet.

The scene was a bit ridiculous. We were sitting in the ornate dining room of the Rosewood, with polished marble and attentive waiters. But I was wearing a T-shirt and Derek a flannel shirt. Still, he seemed perfectly at ease, sitting back and enjoying the view.

I was struck by Derek's candor. He said he wanted to "build a political machine to take over San Francisco" and told me he viewed politics as a matter of "solving an engineering problem." He viewed higher education as "very corrupt," "clubby and flabby." Leaders, he said, didn't "have a very cogent view of what it means to have power."

I nodded and asked questions.

Derek fashioned himself as a polyglot, fluent in the languages of different fields. As a child, he'd been fascinated by the concept of ownership, obsessed with intellectual property. Instead of a sleepaway camp in the summer, Derek borrowed money from his grandmother to go to an intensive course in IP law. He'd discovered a love for tech in the early 2000s and quickly realized that traditional fields were slow to adapt to rapidly changing internet standards. Soon, he was hacking away with a group of like-minded people—"you were there because you were obsessed with it."

It was not entirely clear to me what Derek's company actually did, only that it was successful. He was business facing, and clients paid him lots of money. Derek would underscore this during our walk around the Sand Hill venture capital offices after we ate, dishing out gossip about the firms and their partners as we gawked in empty windows. For the epicenter of the future, I was struck by what a banal place Sand Hill Road was: a bunch of boring strip-mall offices whose apparent main advantage was proximity to Stanford down the hill.

What I remembered most about the afternoon was what Derek told me about his willingness to get ahead, admitting that the first contract his new company had received was to provide tech services for the brutal Libyan dictator Muammar el-Qaddafi. This was said with a smile. He was a startup founder. He did what he had to do.

Toward the end of our lunch, Derek looked over at Gideon, who was wriggling in his chair. He adoringly placed the nine-month-old on his lap. As if struck with the perfect idea, Derek turned to his son. "Do you want to try caviar?" The child, maybe a month or two into eating solid food of any kind, didn't respond. "Open wide," Derek said, while spoon-feeding Gideon black pearls of Rosewood Private Batch Caviar.

This was the world I was giving up.

I'D SAT DOWN FOR MY INTERVIEW WITH JUSTIN, THE HOW TO RULE THE World professor, the same week I broke the first MTL story. The timing couldn't have been much worse. I was in the hot seat reporting, facing the Heap Allocator assignment I ultimately never attempted, and about as sleep deprived as one could be.

I was also going through an existential crisis.

For so long, I'd had a plan: Stanford, technology, building, progress. The MTL investigation had upended all of that.

Justin asked me about my greatest ambitions in life, and I knew what I was supposed to say. I knew he wanted me to talk about starting a company. I knew I was supposed to dream about creating an entirely new sector or "owning this space." I knew the path to "making the world a better place" was supposed to be through entrepreneurship.

"At age eighty, what would cause you to look back and consider your life successful?" Justin asked.

I couldn't answer.

For the first time in my life, I had no clue what I wanted. I didn't know what my ambitions were. Just a few weeks after my TreeHacks interview—when I'd felt perfectly comfortable summoning visions of techno-advancement—I could no longer bring myself to voice familiar lines, and I floundered.

Justin texted me his decision after the interview: "Unfortunately, I can't offer you a spot in the cohort this quarter."

I wasn't cut out to be a Ruler. Instead, I had a new role. To observe.

FOR THE STANFORD INSIDE STANFORD—FOR THE CHOSEN STUDENTS selected for the fast pass to success and status—access is easy. People like Derek find *you*, not the other way around.

A study once determined that VCs fund only one company for every hundred they review. Not so for Stanford's undergraduate elite. VCs seek out this network aggressively, even employing older students as talent spotters. Reputation is everything.

"There are so many different people outside of Stanford trying to network with Stanford students," an accomplished friend once reflected. "Someone could live here for a year without a meal plan, just eating off of free VC dinners," another told me. This was no exaggeration. Once you're in with the right crowd, all sorts of invitations start showing up. "Any VC is begging to shove money down our throat," still another friend, one who took VC money for a startup, said in amazement. Another funded undergrad explained that with the "right résumé" as a company founder, "being in SF is like being a pretty girl in New York: People want to take you out for dinner every single night."

Whole firms have been started with the aim of recruiting and funding Stanford students—the younger the better. Some firms explicitly ask only for freshmen and sophomores. "Our bread and butter is young students," a VC explained to me once while promising a small group of Stanford freshmen and sophomores that if we ever had ideas, their firm would help us out.

It used to be that an early round of investment called a Series A was the first real step in financing your startup. Then investors began obsessing over "seed funding," putting in money even earlier in exchange for a higher stake in a company. Now, early-stage VCs and investors offer "pre-seed funding," often in the form of a SAFE (Simple Agreement for Future Equity) check, a strategy pioneered in 2013 by the famed startup accelerator Y Combinator. As opposed to a typical investment, where firms take a chunk of a company in exchange for their cash, SAFE checks guarantee the VC only the right to buy equity in the future, should a company succeed. If the company fails, a SAFE check never has to be repaid.

The newest new thing by the time I showed up at Stanford was something called *pre-idea* funding. Yup, if you have the right pedigree, the VCs will offer you money without so much as a glimmering of a possible startup in mind. Some Stanford insiders are emailed term sheets by VCs to start whatever company they might want to start—despite never having pitched the investors. (I later received a similar offer myself, with an implied seven-figure commitment, but did not pursue it.)

With the AI boom, getting cash only became easier.

THOSE DESPERATE TO TAP INTO THE STANFORD NETWORK HAVE HAD to become cleverer about how they go after students. Some investors seem to spend more time on campus hanging out with kids—often at the infamous Coupa Café—than with their own families. And an array of increasingly lucrative perks have been dangled in front of students identified as Builders.

Students are often put up in lavish mansions, referred to as "Hacker Houses," although the term can apply to a wide range of accommodations. Summer programs—like the Neo Accelerator/Neo Scholars program or PearX—bring together talented students and give them access to resources and mentors as they work on projects. For these programs, some of which also fork over decent sums directly to those accepted, the promise usually revolves around the tight networks that emerge from the experience. Some of these fellowships explicitly take only Stanford students; others include a few outsiders, usually from MIT or Berkeley. Students have been invited to spend entire summers on yachts or secluded ranches.

Things move quickly. The longer a suitor waits, the likelier the talent will go elsewhere. One friend recalled attending a party with former classmates and chatting with an insider who'd gone to a fast-rising Silicon Valley darling. "Hey, you should consider coming to work with me," the guy said. My friend answered noncommittally. Three days later, he was having coffee with the CEO of the $150 billion–plus company, offered a minimum six-hundred-thousand-dollar salary if he dropped out. He was caught up in the rush. "I felt like I was being swept off my feet," he said. Soon, though, he concluded that the company was shady and turned down the offer. A number of our mutual friends didn't. One by one, they were convinced to drop out and get going. "That's how they recruit," my friend said. "They're assassins."

TO GAIN ACCESS TO UP-AND-COMING TALENT, VC FIRMS ADVERTISE "investing in relationships," often making bizarre pitches to differentiate themselves. Why choose our venture fund? one firm asks. "Dogs have many traits that can be useful at different times . . ." begins the answer. As the first line of its pitch, another firm states: "We talk about how $1B Thunder Lizards are hatched from atomic eggs . . ."

It comes down to a calculus of talent. "Stanford students are much better than anywhere else," Ann Miura-Ko told me. The founder of a VC fund and early backer of companies such as Twitter, Lyft, and Twitch, Miura-Ko began teaching a class at Stanford a few years ago, in part because she would get to know young founders. "I look for super-builders and super-thinkers," she said. And her firm can help them start.

Miura-Ko is impressive. She founded her firm while pregnant and gave her thesis defense six weeks after delivering her baby. People who have gone through her ultra-exclusive Mayfield Fellows program—limited to twelve Stanford students a year—describe her as creative and supportive.

Other investors playing the same game have shadier reputations. One firm is notorious for taking advantage of students, with its founder widely rumored to have raped a young woman. Another firm is run by a man whose volcanic temper is much discussed, and whose vindictive side is an open secret. But nobody ever says anything on the record. Said a fellow VC, "He's protected by the fact that his targets are generally college age, so they don't want to risk their careers." Another company that works exclusively with students and brags about taking no equity and giving money "with no strings attached" is widely viewed as a scam. As an employee of the venture told me, "It's a bullshit factory."

But all of these investors are competing for the attention of the same small group of people.

ACCESS TO THE STANFORD INSIDE STANFORD HAS LITTLE TO DO WITH talent. “It’s totally just vibes,” Boris, an exceedingly networked student, told me once. “You sort of join it freshman year or you don’t.” Again and again, well-placed students echoed this. People “can be like, ‘Oh, I know Alexei, he’s a smart engineer,’ so whoever is receiving that message won’t do the due diligence all the way back,” a student who cofounded a company with a famous entrepreneur three decades his senior told me. “Once you have the trust of one of them, suddenly you have the trust of all of them, because you ask this one to recommend you to that one and you just keep going.” As another student reflected, “You’re treated like royalty if you say the right things.” It’s a closed system, opaque to those who aren’t in the club. You have to make a name for yourself. You have to be someone like Amber Yang.

Amber made the *Forbes* list of 30 Under 30 at age eighteen and had VCs chasing her practically from the moment she arrived on campus. Amber had developed promising technology to address the problem of space junk. Her algorithms could predict the future position of debris with 98 percent accuracy, far better than state-of-the-art NASA models.

“When you’re eighteen and you have that amount of attention, you sort of feel like you don’t have a choice but to say yes,” Amber told me. She felt herself getting sucked in. “I struggled a lot with figuring out what I really wanted versus how people saw me.” She felt like she was going to be trapped before she was even sure whether it was what she wanted to work on. But to say no made her think, “Oh, my God, I’m letting so many people down.”

Unlike so many others, Amber did stake her own path, even turning down the Thiel Fellowship, the program started by Peter Thiel that pays two hundred thousand dollars to students under the age of twenty-two to drop out of college. The Thiel Fellowship allegedly boasts an admissions rate of less than 0.1 percent; for Amber to pass it up was almost unthinkable. She took advantage of the Stanford inside Stanford and made it out the other end without being locked into a yearslong commitment; she had the foresight to see the glitz and glam and instead choose patience, continuing with school long enough to actually discover her interests. Few people in her position can do that.

For Amber, Stanford was a world of opportunity—"I love the Valley, I love Stanford, and I'm, like, the biggest proponent of it," she stressed over coffee one day. But it had shocked her.

She recounted the story of a club she'd helped a friend start. "It was called No Filter, and we would invite a tech CEO to come in every week to a group of thirty people." With access limited, and confidentiality rules in place, No Filter turned into one of those groups on campus where insiders congregate. Noor, a friend of hers who did accept a Thiel Fellowship, "brought in all these people she knew through Thiel," and, because they were an in-demand cohort, VCs willingly paid for Amber and her friend's social club. "There were a few VCs who would just give us—and to them, it was nothing—but they gave us twenty thousand dollars for the quarter to just go out to dinners, and then we'd meet with the VCs." Now Noor runs a company that lets you select what genes you want your child to have. "Sex is for fun," as she puts it. "Embryo screening is for babies."

Most Stanford students don't have the experience Amber and Noor did. No Filter doesn't easily appear in a Google search, even if you know the name. Invite-only is the standard for it and other similar groups. Amber, who eventually chose to become a venture capitalist herself, explained that "from the outside, everyone's looking in and they're like, 'Oh, this person got that job because they're just really great, and it's meritocratic.' And that's what Silicon Valley tells everyone, that it's meritocratic, right? That's not the case." Success, she told me, is about "knowing the right person and being connected in a very specific way."

I WASN'T SURE ABOUT MY OWN PLACE IN THE STANFORD INSIDE Stanford.

TreeHacks was preparing for its big weekend event in mid-February, but I'd gotten so sucked into reporting that I'd been of no real use fundraising. In some ways, I was an active liability. One of the other saplings on the sponsorship team forwarded me an email from a company that had declined to fund the hackathon, saying, "How can Stanford be taken seriously now that its President is under investigation over allegations that he doctored data and images?"

I was still on the list for things, receiving emails with subject lines such as "Private island hackathon—you're invited!" or "HC Fellowship: Up to $250k no strings attached to build." But I was one step removed from the real action.

This crystallized for me one day while returning to campus from lunch with Jesse, one of the people who'd referred me to the How to Rule the World class. We ran into a friend of his.

"Theo, I want you to meet Mischa," said Jesse. "We were in Rule together."

Everyone in the ultra-exclusive How to Rule the World class called it "Rule," and, by introducing me with this secret code word, Jesse intimated that I was in the know.

"Ah, so you're Rule-adjacent," Mischa said, giving me a handshake.

And that was exactly right. I was close enough to know it existed, meaning I possessed a status signifier among the most insider-y of the insider crowd. Yet I couldn't access it myself.

So what if I had?

HOW TO RULE THE WORLD ACCEPTED JUST TWELVE PEOPLE A YEAR. I wanted to figure out what it was like. Eventually, I would convince six Rulers to tell me about their experience.

The first thing I learned was that the class revolved around its despot.

To talk about Rule was to talk about Justin, the egomaniacal CEO who styled himself a professor. His company, like his class, was largely private, focused on the lucrative world of business sales rather than consumer marketing. "Justin looked up a list of the white-collar jobs employing the most people and went after them," one of his students told me. Automation was his bread and butter, imposing ruthless Silicon Valley efficiency on retrograde industries.

He was successful, if hesitant to divulge many details. His company was valued at ten-figures-plus; he told students that he employed people in thirty-five states and was chauffeured wherever he went. Once, he supposedly had sushi flown in on a helicopter. Then again, maybe not. It was hard to tell where the stories ended and the man began. This was an allure he cultivated deliberately, attempting to seem above it all. Justin was also a certified sommelier, a believer in "sexual transmutation," and a self-described "solver of worthy problems."

Early in his Silicon Valley career, while building his first startup, a space-focused venture, Justin had had a falling-out with an influential VC that seemed to color his worldview. Details were hard to come by, but the gist of the story was that Justin and the VC fought because Justin was considering letting another VC lead his next fundraising round. Instead of merely pulling his money, the VC went out of his way to screw over Justin, blacklisting him with other investors and starving the company of cash. After this, Justin "fell into a hole of loneliness," one of his confidants said. Already brash and self-confident, he became "extremely sociopathic," as the confidant put it, and intent on getting what he wanted no matter who stood in his way.

Rule was one way of doing that.

IN PERSON, JUSTIN COULD BE OFF-PUTTING. "HE'S A PRETTY QUIRKY guy," one student said. "His mannerisms are off." As I had seen firsthand,

Justin stares intently at you, eyes unwavering. Perhaps it's a strategy to break you.

Justin was looking for people with "agency," people who betrayed an "action bias." People who actually did things. He betrayed no discomfort asking people he'd just met to discuss their deepest, darkest secrets. He wanted to know about their middle school experiences, their mental frameworks for life, their hobbies.

"I've never been grilled like that in my entire life," said one Ruler.

Idiosyncratic as he was, Justin could also be oddly magnetic. "He commands a room, even though he's not physically imposing," one student recalled. Although a number of the Rulers I spoke to seemed to understand that the class was "insane"—their word, not mine—they couldn't help wanting to be a part of it. He "preyed on our desire for exclusivity," one recalled. Justin, by shrouding himself in mystery, made Rule impossible to resist for the strivers who really did want to rule the world.

THE AURA OF SECRECY MADE IT DESIRABLE; STANFORD'S BEST AND brightest were applying for something even though they had no idea what exactly it was. One student recalled being unable to learn a thing about the course before passing the entrance exam, even from the friend who had referred him. His friend had said, "'Oh, I think you should meet this guy who taught this class that I was in last quarter, and it's super interesting.' I asked for more information. I got nothing."

This, too, had been my experience.

Justin told me he spent eight hours teaching and ninety hours selecting who would be in Rule any given year. It was all about access. Justin was playing the same game as all the other Hangers-On—he'd just found a more creative and effective way of doing it.

The students picked up on this. Janet, who had been in Rule the year before I came to Stanford, told me she eventually concluded that the class's main objective was not so much instruction as selection. "The purpose of Rule," she said, "is to separate who was in and who was out."

TO BE FAIR, JUSTIN DID PICK INTERESTING PEOPLE.

"Everyone was very sharp. *Very* sharp," one student, who didn't otherwise love the class, stressed. The cohort my year included freshmen and sophomores personally funded by Sam Altman or Peter Thiel. Some wanted to "solve aging." Several were in defense tech, working on secret projects with contracts from the government or major companies. Some worked on climate change. One had already started a string of robotics companies and earned a display in a museum. Others worked on commodities trading. Another was Phoebe Gates—daughter of Bill and Melinda—who made her name as a prominent sustainability advocate and cofounded a company with her Stanford roommate.* Together, as undergraduates, they'd already collectively raised millions of dollars for startups—and, of course, had done internships at every possible top company, from classic FAANG behemoths (Facebook, Apple, Amazon, Netflix, Google), to Jane Street, the quantitative trading firm that pays interns hundreds of thousands of dollars, to top-flight VCs.

Several people found the group daunting at first. "I felt an unsafe amount of impostor syndrome," Janet lamented, in part "because a lot of them already knew each other, and I kind of got added as a last-minute addition, maybe in part because they needed more women. I just remember being insanely intimidated by these people who had sold companies, who had run VCs, who had done all of these incredible things."

She didn't know that many of the others felt the same fear. Justin prized openness, sure, but also competitiveness.

Arjun, who was one of those serial startup founders, walked into the room and felt his breath rise in his chest. "I felt like the dumbest

*When I reached her, Phoebe Gates wrote that she "would rather not speak on the class."

person," he told me. "My impression of the people in that room was very much 'Oh yeah, these are people who are into some pretty insane stuff.'" (Arjun, to be clear, has never once been the dumbest person in a room.)

EACH WEEK DURING THE WINTER QUARTER, STUDENTS WOULD GATHER in a Stanford building overlooking the wide expanse of Lake Lagunita. Justin would bring a PowerPoint presentation and expound on the hidden path to success.

"The overriding theme of the class is to exceed the limits of your conceivable ambition," a Ruler named Billy told me. Justin would bring in a different topic each time, always coming back to the same core point: "For a select group of people—those with increased agency—a great amount of value can be extracted from the people around you."

He liked teaching about something called the "multipolar trap," the notion that "people who undercut in cost most always win," and how to avoid it. He also lectured on negotiation and "beating" your opponent.

While the class was billed as a discussion seminar, it was really The Justin Show. "Each class wound up being more of a lecture married to a Q and A than a seminar," one student recalled. And Justin expected rapt attention. He wouldn't allow phones in the classroom. Still, only a few listened intently; Justin's material, while argued fervently, was not all that original.

"It was a composite of a lot of frameworks I think are smart," Boris, one of Justin's bigger fans, said. "Some effective altruism, some stuff from Peter Thiel, some stuff from Paul Graham. He was explaining a very specific outlook on the world, which I think is characteristic of Silicon Valley around 2015." Much of it had to do with his concept of expected value, his guiding star for decision-making.

Billy explained Justin's thinking with an anecdote. Luxottica, a little-known Italian company, controls the eyewear industry. Ray-Ban, Oakley, Prada, Ralph Lauren, Armani, Bulgari, Chanel, Coach, Dolce & Gabbana, and more—Luxottica either owns them or manufactures their frames. In 2014, it controlled more than 80 percent of the major brands in the global eyeglasses industry. But Luxottica also owns the retailers—Sunglass Hut, LensCrafters, Glasses.com, Target Optical, Vision Express, and many others. And it owns eye doctors as well, through EyeMed, which proclaims itself "America's largest vision network." With consumers none the wiser, Luxottica uses this extensive portfolio to set prices. Markups can exceed 1,000 percent, with designer frames frequently costing more than five hundred dollars. Luxottica rakes in tens of billions of dollars a year.

"Under the Justin framework, that could be considered benevolent," Billy said. For Justin, "it doesn't matter how you get there if it's a net positive"—and "Luxottica helps people produce value by seeing." So yes, the Rulers were being taught one of the oldest themes in the world for those who are expected to be among life's biggest winners: The ends justify the means.

MANY OF JUSTIN'S CLASSES REVOLVED AROUND THE EXTRACTION OF value from others.

"He believes deeply that he can influence almost anyone to a great degree, a really great degree," one Ruler told me.

Janet took this to heart. "One of the big things I picked up is that there are ways to influence people where it doesn't seem inherently obvious that you're doing so." Justin taught her tactics—how to humor people, when to be self-deprecating, and so on. "There are things people do in conversation," Janet learned, "that seem super harmless and almost accidental, but they're not. They're actually pretty intentional, for getting somewhere, for framing a conversation a certain way, for getting them to make you feel really close to them." Justin had "thought through all those things—honestly kind of like a sociopath."

Janet was one of the believers. Justin, as everyone acknowledged, was polarizing: "You either love him or hate him" was a phrase I heard repeatedly. This was in part because he had "a very extremist view on a lot of things," said one Ruler. Justin "was very contrarian, very willing to say, 'Everyone is doing this and it's completely wrong.'" A few students became his mentees, frequently soliciting his advice. Carl, a sophomore, decided to "hole up for the summer and come up with a billion-dollar company" because of Justin.

Still, others were put off by him. Especially some of the women. Justin hit on several of his female pupils, fuzzing the boundary between older professor and peer, according to several students. Basically every person I spoke with, including Justin's defenders, acknowledged that he behaved weirdly around women.*

AFTER TAKING RULE—AND MAKING "SOME OF MY BEST FRIENDS"—Janet fashioned herself into one of the foremost Builders in her Stanford class. She cultivated an image of extreme competence, optimism, and ideological commitment to changing the world. And people loved it.

Bright and well connected, Janet learned to get her way. She persuaded a VC to pay for her and her friends to live in a $6 million mansion—a perk she branded as a "women in tech" venture. In her words, "with VCs, it's like you kind of are taught to lie," to present yourself as aligned with their interests. Soon, she dropped out of Stanford, raising a huge amount of money for a new startup. Janet had a glitzy launch. Invites went out via an AI voicemail to your phone. There was an ice sculpture, a second party, in Hollywood, with views across Los Angeles, praise from the top minds in Silicon Valley, a separate blowout birthday party (with her Rule friends) at another fabulous mansion offered up by an admiring tech figure. "The VCs, they identify two kids, maybe one kid, a year, and are like, 'This person is going to make a Unicorn,'" Janet said. "These people were like, 'Oh, you know, Janet's building a lot of cool things, yeah, she's putting them out in the world.'" Soon,

*Justin did not respond to requests for comments for this book.

she was being invited back to speak with Stanford classes about her success.

When Janet's startup launched, the polished demonstration video showcased incredible capabilities. The actual tech she'd developed could do none of it. Facing internal discontent, she fired her entire team and started over, this time without any Stanford kids who might've heard murmurs.

Janet had been riding high. The first check for her company had come from an angel investor the year before. "I literally biked to someone's office, and he—without even asking what my situation was, whether I was still in school, whether I'd raise [a fundraising round]—said, 'All right, here's your term sheet.'" She had the reputation, she told me, and knew it "wasn't fair," but why not go for it?

Janet's reputation was inflated, according to friends, coworkers, and fellow Builders who privately expressed concerns while publicly lauding her. She'd raised money off the premise that she was an exceptional coder, more talented than nearly anyone else at Stanford, but a friend told me that Janet had struggled in the core computer science curriculum. In one class, Janet had faced an honor code sanction after turning in an assignment that was identical to another student's. (Cheating in CS classes is rampant, but falling under suspicion for it is rare. Of the dozen or so cases of blatant cheating I witnessed in CS classes, not one was flagged.)

Janet had come to Stanford with chutzpah, smarts, and what I believe to be a genuine commitment to innovation. She bemoaned the many fakers who sought only money, and was a true worshipper of tech. But, in Rule and elsewhere, Janet learned how to play the game as successfully as any other. She learned to cut corners. An East Coaster, she grew apart from her family. They thought Stanford "completely changed me," Janet said. Her priorities were no longer theirs. "They're different from me," Janet said, "and they don't understand it at all. They, like, genuinely don't get it. We're not operating in the same sphere right now.

We're not in the same world." Eventually, she stopped talking to them about her company and her achievements.

NOT ALL OF STANFORD—EVEN INSIDER STANFORD—IS LIKE THAT.

The most famous Stanford entrepreneurship program is Lean LaunchPad, a class that has been run since 2010 by Steve Blank, a serial entrepreneur who developed the now-ubiquitous "lean startup" methodology used by thousands of companies. In ten weeks, teams of students develop a company from idea to fundable startup. Then they pitch it to investors brought in by Blank and his colleagues. It is extremely selective, extremely rigorous, and, as the name implies, a launchpad to Silicon Valley success.

If Rule is the dark side of Stanford, LaunchPad is its sunnier sibling. Theoretically the two classes may be somewhat aligned—they each ask the question "How do you succeed?" and provide students a network to do so—but in practice, they couldn't be more different. Rule teaches manipulation, domination, the prioritization of the self above all else. LaunchPad hearkens back to a view of innovation focused less on personal gain than on building something new, something that helps improve the world. The course forces students to spend time with ten to fifteen customers a week and teaches fanaticism about creating products that are actually useful—as opposed to the attention-grabbing, substance-free companies currently springing up by the dozen.

Blank has been doing this a long time and seen Silicon Valley's culture change now that everyone comes to Stanford thinking they just might be the next billionaire dropout. "We've lost the moral compass for what we invest into," he told me. "We've lost the sense of shame and the sense of purpose."

The campus is so suffused with entrepreneurial ambition today, he has come to believe, that it's become even harder to spot the actual geniuses. "Stanford is an incubator with dorms," Blank said. But "the true founders—not the ones who want to make a lot of money or do it because their roommates want to do it—are closer to artists than to any other profession." They "see things that other people don't. They hear things others don't. And they're driven to take that vision and turn it into physical reality. You know who else does that? Painters do that, sculptors do that, poets do that, playwrights do that." He took the comparison to its logical conclusion: "Most paintings are failures. Most songs suck. Novels aren't often bestsellers. So the nature of an artist is you fail most of the time, yet you're tenacious and you're resilient."

These people exist, but they're rare. "Turns out," Blank said, "one hundred percent of entrepreneurs think they're visionaries. The data say ninety-nine percent aren't."

This was a reality echoed by John Hennessy, the former Stanford president, when we met for coffee one morning in a sleek, award-winning building, one of dozens he'd helped erect at the university during his tenure. "There are hundreds of students on our campus who think they're going to build the next great AI company," Hennessy said. "Yeah, maybe one of them will. But not hundreds."

Hennessy ushered in much of the Stanford innovation ecosystem that enabled undergrads to raise towering sums. Yet he felt that something was awry today. Students "look at Steve Jobs, Mark Zuckerberg, and Bill Gates and conclude that dropping out is the most brilliant thing," Hennessy told me. "This is an incorrect assumption."

For all the effort by Silicon Valley to identify talented teenagers and pluck them from Stanford's campus directly to work, he pointed out, "if you look at the most successful startups that have spun out, they were graduate students, not undergrads." The mythology of the brilliant dropout founder doesn't reflect reality, he argued. "I think we want to talk about what went wrong with Theranos," Hennessy said. Elizabeth Holmes had started the blood-prick startup as a Stanford sophomore, when Hennessy was three years into his term as president; he watched it all fall apart during his final year in office. "The founder-CEO model implies that you have a young founder who doesn't really know how to be CEO," Hennessy said. When vested with power, and guided by ego, "that's often the failure that occurs."

STUDENTS AREN'T SOLELY RESPONSIBLE FOR SUCCUMBING TO SILICON Valley's seductions. Much of the responsibility lies with those who enable them.

One of the dirty truths about Silicon Valley is that most VCs suck at their jobs. About 2 percent of VC firms generate 95 percent of the industry's returns. The average VC firm does not outperform the average stock. And many of them seem to be simply guessing—or, more accurately, going where they see a group headed.

Right now the stampede is toward anything with "AI" in the pitch. Before AI, it was crypto. Before crypto, it was virtual reality. And so on. The VC model depends on a few colossal successes outweighing the many failures. Investors buy into hype cycles, knowing that the next Google will set them up for life. There seems to be more money now than ever, and more of it focused on a mythologized view of a young founder. Facebook was originally launched on a shoestring budget, and a falling-out between Mark Zuckerberg and Eduardo Saverin—Zuckerberg's classmate and cofounder who provided the company's initial funding—eventually turned into a dispute worth tens of billions of dollars, thanks to Saverin's original fifteen-thousand-dollar stake.

Nowadays, Stanford clubs will spend twice that on a party.

TODAY'S STANFORD INSIDER WORLD HASN'T BEEN AROUND ALL THAT long; it is built on the notion of replicating the success of people who attended what was, even just a few years ago, a very different university.

Sam Altman, a regular adviser to young students known on campus by the mononym Sama, dropped out of Stanford to create a startup. As president of Y Combinator and now CEO of OpenAI, he has nevertheless maintained a very close relationship to the community. When he was a student, Altman told me, he "had actually been fairly disappointed" that there weren't more opportunities for young entrepreneurs. So, he said to himself, "If I'm ever in a position to help the Stanford community with more startup stuff, I will."

Now he hosts dinners, texts budding founders, and lobs an investment their way if they need it or offers them a job working for him if it's time to move on.

When I asked Altman, who left Stanford in 2005, the year I was born, about the lavish parties and VC wining and dining and insider excesses, he paused for a minute. "It was twenty years ago when I was there, and it was a very different time in the world. None of that stuff happened. No VCs were showing up taking people to dinner. There was nothing even close to the idea that clearly exists now of the VC circuit, where the same people go to every event." He continued, "I've heard there's these crazy luxurious trips now and all of this stuff. And it sounds very awesome. But that didn't exist at all when I was there."

He wondered if maybe it was a bad thing. "I have heard from some of the people who work at OpenAI and went to Stanford that they're very skeptical of the people that are doing the VC dinner circuit, and they tend to not be the really talented Builders. It tends to be a big anti-signal," Altman said. "But I don't know."

I DIDN'T KNOW, EITHER. THE FURTHER I DELVED INTO STANFORD'S INNER worlds, the more uncertain I was. Parts of the university—inhabited by the Steve Blanks and Amber Yangs—felt genuinely committed to progress, advancement, and ethics. Then again, some of the same people I heard expressing the best motivations about using technology to save the world, I witnessed behaving in diametrically opposed ways.

Who was a pretender? Who was really who they said they were?

Just a few months into my first year at Stanford, I could no longer really tell.

CHAPTER 7

DUCK SYNDROME

Around this time, things began to fall apart for me.

First it was Lily. She was my girlfriend. And then she was gone. After months of waiting for me to get my act together, Lily had had enough. We both recognized that things weren't working. I wasn't responding to messages, and even when we did talk, I found myself so distracted that whole friend-group-drama subplots would pass me by before I even registered the names. So, via FaceTime, we clinically beheaded the romantic relationship we'd once viewed as timeless.

I knew most high school–college couples who try the long-distance thing break up a few months in. At Stanford, some students called it the Turkey Drop because it so often happens around Thanksgiving. I'd hoped that we were somehow different, that we could make it work even though so many others fail—well, I was wrong. Just like everyone else who's gone through the same thing, Lily and I quickly found ourselves immersed in different worlds, thousands of miles apart and just as emotionally distant.

Technically I did the breaking up, but that really is a technicality. First, Lily broached the idea of taking a "break." I assented, and we did . . . for a week, before she took it back and we decided to give it another go. But we were attached to what had been, to the folie à deux that had convinced us of our own exceptionalism. Not long after, I told Lily I still didn't think it was working. So it ended. And that was that for another week, until I came crawling back to her, begging for another chance. Finally, Lily put her foot down. The breakup would stand, like an uneasy ceasefire morphed into a wary full-time truce, and I thanked Lily for having the backbone to break the cycle before it did too much damage. We hung up and that was the end of it, a phone screen fading to black.

I HAD A LOT OF TIME TO THINK ABOUT THIS, BECAUSE STANFORD, HOPing to avoid a COVID flare-up later in winter quarter, locked us all in a preventative quarantine.

COVID was still very much a thing in January 2023, and I didn't really give the lockdown a second thought. Like so many of us almost exactly three years after coronavirus landed in the United States, I'd grown used to the idea that simply being in a shared space could be dangerous.

People my age had been ripped from our sophomore year of high school into isolation. So, like everyone, we adapted. I organized virtual Netflix parties with friends and we played Among Us, the then-inescapable game of deception, in which a space crew has to ferret out the "impostors" before the "normal" animated characters can be fully dispatched, picked off one by one by the innocent-looking murderers.

I was lucky to have been spared the worst of COVID, but it was undeniably disruptive. In the middle of the pandemic, I ended up starting at a new high school virtually (yeah, that was weird) and never really had the chance to say goodbye to some of my friends from my old school. By the time COVID put my grandfather in the hospital and sent him spiraling toward his death, just before I arrived at college, I was thoroughly done with the virus and wanted never to think of it again. I think most people felt the same. Still, even unacknowledged, the pandemic clearly took a toll on my Stanford classmates.

We were worse at math than we should've been, unused to the workload that had been expected pre-pandemic. We'd also, on the whole, reckoned with more personal loss than the college freshmen right before us. Even after vaccines, life on campus did not return to a pre-pandemic equilibrium. The Stanford experience described to me before the 2020 lockdown was markedly different, and students who experienced both before and after characterized the difference as a wholesale transformation. The already ongoing administrative War on Fun was supercharged. Traditional community hubs, some decades old, disappeared for good. So did institutional knowledge built up by successive generations of students and their mentors—about how to run clubs, how to organize events, how to, in effect, be a college student.

We didn't know how to talk to one another coming out of high school. We'd been so cocooned in silos on the internet that live human interaction seemed utterly foreign. Social anxiety became widespread, beyond even the neuroticism you might expect from such a high-achieving group of social rejects. Mine was the generation of "situationships" and "brain rot," more comfortable in a digital world than the real one. In part because people my age learned how to be activists from Instagram, and because consumption of quality news content was so low, we tended to speak past one another when we argued. The divide between men and women in my generation on political topics was greater by some metrics than the gender divide among any previous generation in the history of American polling. The internet enabled us to live in alternate realities.

As I lay alone in my dorm room that winter, I ruminated. For a while my bond with Lily helped push me out of myopia. With relationships among people my age at an all-time low, not everyone got to have that. And now I didn't, either.

THE WORK WASN'T SAVING ME FROM MYSELF. IN FACT, I'D STALLED. FOR the past month, I'd been in the hot seat, working on a new story for *The*

Daily almost every day—sometimes several. Now, as I tried to get the larger MTL story that had eluded me, I was finding roadblock after roadblock. Unable to publish, I felt withdrawal. As any journalist who's found themselves in the middle of an intense story will tell you, the adrenaline rush is addictive. You sacrifice everything for the story because, as the late *Washington Post* publisher Philip Graham famously put it, you're writing "the first rough draft of history." For this, I gave up Heap Allocator, I sacrificed my relationship, I stopped attending social events.

My relationship with campus was also beginning to transform. At first, other students had rooted for me, making memes, cheering me on. On the Stanford social media site Fizz, my name was everywhere—posts like "Theo does it again folks 🔥🔥" would garner more than five hundred upvotes. One post that read "How did I not realize that the William Curry articles and the MTL scandal articles were all written by Theo Baker . . . mf's gonna single-handedly take down Stanford admin" got twenty-five hundred upvotes. An image purporting to show me slapping MTL captioned "Every. Single. Day. 🐐" received fourteen hundred upvotes. You get the gist. Then, overnight, it changed.

When I followed up on my Stan Cohen story with a piece documenting how Stanford had made a provably false statement in response to my queries, the reaction was night-and-day different. People started fretting that I was "devaluing a Stanford degree" by making the school look bad. "Abolish Theo Baker" one post read. "Maybe one day Theo Baker will write something positive about Stanford," said another user. The critiques weren't really substantive—I'm sure that most of the people hadn't even read any of my pieces, which was no doubt true of many of those praising me, too. It came from vibes, perception. "Honestly, Theo Baker is not good journalism. This latest article is total sensationalism. Sad to see the state our student newspaper is in, losing so much credibility among students and faculty" read a popular post. Yet another person complained, "He honestly has got to stop. . . . I'm all for holding admin accountable but there is definitely a much better forum for this—there should also be an investigation into how ONE person is able to get all of this information. What is the end goal?"

Not even four months into my freshman year, I'd suddenly become polarizing. People treated me like a zoo animal, a campus curiosity. Some started writing graphic sexual fan fiction in which Marc Tessier-Lavigne, age sixty-three, had intercourse with me, a minor. People messaged me asking if they could buy my used tissue paper. (Which, what the fuck?) A handful of random people showed up outside my dorm room door, gossiping, "It's that kid!" Quarantined inside, I heard every word through the thin walls. Still others began trying to invade my personal life.

I'd started talking to another freshman over winter break when he slid up on one of my Instagram stories to discuss literature. We messaged back and forth at great length and he seemed keen to learn about how I'd grown up and what I was interested in. We talked about Sylvia Plath and czarist Russia and American politics. I was grateful for the company and enjoyed our exchanges. He proposed meeting up after quarantine ended. He didn't show. In fact, as I learned later from people who lived with him, the whole thing had been an act, a dare to see whether he could gain my confidence. Well, he had, and as a result I felt shockingly disturbed, naked. He'd lied to my face and I'd naïvely gone right along with it. Now I had to consider people's motivations in every casual interaction. I was crushed.

College is about reinvention. Like others, I'd hoped to leave behind the baggage of high school and begin anew with people who didn't know me. Except, only four months in, that was over. Nearly every person I would meet now would already have an opinion of me. I cannot describe how depressing that felt, that at seventeen I'd already lost the chance to be seen as a blank slate.

As I was just beginning my second quarter at Stanford, a sense of isolation crept in. I hadn't had time to make real friends. Was there really a place for me at Stanford? Would I always be some form of *other*?

I wanted to call Lily, but I restrained myself. At the end of the day, the only thing to do was to keep working. That's what I'd always been taught.

QUARANTINE ENDED A COUPLE OF DAYS BEFORE MY BIRTHDAY IN JANuary. I was turning eighteen and, frankly, dreaded it. I hate birthdays. Thankfully, my best friend from high school, Frank, was flying in to spend the weekend with me.

Before his arrival, I tried to make progress investigating Tessier-Lavigne's work. I was trawling through decades of press clippings, legal briefs, and SEC filings, piecing together a portrait of the man whose labs harbored secrets that I keenly wished to understand. I collected countless anecdotes I would never write about, stories that had nothing to do with his labs and research but that nevertheless helped me to understand Tessier-Lavigne as a person.

It was a slog. There were leads and rumors that didn't check out and some things I didn't dare pursue. I learned that Tessier-Lavigne had left his lab's Slack unsecured—if I used the "join" link, I could access all of their messages. But I didn't. It didn't feel right, and besides, I had to make sure my conduct was unimpeachable, to ensure that Tessier-Lavigne and his surrogates couldn't paint me as a rogue teen with a vendetta. I was in it for the story, not the man, and if what I found exonerated him, I was eager to publish that—frankly, I hoped this would be the case. I wanted to think highly of Tessier-Lavigne, the leader of the school I'd just joined as an idealistic student. I didn't want a skeleton in the closet. But I would check all the closets, because if I didn't, maybe no one else would.

ON JANUARY 10, MY INVESTIGATION GROUND TO A HALT; SLOW GOING became a hard stop, and my stall became a spiral.

I was lying on the edge of my bed, head hanging off the side, as I delayed getting up. It was the first day of classes, but I'd discovered an old profile of MTL the night before and stayed up late writing down and researching all the friends, colleagues, competitors, and admirers mentioned. I had a lot to learn—each of them had a résumé hundreds of pages long and a well-defined reputation.

Since I'd only gotten a few hours of sleep, I allowed myself the luxury of a slow start to the day. I opened Twitter and scrolled. And then I saw a familiar name next to some very unfamiliar words: "I am so shocked and so sad to hear about the tragic death of Blake Hounshell," the tweet read. My eyes clouded with tears before I even finished reading. "What the fuck?" I asked aloud to no one in particular. How could he be dead?

As a child, your life changes rapidly. Circumstances shift, your limbs extend, friends flash in and out; step by step, the world begins to reveal itself, and you cast about trying to find your place in it. Few things remain constant. Thus the people who make up the small cast of permanent characters in your life take on particular significance. You may not see them every day, but to a child, these anchor people provide stability.

My grandfather was one of those anchor people. So was Blake.

Blake was my mother's closest professional friend and partner for almost my entire life, working with my mom to rejuvenate *Foreign Policy* magazine, starting when I was three years old; the two then went on to found *Politico Magazine*, and, eventually, to run all of *Politico*. He was one of the most brilliant people I'd ever met; he was also a damn good guy.

An only child in a city of adults, I spent my time growing up immersed in my parents' world, soaking up dinner conversations about omnibus bills and nuclear nonproliferation. To their immense credit, my parents always included me. And I leapt at this opportunity.

For most of my life, I didn't fit in well at school. (Surprise, surprise!) I was the only person who'd skipped a grade, and wasn't even five feet tall by the time I entered high school. Kids can be vicious to anyone who presents differently, I learned. In fourth grade, a classmate, unprompted, came up to me and shoved me so hard to the ground that I cracked my head and was out of school with a concussion for a full month. In fifth grade, I was stuffed in a garbage can and shoved down the stairs. In sixth grade, I was locked in a locker, rescued by a burly hockey player friend who protected me on more than one occasion. I avoided the locker room after that.

In my parents' world, I found refuge. Their friends were authors and dissidents; they'd been to war zones and stood up to dictators. They were always reading something interesting or citing some wonky policy report. Some of the kids at school didn't know what their parents did for a living—not me. Journalists are on call 24/7, and, since both of my parents are deeply immersed in their work and share the same passionate interests, their work and life are one. They let me experience it, too.

I have vivid early memories of lying on my mother's lap in bed as she edited articles and asked me about headlines. My dad would sit me down in the old rocking chair that my great-grandmother had delivered to our house during a snowstorm a few nights after I was born and tell me stories about the Iran-Contra scandal or Rutherford B. Hayes's 1876 contested election. He always answered my questions.

I began bartending at my parents' parties when I was in grade school, sitting behind the makeshift bar and pouring wine from bottles the size of my torso. I've long thought that the best measure of a person is how they treat someone who cannot benefit them, and as a tiny kid, I definitely fit into this category. Plenty of adults would ignore me, even if I spoke to them. They had no time for me. Others would be short or rude. Then there were the few who would go out of their way to be kind to me, to speak to me as a human being. That was Blake.

On snow days or when I had other excuses to visit the office, I would hound Blake with constant questions and he'd lean back, answer, and then ask me something in return, no matter how busy he was. When he and my mom went into meetings, Blake set me up to watch videos on his computer. He was gruffly hilarious, dizzyingly intelligent, and kind in a profoundly rare way. He never looked down on me. When his eyes scanned a room, Blake would *see* me.

One time at a book party when I was eight or so, Blake brought a bottle of whiskey as a gift for my parents, who were hosting. I'd never really seen hard liquor before. So, when he asked if I'd pour him a drink, I dutifully filled a tall glass to the top as if it were a beer. Instead of laughing or making fun of me, Blake gamely took the giant glass and nursed it the rest of the night. It was a story that stuck, one we recounted for years. In fact, I'd just been talking about it with my parents over winter break.

On New Year's Day, my parents and I had hosted brunch for a couple of dozen friends. Of all the people coming, I told my parents, I was most excited to see Blake. It had been a while and I missed him. I volunteered to do the cooking and spent most of the party stuck at the stove. Toward the end, I finally managed to catch Blake. We talked about Stanford and politics while his young children, David and Astrid, whom I'd known since their births, ran around. Just as he was leaving the house, I called out what I'd wanted to say from the very beginning: "I hope things get better." Because he and my mother were close confidants, I knew that Blake had been struggling with a new job and the ongoing aftershocks of a stroke a couple of years before. I think my comment caught him off guard, and since he was being dragged out the door, he didn't have time to respond. In the end, those were the last words I ever said to him.

Blake had plans to come over for dinner with my parents a week later. But he didn't make it. Just a few hours before, Blake jumped off a bridge barely three blocks away.

I LEARNED THIS FROM TWITTER. IN THE FEW HOURS SINCE IT HAD happened, shock and grief had spread like wildfire. Hundreds of people were sharing stories about Blake and his kindness. When *Politico* dedicated its Playbook newsletter to Blake the next morning, the collected tributes stretched more than eleven pages when printed out.

After seeing the tweet, I called my parents. "Why didn't you tell me?" I asked, barely one step away from bawling. My dad's voice faltered as he replied. "We didn't know how you'd respond," he said. Because it was suicide. He and my mom had been with Sandy, Blake's widow, for the past few hours. They were trying to console her, of course, but also having to take care of the shitstorm that happens when someone departs prematurely. They'd helped write a statement for the family to issue, knowing that in the journalism world Blake's death could only remain quiet for so long, and they were charting next steps.

I cried over the phone. I couldn't imagine what they were going through. I told my dad to go—they had more important things to do—and hung up. Then I curled up under the sheets and tried to process the jumble of feelings. Initially, I just focused on the anguish of loss. First my grandfather, then Blake. They were constants, not people who could disappear in an instant. Soon, though, I began feeling guilt. Why was I entitled to this grief? Sure, I'd known Blake my whole life, but not like my mother had, not like his colleagues had. Had I earned the right to be as torn up as I was? Hell, my mom had lost both her dad and one of her closest friends, and she was putting on a brave face. Why couldn't I do the same?

And then there was a whole other set of feelings. Because it was a suicide.

I WAS JUST THIRTEEN WHEN I HAD TO TALK A FRIEND DOWN FROM SUICIDE for the first time. Several of my high school friends attempted suicide or came close, ending up in psychiatric wards or simply suffering alone. This disease had seemed to dominate everything around me.

Suicide is endemic to my generation. The most recent data suggest that nearly 30 percent of high school students experience depression, and roughly a fifth have seriously contemplated suicide. Nearly 10 percent have attempted it. While mental health is not a new problem, it seems to be striking the youngest generations in a particularly cruel way: Suicides among ten- to twenty-four-year-olds increased 62 percent between 2007 and 2021.

It is now the leading cause of preventable death among teenagers.

One suicide alone is enough to wrack a community. But, especially among kids, a suicide can also serve as a contagion, opening a dam for more deaths to follow. This had happened in Palo Alto several times. In 2009–10, five high schoolers in the small city around Stanford took their own lives, one after another. Another suicide cluster occurred in 2015—four more students in short order. For a community that prided itself on excellence and achievement—one of the most moneyed and successful school districts in the world, and a direct pipeline to Stanford—this had been devastating.

Coming to Stanford did not alleviate the problem. Students raised in a cult of stress and overexpectation found themselves unable to rewrite their programming.

The Stanford mental health crisis had a particular manifestation: Duck Syndrome. It was a term coined at the university to describe the shocking divergence between projected experience and lived experience. At Stanford, smiling, vital students appeared to glide across the water, serene, presenting effortless achievement. But beneath the surface, their legs, like a duck's, paddled desperately, relentlessly, just to keep afloat.

The year before I arrived, four students at Stanford took their own lives. It should've been a wake-up call for the school, definitive proof that, no, the kids were not all right. But nothing really had changed. Mental health support remained abysmal, with school psychologists inaccessible for months and limited in their ability to help or schedule regular appointments.

THERE WAS A CRUELTY INHERENT TO STANFORD'S CULTURAL INSISTENCE on appearance. What happened to Katie Meyer is a perfect example of this.

Hailed as representing the best of Stanford—the captain of the women's soccer team who was decisive in winning an NCAA championship; perfect grades; law school bound and beloved by her community—Meyer was sent an email late at night in the winter of 2022, saying that her degree was being placed on hold over an incident six months earlier in which she spilled coffee (she said accidentally) on a football player who'd allegedly sexually assaulted her teammate. Meyer was a perfectionist in all things; she didn't drink, she didn't speed, she considered an A-minus failure. These were all the traits that had made her the perfect Stanford student. But they also made her vulnerable. Thinking that her entire future had just been ripped away, and with no resources available to console her, Meyer took her own life.

It had been a gut-wrenching moment for the community, just a few months before I arrived. Then Meyer's parents learned the circumstances behind her suicide and sued the school for wrongful death. In turn, Stanford blamed the parents. My first fall on campus, twelve different colleges honored Katie Meyer; Stanford was not one of them. At the women's soccer "mental health night," her name went unmentioned.

It's not just that Stanford wanted to avoid confronting things that looked bad; even the good stuff had to appear better. As one professor wisely put it to me, "Stanford has a culture of overclaiming. We take the same result and blow it up bigger than it would be somewhere else." Beginning the second of my freshman year's three terms, I could see Stanford's crippling relationship to perfection more clearly each day.

WHEN FRANK, MY BEST FRIEND FROM HOME, ARRIVED AT MY DORM the day after Blake's death, I greeted him with a shaky hug. My head hurt, my body felt a little numb, but in the familiar warmth of Frank's signature fleece, the world stopped spinning.

I showed off my new surroundings to Frank: Lake Lagunita, filling up with water for the first time in years due to excess rainfall; my dorm, Alondra, with its peeling walls and stark lighting; and the Daily

House, where it turned out that Sam and a few other staffers had arranged a surprise birthday party for me. They'd put together a presentation with mock quotes from people touched by my reporting, some of which were heartfelt comments from editors and colleagues, while others were spoofs of MTL or the War on Fun czar or the Davis Wright Tremaine lawyers complaining about "the problems you cause for *The Stanford Daily*."

It was a genuinely kind gesture, one that made me laugh and one that was far more meaningful than they could've known. Blake had always made me laugh in the newsroom. The childhood comfort I'd felt whenever he was around—maybe I'd found some of it here, too.

CHAPTER 8

HARRIET THE SPY

Marc Tessier-Lavigne is a tall man with sharp cheekbones and an unwavering affect. He doesn't blink, he doesn't shift about. He doesn't speak a word he does not intend. In public, at least.

His is a carefully curated presentation—neat hair, perfect suits, a practiced smile—that projects, above all else, rationality. Long before his tenure as Stanford's president came under scrutiny, students characterized MTL as robotic. As I researched Tessier-Lavigne, one video stuck out: a conversation with Ruth Porat, then the chief financial officer of Alphabet/Google, that was released as his introduction to the Stanford community in 2016. "You might say I'm a little bit proper and perhaps formal at times," Tessier-Lavigne said, enunciating every syllable. "They say that the way you can spot a Canadian on a crowded street is to look for the person who's saying please and thank you to the ATM machine. I'm that person."

Then came my favorite part.

"But don't get me wrong," Tessier-Lavigne told Porat, eyes wide and unblinking. "Although I can be a little proper at times, I'm very approachable. I love interacting," he said, pausing before adding, "with people."

Years before I arrived on campus, two Stanford professors separately began using Tessier-Lavigne's public statements as examples of how *not* to communicate, instructing students to ignore their president's example. (Neither, apparently, knew about the other. One emailed MTL in 2020—"I feel compelled to tell you, as a heads-up, that I have begun using emails like the one below as examples of how NOT to write"—but never heard back.) In public speeches, Tessier-Lavigne often used platitudes and avoided specifics, eschewing flair in favor of predictability. I hadn't even remembered that MTL spoke at my convocation, not a month before I started reporting about him.

In private, Tessier-Lavigne could be warm to those he favored, I learned, and he was talented at charming powerful figures, such as those on the Stanford board. According to people involved with the presidential search committee that vetted him in the fall of 2015, Tessier-Lavigne had been the only candidate to actively campaign for the role, managing, especially, to win over Isaac Stein, chair of the search committee, and Steve and Roberta Denning, wealthy and dedicated Stanford patrons. (Steve was chair of the Stanford board of trustees and served on the search committee; after he became ill, Roberta stepped into his seat on the board while Jerry Yang took over as chair.) They were especially taken with Tessier-Lavigne's ability, while president of Rockefeller University, to convince New York City to allow a $500 million construction project over FDR Drive and sweet-talk donors into backing Rockefeller's most expensive project ever.

To some, Tessier-Lavigne was a real mentor, shaping the careers of fledgling scientists and staying in touch even after they left his labs. Unlike some in positions of power in Big Science, Tessier-Lavigne wasn't known to hit on his students, nor would he make the kind of racist or misogynistic jokes that can be common in neuroscience's older, white, male upper echelons.

Yet Tessier-Lavigne, unexpectedly, was capable of immense rage. "Really?" I'd asked a source the first time this came up in an interview. A longtime colleague of MTL, the source was vehement, insisting, "I know how fucking vindictive he can be." When I broached this with an old friend of Tessier-Lavigne's, he laughed: "Let's just say you don't want to cross him. Though I guess you already have." Canadian polite, as Tessier-Lavigne had put it in his video, did not make him Canadian nice.

THE TRAIT THAT BOTH ALLIES AND OPPONENTS AGREED ON UNANImously as I did more reporting was Tessier-Lavigne's ambition. Singular ambition. From the start, he'd been "a man in a hurry," an early collaborator of his told me. He was "always looking for the next thing."

Opinions differ on whether he merited the description of "brilliance." The titans of the field tended to be more judgmental, although I assume few people meet their standards. But Tessier-Lavigne was clearly an impressive scientific mind—dedicated, thoughtful, probing. In that sense, then, he was no fake: He genuinely produced excellent science. For three years after opening his lab at UCSF, Tessier-Lavigne and his team methodically searched for the unidentified chemical attractant that governed axon guidance, painstaking research that involved more than twenty-five thousand embryonic chick brains. In 1994, they revealed to the world their discovery: the netrin, named for the Sanskrit word *netr*, or "one who guides."

The whole subsequent field of research that developed from this breakthrough rocketed Tessier-Lavigne to scientific stardom. He wasn't at the top of the food chain yet, but seemed destined to get there. Suddenly, MTL had his first real taste of attention. He also got his first taste of the money in the lucrative biotech industry. Things began to change in his lab. This is when, colleagues said, the problems began to creep in.

THE OFFICIAL STANFORD INVESTIGATION OF MTL BEGAN IN EARNEST in mid-January 2023, with the announcement of a scientific panel to advise the Stanford board. No, actually the scientific panel would report to the special committee of the board. Well, sort of. It would report to Mark Filip, the lawyer, who would report to the special committee, which would report to the full board. Who exactly was in control of what remained unclear, as did the question of what would be disclosed to the public.

I sent over a litany of questions to Aidan Ryan, the Edelman crisis communications flack enlisted by the board, hoping for clarification. And I refreshed myself on how our previous interview had gone:

"What results exactly are going to be released to the community in terms of the findings of the committee?" He couldn't say.

"What specifically is the board investigating? Is it his whole CV or just the papers that have been so far identified?" Ryan wouldn't elaborate beyond the board's statement, announcing "a review of issues relating to academic articles in which Stanford President Marc Tessier-Lavigne is a listed author."

Did Felix Baker, the trustee with the stake in Tessier-Lavigne's company, "reveal his financial investments before being placed on the committee?" Ryan: "You know, I don't have an answer for that. I can try to chase that down."

You get the gist.

The only interesting part of the interview had come at the end. Tessier-Lavigne's initial defense included this alibi for some of the papers now being questioned: "President Tessier-Lavigne was included as an author on these publications solely to recognize his contribution in providing necessary reagents for the research by other authors. He was not involved in any way in the generation or presentation of the panels that have been queried."

Several scientists had written me to point out that Stanford's Research Handbook, in effect since the 1980s, contains this portion:

> There is a tight coupling between authorship and responsibility. Let us suppose that the name of a faculty member has been included on a paper resulting from the relatively independent ex-

> periments done by a student or fellow. If the data are then shown to be faulty, or worse, invented . . . the faculty member is responsible. . . . Faculty members are generally responsible for the scholarly conduct of staff and students involved in their research enterprises. When one assumes coauthorship, a still higher duty of certainty prevails. The defense of minimal participation in work done in one's laboratory is generally questionable; surely it is entirely inapplicable when one is coauthor of the disputed work.

The scientific world has long debated what level of responsibility coauthorship entails. For one category of paper—where it was by now fairly clear that MTL's lab had been the source of the fraud, and he was the senior or corresponding author with full responsibility—he was certainly at least somewhat on the hook, although even then opinions diverged. On some of the other papers, though, Tessier-Lavigne's defense was that he had nothing really to do with the study.

This is a practice known as gift authorship, where a more senior scientist is included as an author despite minimal contribution, typically because their name will help get a paper published. This behavior occurs on a spectrum—some scientists literally have nothing to do with the research, others may have provided some insight but not worked on the actual experiments—and can allow famous researchers to take credit for major advances they had little to do with, while disclaiming responsibility should something bad result.

This, theoretically, is frowned upon. Yale's policy, for example, states, "Individuals do not satisfy the criteria for authorship merely because they have made possible the conduct of the research and/or the preparation of the manuscript. . . . Nor should 'gift' co-authorship be conferred on those whose only contributions have been . . . to provide a valuable reagent." In defending himself against the specter of research misconduct, this is exactly what Tessier-Lavigne had admitted doing—he "was included as an author on these publications solely to recognize his contribution in providing necessary reagents for the research by other authors," according to the original statement defending him.

Now, this was clearly much less severe than actually falsifying research or ordering others to do so. And it's true that Tessier-Lavigne was far from alone in this behavior. Scientific publishing is a major undertaking, often orchestrated by large international teams, and there's a stark difference in responsibility between being a middle author and being the first or senior author.

For all those reasons, I had focused on research over which Tessier-Lavigne had direct oversight. Still, it interested me to see how Stanford would react to MTL's admission. Stanford had a policy on the books saying you could not simply disclaim responsibility by saying you were just a coauthor—a policy written, I might add, by a former Stanford president, Donald Kennedy, in the 1980s. Kennedy was himself a neurobiologist and former FDA commissioner, and would go on to serve as editor in chief of *Science* at the time when the suspect Tessier-Lavigne papers in *Science* were published. How would Stanford apply this policy?

I'd asked Aidan Ryan at the end of our last interview whether Stanford would utilize the standards established in the Research Policy Handbook in its review of Tessier-Lavigne's behavior.

"We don't know what it has turned up yet. So we don't know what would be relevant," he said.

"So," I asked, "there's a situation in which the university wouldn't apply the same policies to Tessier-Lavigne that are applied to other scientists here?"

Ryan replied, "No, I certainly wouldn't say that. What I'm saying is that the review is just getting underway, so it's too early at this point to say what standards might apply given we're not totally sure what we're looking at yet. . . . What I'm saying is that the findings themselves will determine what standards apply."

In other words, they were making it up as they went along.

A MONTH AND A HALF AFTER RYAN AND I LAST SPOKE, THE STANFORD investigation still had no projected budget, no projected timeline, no specific scope, and, most important, no commitment to releasing any results.

At least there were scientists now: Shirley Tilghman, former president of Princeton and a well-regarded molecular biologist; Steve Hyman, a neuroscientist who'd served as Harvard's provost; Randy Schekman, co-recipient of the 2013 Nobel Prize for his work in cell biology; Hollis Cline, director of the Scripps Research Institute neuroscience center; and Kafui Dzirasa, a rising star in the Duke neurobiology department and the only non-administrator among the investigators.

They were an impressive group. Each of them belonged to the National Academy of Sciences or the National Academy of Medicine. Colleagues and friends I interviewed described them as people of high integrity and leaders in their respective fields. Yet despite their stellar academic backgrounds, it was not entirely clear how much experience they had in investigating research misconduct or assessing image manipulation. As before, when I requested interviews with the scientists or board members involved in the review, I was rebuffed.

Theoretically, the Research Policy Handbook required misconduct inquiries to be completed within sixty days, but the trustees had created their own process. It made sense to me that following the handbook and assigning the investigation to Tessier-Lavigne's subordinate, the dean of research, as would be standard procedure for a professor, would be untenable. But the board had done, frankly, a terrible job in communicating this at the start, and to some outsiders, including whistleblowers and sleuths, this made the investigation seem less independent, not more. Elisabeth Bik wrote to me at the time, "With a person of their own board involved, whom they presumably know very well and might have had a beer with . . . it is hard to imagine that this can be done in an objective way. No matter the outcome, people will wonder if the president's role at the university might have played a role in the severeness of the final report."

This concern wasn't entirely without merit. According to one trustee's recollection after the conclusion of the investigation, the board at first felt, "This can't be right, we have a world-class scientist here and a freshman reporter during their first quarter. So we're going to stand by the president, and say we're looking into it because we have to, but we didn't think it was serious." Another member of the board later summed up their thinking at this time, saying the trustees thought it necessary "to defend the president in order to serve the institution the best as a part of their job." Not everyone felt that way, but at the time, I had no way of knowing it.

I certainly didn't feel that I could count on Stanford to come clean if something needed exposing. That wasn't really its playbook. When Stanford commissioned a misconduct investigation into the head football coach, Troy Taylor, he was let off with a warning. When a second investigation within a year determined that there was "an ongoing pattern of concerning behavior by Coach Taylor," including abusive and inappropriate treatment of employees, particularly women, the university said nothing and allowed Taylor to stay. Only after ESPN uncovered the existence of the investigations was he fired. (Taylor is now suing ESPN.) When Joseph Bankman and Barbara Fried were accused of aiding their son's multibillion-dollar deception and improperly accepting funds in the eight-figure range, Stanford, again, said nothing. The university allowed Bankman to stay on the faculty despite violating Stanford's policy on maximum leaves of absence, a policy so strictly applied that violation even due to a serious illness like cancer typically results in the revocation of tenure. When Stan Cohen was found liable for fraud in that $29 million lawsuit, you already know what happened. And even if Stanford found something and held Tessier-Lavigne accountable for a hypothetical transgression, that wasn't a guarantee that we'd ever see the findings. For example, when a former dean of freshmen was investigated and found to have maintained a coercive sexual relationship with a student, she was allowed to leave with a cover story and no mention of any misconduct. (I met this woman before her case was publicly reported years after it occurred. Her first question to me and the friend I was standing next to was about whether we were having sex.)

A famous historical cover-up is even baked into Stanford's origin story—when Jane Stanford, cofounder of the university in 1891, was murdered, David Starr Jordan, its first president, buried the truth. With MTL, I didn't know what the university would find, but I knew that the only way to be certain it was found was to keep digging, not to place blind faith in an institution with a blemished record in the whole truth department.

I'D GOTTEN INTO THE GROOVE INVESTIGATING. I WAS THINKING ABOUT it every hour of every day, trying to piece together the story. This was an investigation that spanned several decades; a number of the suspect papers had been published before I was even born. It was crazy to think that I was going to ferret out secrets that had lain dormant for so long. And yet, I couldn't help it.

I'd always loved investigating. My favorite stories growing up were the swashbuckling adventures of Tintin and, especially when I was little, Harriet the Spy. Harriet was a snoop. She was an eleven-year-old with a penchant for intrigue, always trying to figure out what was happening around her.

I'd tried to copy that approach. In grade school, I was especially proud that I knew the names of every person in my school and kept imaginary flash cards in my head with facts about each of them. Whenever I walked into a bank, I always counted all the security cameras. I had no intention of stealing anything; I just wanted to know how the system worked. For the same reason, I found myself corresponding with a Vermont lumber supplier at age nine (I wanted to know how they got their hardwood so wide) and a Swedish camera manufacturer at age eleven (I wanted to know if the sensor they used was identical to their Danish competitor's, because they shared the same specifications and were made by the same Japanese third party). I was obsessed with figuring things out, even when they were well above my pay grade. (Unpaid.)

In that sense, then, journalism was something of a natural fit. People had tried to tell me this before. In my senior year of high school, I'd shown up to get my portrait taken for the yearbook and the first words out of the photographer's mouth were "Oh, you're either going to be a writer or a historian." At the time, I silently fumed, since I was in the midst of applying to Stanford and my whole identity was wrapped up in coding. A few months later, Lily made a wager with me: "I bet you're going to do some kind of journalism in the future," she said. I strenuously disagreed and took the bet.

Now, though, I'd given in. Investigating wasn't so much a choice as it was a requirement of my personality. I needed to do it. And as I continued to pursue the MTL story, a *Harriet the Spy* exchange came back to me.

"I want to know everything, everything," Harriet screeched. "Everything in the world, everything, everything. I will be a spy and know everything."

"It won't do you a bit of good to know everything," responded Harriet's mentor, Ole Golly, "if you don't do anything with it."

I set my status in the *Stanford Daily* Slack as "pretending to be Harriet the Spy" and dedicated myself—for the first time in my life—to doing something with the information I sought.

INSIDERS WITH KNOWLEDGE OF HIS LAB TOLD ME THAT TESSIER-Lavigne's research ethos seemed to have shifted in the late nineties. "He was becoming sort of royal, hands off, becoming a little distant from the day-to-day," a colleague recalled. People "were afraid to talk to him." Tessier-Lavigne's partnership with Cori Bargmann, who opened her UCSF lab at the same time as MTL in 1991, had been described as unusually open, with the two research groups sharing space, personnel, and ideas. Yet over time Tessier-Lavigne "became terrified that someone would swoop in and steal his research," said an early associate. He seemed to grow distrustful—and others started to distrust him.

Tessier-Lavigne collaborated extensively with a lab run by Corey Goodman, and the two would go on to found a company together and share the prestigious Gruber Prize. In 1997, a group of scientists in Goodman's lab became convinced that MTL had taken one of the reagents they'd developed without permission and beaten them to publication on the research they were working on. (Tessier-Lavigne denies that the reagent was taken without permission.) The result was one of Tessier-Lavigne's most significant papers, which would go on to be cited over one thousand times. Goodman and Tessier-Lavigne continued to collaborate, but members of the lab group remained suspicious, and MTL was never again seen in the same way.

IN 1999, THE FIRST PAPER WITH FALSIFIED PANELS FOR WHICH TESSIER-Lavigne served as senior author was published in *Cell*, followed by two others in 2001, this time in *Science*. That same year, Tessier-Lavigne was brought to Stanford by Sue McConnell (who two decades later would help marshal his defense). Tessier-Lavigne opened a lab and made use of significant funding, before decamping to Genentech after less than two years at the university to take a position offered by McConnell's husband, Richard Scheller. Having assumed the new post of senior vice president, research drug discovery, Tessier-Lavigne nevertheless remained "on leave" at Stanford for the maximum two years allowed, the same amount of time he'd been an active faculty member. This left a bad taste in the mouths of some colleagues, several of whom made a point of telling me the story some twenty years later. In their view, Tessier-Lavigne had been nakedly careerist, leaving Stanford hanging as he took a leave without giving up his faculty position or his laboratory space, even as he apparently had no intention of returning.

At Genentech, Tessier-Lavigne and Scheller became something of an unlikely duo. They were "Boy Scout and Bad Boy," as one insider put it. MTL was extremely buttoned down, measured, controlled. He never drank to excess and encouraged people to think politically and keep their mouths shut. Scheller was outspoken and wilder, with a reputation for taking drugs, listening to hard rock, and engaging in rampant womanizing, according to four people with knowledge of the dynamics.

Less than a year into his time at Genentech, another falsified study with Tessier-Lavigne's name listed as senior author was published in *Nature*. However, the story didn't stop there, at least not according to an anonymous letter I'd received soon after the publication of my initial investigation. Instead, apparently, there'd been a far more serious offense in 2009, the details of which I'd been searching for since the beginning of December. But no one would talk. Yet.

I'D BEEN SLOWLY ASSEMBLING A LIST OF PEOPLE WHO MIGHT KNOW something. People either ignored me or gave some excuse and got off the phone as quickly as possible. But, miraculously, one Genentech executive eventually told me that he was willing to chat—as long as it was in person. I was thrilled, if nervous.

I hadn't given any details when reaching out to him, writing only my name, my affiliation with *The Stanford Daily*, and a short note: "I was wondering if you had a few minutes to talk about your time at Genentech. I have a few specific questions that I'd love to get your perspective on." By now, since I was reaching out to so many people on company emails or through secretaries at Genentech and other biotech companies, I made a point of not including information that could set off alarm bells in automated email monitoring software. I didn't even include Tessier-Lavigne's name. But this scientist responded immediately with a time and a place, and the meeting was set for a few days later.

I TRIED TO KEEP MY EXPECTATIONS LOW—THE GUY MIGHT KNOW nothing—and went about my life.

We were studying Dante's *Inferno* in SLE, and later that day all of us made a required outing to one of Stanford's art museums, the Cantor Arts Center, and its imposing, twenty-foot-tall *Gates of Hell*, the iconic Rodin sculpture based on the *Divine Comedy*.* It was a beautiful day, classic Northern California T-shirt-and-jeans weather, with warm rays of light bouncing off the gleaming metal. Students were laughing, smiling, leaning in close and noting the intricate details Rodin had so painstakingly worked into the defining project of his career. The vibes were great—and left me queasy.

This was the first time in months that I'd been with the full SLE group other than at a lecture. Everyone now seemed to have a little clique, groups that had developed shared inside jokes and easy chemistry; some people I'd last observed furtively holding hands late at night when they thought no one could see or sneaking longing glances during section now avoided each other like the plague. Others who hadn't even known each other the last time we were all together were now inseparable. The social dynamics, uncertain and unwritten when I'd joined the program, were now codified. I'd missed out on the process.

That night, at a private dinner hosted by a tech investor, I felt even less at home. Over arancini paid for by the oddball Silicon Valley dude bro, students talked about their B2B SaaS startups and how Sam Bankman-Fried, arrest notwithstanding, was "directionally correct." They lamented that, as one crypto savant put it, "building is halted now, people are just worried about legality and trying to figure out, 'How do I get around this?'" The host was Cory, a gangly man who prided himself

*Stanford's is one of several casts. The original plaster mold sits in the Musée D'Orsay in Paris, France. According to the university, the Cantor Arts Center possesses the largest collection of Rodin sculptures aside from the Musée Rodin, also in Paris; however, this is a contested claim.

on "grind culture" and viewed the number of all-nighters pulled in a week as the most valuable metric of success. At the dinner, when he stood up and announced that "the next trillion-dollar company is in this room for sure," people erupted with "Hear, hear!" Also, Cory said, the cofounder of YouTube had decided to join at the last minute and wanted to hear our ideas. Why not?

The guests did have big ideas, of course. When I asked my interlocutor across the table, he professed his grand ambition: "I want to build a city." I half laughed, unsure how to respond. What do you say to a twenty-year-old who wants to build a city?

Most people at the table knew one another, having attended many such events with Cory and others like him. I got a ride back from the restaurant in the car of an engineer with a sharp mind who was doing cutting-edge research. In the car, he spilled AI tea. One paper his friend worked on, he said, "was all fudged." After dishing about another startup founder, he laughed. "This came through some back doors," he confided. Shouldn't he be more careful telling everyone about it, then? I wondered. But, of course, he didn't feel the need to be—we were part of the club.

It's a funny fact about Silicon Valley, where secrecy is worshipped. Rob Reich, the Stanford professor and tech ethics expert, often repeats his story of meeting with a freshman who expressed a passion for tech. "That's wonderful," Reich told the kid. "Is there anything in particular you want to work on?" The frosh responded enthusiastically. "Yeah, I have this great startup idea!" And what was it, Reich queried. "Oh," the kid said with complete sincerity, "if you want me to tell you, you're going to have to sign an NDA." A nondisclosure agreement just to hear his probably half-baked idea. Reich had relayed this incident to me a few months prior over coffee, just days after the incident in CS107 when my classmates didn't raise their hands to signal any interest in ethics; now, I was starting to experience this mindset, too. Not long after, a friend would ask me to sign an NDA just to come to a party with him.

This secrecy, though, is paradoxically paired with often breathtaking admissions of wrongdoing, shared liberally among people in the know. If loose lips do sink ships, Silicon Valley's fleet of yachts and assorted pleasure craft should by now be sitting on the ocean floor, next to the *Titanic* and the OceanGate submersible. An astonishing amount of what is known to the "insider" is never revealed to the broader public, nor pursued by the outgunned, underdeveloped Silicon Valley press corps.

THE NEXT NIGHT, A VC CAME TO VISIT OUR TREEHACKS MEETING. WITH the event just around the corner, we were ramping up our efforts frantically. I was trying to make up for my failure to help while working on the MTL story by putting in the hours now. Like everyone else, I'd gamely reviewed hundreds of applications over winter break. Now that we were back, I was dealing with financial sponsors full-time and helping arrange dozens of workshops and booths that we would set up during the two-and-a-half-day event.

At this night's meeting of the full TreeHacks team, the VC stopped by to meet us and let us know that any ideas we had for companies of our own were welcome. "Our bread and butter is young students," she underlined, as we munched on catered "menage a trois" sandwiches.

By 1:00 a.m., when the student center where we met closed, only the two codirectors, Vedant and Sara, as well as Jessica and I, were left. We still had mountains of issues to tackle, but Stanford, suburban school that it is, shuts down early. I volunteered use of the Daily House, since I had key card access.

Nobody else was there, and we set up in the conference room downstairs. It was weird. For some time, I felt like I'd managed to separate my reporting life from my tech life, but now the two worlds intersected. You know when you see someone where they're not supposed to be? We sat in chairs I'd used so many times for reporting, lobbing around gobs of money that journalists never get to see and plotting how to serve the kind of corporate sponsors a reporter might normally be investigating.

("Oh! Are we fucking over [company] again?" Sara said at one point, gleefully.)

Toward the end of the night, as Vedant played horrible bass-boosted music, we talked about the team, our friends, who had met expectations, who hadn't. Vedant turned to me and said, almost sadly, "You know, I thought you were the best of all the interviews." The subtext was left unsaid. I hadn't been the team member I promised to be. I'd been too busy playing reporter.

MY INTERVIEW WITH THE GENENTECH EXECUTIVE WAS TO BE HELD off campus. Like a good Stanford student, I dutifully hopped on my bike and navigated a series of narrow roads pockmarked with stop signs to get there.

I was just rounding a corner only a few hundred feet from our rendezvous when a blue Volkswagen ID.4 turned the bend, coming the opposite direction. And I promptly fell off my bike. Because the driver was Marc Tessier-Lavigne.

I'd never seen Tessier-Lavigne in person, apart from convocation, where I clearly hadn't paid attention. Suddenly, here he was, at the very moment I'd hoped to finally crack this case wide open—coming, it seemed, from *the very place where I was supposed to meet my secret source*!

It seemed so implausible, so ludicrous, that instead of paying attention to my turn, I'd craned my neck to stare directly at Tessier-Lavigne, smashing into the curb. Thankfully, aside from a bit of a wedgie, I was fine. As I eyed the sensible midrange electric vehicle, Tessier-Lavigne paid me no attention and drove out of sight.

My nerves had already been pumping, but this sent me over the edge. I feared I was somehow being set up, though I couldn't imagine how.

As I got back on my bike, I texted Sam, still reeling. "Just biked past Marc Tessier-Lavigne lol."

Sam got back in a flash. "He's out and about? Wild. Where. Should've tried to ask a question haha."

"I can't I'm on the way to the Genentech h interview," I texted, the extra *h* due to some one-handed-biking finger slippage. (Given that I'd just fallen off, I can't tell you why I got back on my bike and began texting, apart from having too much adrenaline in my system to think straight.)

I went into the interview expecting the worst, confident that my whole reporting process had been blown.

I walked out hours later in a different universe.

I texted Sam: "jackpot."

CHAPTER 9

[[NOT FOR DISTRIBUTION]]

In 2009, Marc Tessier-Lavigne seemed to have accomplished a miracle: He'd found the likely cause of neural degeneration in Alzheimer's patients.

Billions of dollars had been spent and countless avenues exhausted in studying Alzheimer's, and now Tessier-Lavigne—whose research expertise was primarily in brain development, not neurodegenerative disease—seemed on his first attempt to have found the culprit that eluded so many others. He was already a top executive in charge of hundreds of scientists. To have managed such a large organization while also producing such groundbreaking research himself was astonishing.

When Tessier-Lavigne unveiled his findings for the first time internally, at a Genentech retreat in Lake Tahoe, the room was stunned. "This came out of nowhere," one attendee told me. Another senior executive in the room said, "We all thought, holy shit. This is Nobel Prize stuff." Tessier-Lavigne, cool and collected, walked through each of the discoveries he had made, and executives openly speculated about what the consequences would be. "It was the miracle result," said one executive.

For years, Alzheimer's researchers had focused on the so-called amyloid hypothesis—the idea that the buildup of amyloid-beta is the key driver of the deadly disease. Amyloid-beta is a peptide derived from the larger amyloid precursor protein (APP), and the brains of Alzheimer's patients are filled with plaques made up of the amyloid-beta peptides. Still, despite numerous attempts since the inception of the amyloid theory in 1991, not a single drug has been shown to produce anything more than modest improvement. Tessier-Lavigne proposed a novel target: not amyloid-beta, but N-APP, a neighboring fragment of the larger APP protein.

Tessier-Lavigne's research, published February 19, 2009, in the prestigious journal *Nature*, identified a pathway by which N-APP bound to the protein death receptor 6 (DR6), triggering apoptosis—or, in plain English, "cellular suicide"—through another protein called caspase 6. Apoptosis is a necessary process, allowing the brain to eliminate damaged or unwanted cells. But it was this pathway, Tessier-Lavigne proposed, that was hijacked by Alzheimer's, leading to the neurodegeneration suffered by victims of the disease.

The paper was a hit.

"The Alzheimer's research community is buzzing," *Nature*'s news wing wrote a month after its release. Paul Greengard, a Nobel laureate, proclaimed, "It's going to have a major impact on the Alzheimer's field." Almost every major news outlet wrote about the research, lavishing Tessier-Lavigne with positive coverage. Bloomberg's headline: GENENTECH FINDS ALZHEIMER'S 'DEATH RECEPTOR' TARGET FOR DRUGS. Reuters: ALZHEIMER'S MAY HIJACK CHEMICAL MECHANISM. The *Los Angeles Times*: NEW THEORY ON ALZHEIMER'S.

Tessier-Lavigne, speaking to *The Wall Street Journal*, explained his discovery: "Alzheimer's is not just bad luck, but rather it is the activation of a pathway that is there for development purposes. [This study] suggests a different way of looking at Alzheimer's disease." And different it was. "Whereas amyloid-beta has been the subject of a great deal of work because of its clear role in plaque formation, N-APP has been ignored because it was thought to be trimmed off and thus not play any role in Alzheimer's Disease," a writer for an industry publication wrote in its cover story on Tessier-Lavigne and the new study. "The N-APP molecule used to be seen as a bit of unimportant debris released by the splitting of APP," the *San Francisco Chronicle* wrote. Not anymore.

Genentech filed numerous patents based on the paper and called it "groundbreaking basic research about an entirely new way of looking at the cause of Alzheimer's disease" in its annual letter to shareholders. "Because of this research," Genentech said, "we are working to develop both antibodies and small molecules that may attack Alzheimer's from a novel entry point and help the millions of people who currently suffer from this devastating disease."

But none of that would come to fruition. Because, after several failed attempts to reproduce the research, Genentech opened an internal review—and, according to seven people with knowledge of the incident, found that the Alzheimer's paper had relied on fabricated data.*

I LEARNED DETAILS OF THIS INCIDENT FOR THE FIRST TIME THE DAY of the bike accident, from the Genentech scientist and executive who became the first to speak with me despite an NDA.

When I walked in the door, my source started talking right away. He clearly had a lot to get off his chest. "I'm surprised at the stuff that's been out there because it's just the very tip of the iceberg," he told me. He then detailed three incidents of alleged misconduct at Genentech, the Alzheimer's paper being the most significant. This was not only because of the prominence of the study, he explained, but because of what had happened afterward. Because Tessier-Lavigne, my source told me, had deliberately kept word of the paper's apparent manipulation from coming out.

*Marc Tessier-Lavigne's response is described in detail in the subsequent chapter and in this book's notes.

By 2011, two years after the publication of the Alzheimer's paper, experts had begun to raise alarms because the study could not be reproduced. Many factors can cause a study to be irreproducible, but with suspicions raised both internally and within other organizations that attempted to verify the results, Genentech's Research Review Committee—the company's governing body of top executives—decided to open an internal inquiry into the research program.

There were some issues in the *Nature* paper that were clear from the published record alone. For one, the study didn't include a robust statistical analysis of its findings, and the number of samples was abnormally low, independent experts told me. Plus, the experiments themselves showed an extremely low degree of variation. This alone was not enough to come to a conclusion. But other issues, including two duplicated control slides, an incorrectly spliced blot, and two apparently identical lanes within separate blots raised further concern.

The Genentech inquiry, as I would eventually learn, didn't stop at the published record. Experienced scientists within the company were assigned to re-create the underlying experiments, while interviews were conducted with lab technicians and requests were made to review the original data. What they found, according to all seven people who had knowledge of the review at the time, was conclusive: "None of us believed that these data were true by the time people had attempted to reproduce it," one member of the committee told me. The paper had been "faked," utilizing "made-up" figures as evidence, he said.

Although Tessier-Lavigne had departed the company earlier in 2011 to serve as president of Rockefeller University, he was summoned back to California to account for the suspicious research. He was encouraged to retract the study. "Our interest is really in Genentech's credibility," an executive involved in the review told me, "and if that meant we had to go retract papers publicly, so be it. Marc's interest was—is—to try to keep it quiet."

Instead of retracting the paper, Tessier-Lavigne opted to publish two

STANFORD IS SUPPOSED
★★★ TO LOOK PERFECT. ★★★

I was a lifelong tech lover and Stanford acolyte.

My parents dropped me off at Alondra ("the Nerd Dorm") on September 20, 2022. I was excited, nervous, and a bit sore from lugging around boxes.

I quickly learned that the regular rules didn't apply out here. Coming across a Ferrari with license plate "FALIURE" my first weekend underscored this.

Stanford sees itself as quirky. Graduation begins with the Wacky Walk, where students process in outlandish getups.

At my first Stanford frat party, I learned that students were now required to recite consent pledges and land acknowledgments to get in the door.

I joined *The Daily* to investigate Stanford's increasing corporatization.

Shortly after finishing my first article on October 25, 2022, just after midnight.

The Stanford Tree mascot was suspended for protesting the War on Fun.

Marc Tessier-Lavigne darts across Main Quad on February 7, 2023, minutes after receiving questions about a famous Alzheimer's study he coauthored. He did not respond to the questions; instead, his lawyer sought to prevent publication of the article.

Sam Catania, my editor at *The Daily*, and I became bonded for life by the experience of investigating the president.

Elisabeth Bik, the super-sleuth who has reviewed more than one hundred thousand scientific studies for doctored data, became my first crucial source.

Luxury retreats and mansion parties are standard for Silicon Valley's favored teenagers.

"A yacht party is like a central Stanford experience," one friend advised me. With money from VCs, students host nights on San Francisco Bay regularly.

TreeHacks spends hundreds of thousands of dollars on a weekend of hacking projects, with up to seventeen hundred contestants.

Nestled by the library, Coupa Café is the unassuming meeting place for investors, students, professors, talent scouts, and just about everyone else.

The Stanford Highly Incompetent Team (S.H.I.T.) labored in the lowest level of an underground garage to assemble two race cars for the 24 Hours of LeMons.

I visited Frank, my best friend from high school, and Lily, my ex-girlfriend, after the Polk Award ceremony.

The Structured Liberal Education (SLE) program on a field trip to *The Gates of Hell*. Our sweatshirts bore a quote from Aeschylus: "Suffer into truth."

subsequent studies in lower-readership journals that effectively walked back the Alzheimer's paper's main claims without admitting any doubts about the original study. Genentech, uneasily, papered the whole thing over.

THE BRUNT OF THE WORK OF THE ORIGINAL STUDY HAD BEEN CONducted by Anatoly Nikolaev, a postdoctoral scholar in Tessier-Lavigne's lab, fresh off a Columbia PhD. He was listed as its first author, with two Salk Institute scientists who conducted a retinotectal analysis given middle authorship, and Tessier-Lavigne named as corresponding author. MTL "supervised or co-supervised all experiments, and co-wrote the paper," the paper said, but it was Nikolaev who'd actually generated the results, as is typical between the senior author and his lab member.

Nikolaev was described to me as an up-and-comer at Genentech, celebrated as the perfect example of how its postdoctoral program was supposed to function. One senior scientist at the time recalled that following publication of the *Nature* study, he was "invited to a meeting with the new rising star scientist at Genentech, Anatoly." He was told that Nikolaev had found "the involvement of a very specific protein in Alzheimer's disease," and "the company immediately initiated a drug discovery program around that protein." The senior scientist I spoke to was assigned to lead that team.

In the wake of the *Nature* study, both Nikolaev and Tessier-Lavigne received promotions. Nikolaev was hired as a full-fledged scientist, a coveted role for a young researcher in a field with too few positions to go around, and Tessier-Lavigne was promoted to chief scientific officer, in charge of fourteen hundred scientists. Then came the internal review.

The senior scientist and his team developing drugs based on the protein were abruptly reassigned. He was told that "lab data had been falsified"—in those exact words, he emphasized to me. And Nikolaev, the rising-star Columbia PhD who had published one of the most highly cited Alzheimer's papers of the decade, "was disappeared," in the words of one executive. Once considered an emblematic success, Nikolaev departed the field of biotech entirely after the internal review, winding up taking classes at a community college in Michigan and, eventually, becoming a low-profile radiation oncologist in Florida.

Details of the internal review were kept secret. When findings of the inquiry were disclosed in one meeting of the Genentech Research Review Committee, they were read out loud directly from a report rather than being physically distributed, so as not to generate a paper trail, according to one attendee. This wasn't entirely unusual for the committee, which could be hyperconscious of what it recorded; another member of the committee, in illustrating the point, described to me how the minutes of their meetings were "highly edited." In recording one meeting, this executive remembered, "one person had written that such and such might be a good target for such and such disease, and the first edit was the insertion of the word 'not' into that statement."

People involved with the internal review were disturbed by its findings. "I don't think anyone at Genentech would be interested in this becoming public," one senior scientist told me, adding, "It's a dent in the reputation." Another senior scientist said that withdrawing the paper would have been viewed as "sullying Marc's/Genentech's reputation" and that MTL refused to do so when urged on several occasions by several emissaries. "Instead of stopping it and saying, 'Okay, hold it here. We got something, we've got to look into it,' what Tessier-Lavigne did was walk around behind Anatoly with a broom and sweep up the footprints in the dirt," one member of the review committee told me.

Since Tessier-Lavigne was the one who ultimately chose whether to retract the paper, Genentech executives contented themselves with canceling the research program based on the study and "instituting a program within the company to address these problems," said the scientist who'd been assigned to develop drugs based on the study's findings. Genentech recruited a research misconduct expert, David Vaux, to lead several sessions with its scientists about, in the words of one executive, "why not to falsify data" and "how to identify falsified research."

When I reached him, Vaux confirmed that he had been brought in several times, beginning in May 2012. "My hosts at Genentech did not tell me why they asked me, but of course I had my suspicions," Vaux told me. "I did not ask them directly. They also made attendance universal and compulsory, and asked me to give the talk several times, because no auditorium was big enough to hold all their staff at once." A well-known researcher and member of the Center for Scientific Integrity, Vaux told me that he'd given versions of the talk at several institutions, but that one aspect of his presentation was modified: "Genentech also asked me to include one slide of theirs, which was an external phone number, so that anyone with concerns could speak up anonymously."

FOR MORE THAN A DECADE AFTERWARD, NOTHING ABOUT THE INTERnal review ever became public. People told me they were too scared to talk. Nearly all of my sources were governed by restrictive nondisclosure agreements, and even if they hadn't been, the price for speaking out was too steep. Scientific whistleblowers almost as a rule become unemployable, ostracized by friends and peers. People in a position to know what had happened with Tessier-Lavigne were also generally closely tied to him—science at that level is a small field, with numerous professional and personal intersections.

In the weeks that followed that breakthrough meeting with the Genentech executive, I slowly, painstakingly collected more accounts, probing potential sources over email and phone, in coffee shops, living rooms, and offices. I did not prompt them with what I had already heard; instead, I asked open-ended questions and allowed them to recount their own memories before following up on the details they gave. Each of the sources I spoke with over the next month—ultimately four people who served as senior figures at Genentech at the time of the internal review—independently relayed the same story. They remembered the same sequence of events, the same timing, the same details. Each one, of course, knew parts that the others didn't, but I was encouraged that their accounts lined up well even though none of them was in contact with any of the others.

I dug to find conflicts of interest or anything else that might compromise the credibility of my sources. I also sought to test them, occasionally asking leading questions I knew to be false to see whether they would agree. They didn't. In fact, the sources I spoke to the most betrayed a deep ambivalence about cooperating. This had been a theme from the first interview, which I'd recorded in a memo immediately afterward: "My source was clearly conflicted about speaking with me. 'I considered just responding to your email and saying I didn't know anything,' he said at one point. . . . Yet his concern for the scientific record won him over. 'I want the right thing to happen here,' he said."

Of Tessier-Lavigne himself, that source displayed uncertainty. "He stressed that he didn't know what the right outcome was," I recorded in the memo. "He was unclear what should happen to Tessier-Lavigne." In what would become hours and hours of conversations, we would return to this topic repeatedly. Most of my sources offered deeply anguished views of Tessier-Lavigne. Many were still friends with him, or at least friendly. The only thing they all seemed certain of was that the paper should've been retracted a decade earlier, and the fact that it hadn't been left the scientific record tarnished.

The scientific record, to the many scientists who make this their priority, is sacrosanct. Protecting and upholding it is of utmost importance. After all, scientific discoveries necessarily build on one another. Ignoring a rotten foundation can have unforeseen consequences. This is why so many scientists told me that they viewed research misconduct as an affront to their values, and even a betrayal. As a 2009 report from the National Academy of Sciences put it, fabrication flies in the face of "fundamental research standards and basic societal values. These actions are seen as the worst violations of scientific standards because they undermine the trust on which science is based." (Tessier-Lavigne has been a member of the National Academy of Sciences since 2005.)

Because the Alzheimer's paper had never been retracted and Tessier-Lavigne's record remained unmarred, he was able to segue into positions of higher acclaim, making a significant amount of money in the process. When *The New York Times* reported his appointment as president of Rockefeller, it referred to the *Nature* paper as his crowning achievement. He continued to cite the paper after he was informed of the Genentech internal review's findings, including in a National Institutes of Health grant application from 2014 that I obtained. Ultimately, the study garnered more than thirteen hundred citations.

Soon after the conclusion of the Genentech review and his refusal to retract the paper, MTL joined the board of Regeneron, the pharmaceutical company, where he became chair of the compensation committee; he and his fellow directors would be paid more than any other corporate board in the S&P 500. (He, Regeneron, and others faced a class action lawsuit over this and settled out of court.) Tessier-Lavigne ultimately made more than $80 million from serving on the Regeneron board. He earned much more than that from Denali, a company he co-founded in 2015 with two Genentech alums that launched with the highest-ever initial funding round for a biotech company, $217 million. The only "reason for the overstuffed purse" given by *Forbes*: "One co-founder, Denali's chairman of the board of directors, is Marc Tessier-Lavigne, a well-known neuroscientist and president of Rockefeller University in New York. He served as Genentech's head of drug research during its legendary run in the late 2000s." In 2017, Denali pulled off the largest biotech initial public offering of the year, and reached a market capitalization of around $10 billion in 2020.

After scouring decades of SEC filings and other records from a dozen companies, I estimate Tessier-Lavigne's current net worth to be north of $500 million—or, roughly, the net worths of the CEOs of Ford, Coca-Cola, and Bank of America combined. Or George Clooney's and Sabrina Carpenter's net worths combined. The point is: He got very, very rich, mostly during the period when the results of the Genentech internal review sat buried.

BY FEBRUARY 3, I WAS READY TO WRITE MY FIRST DRAFT OF THE ARTIcle. I sat down around 11:00 a.m., claiming one of the wooden tables in the Alondra dining hall, which doubles as a lounge, common space, and classroom. I opened a new Google Doc, which I labeled "[[NOT FOR DISTRIBUTION]]." It was a reflection of how paranoid I was about revealing this weighty story to anyone. By the time I looked up from my laptop, it was dark out and my watch read 3:18 a.m. I'd missed lunch, I'd missed dinner, I'd missed a birthday celebration for one of my dorm mates, all of which had presumably occurred around me in the same room without my noticing. But my first draft was done.

The next morning, I distributed the six-thousand-word [[NOT FOR DISTRIBUTION]] file for the first time, sending it to Tracy Jan, the *Washington Post* science editor who sat on *The Daily*'s board. After our previous work together on the first big MTL story, I trusted Tracy implicitly. My other adviser would be Glenn Kramon, a Stanford grad who'd served as the legendary business editor and assistant managing editor of *The New York Times* before coming west to teach at Stanford's business school. I'd reached out to Glenn in December, when someone on the George Polk Award nominating committee had emailed Sam asking us to submit our work; I asked Glenn if he might help us assemble our entry. The George Polk Award is a big-boy prize for professional journalists, and I thought we had no shot at winning. But I wanted to put our best foot forward. Although we'd never met, Glenn agreed to help and began advising me because, he later put it, "as a journalist I wanted to help him get to the bottom of the story, and as someone who has loved Stanford for fifty-two years I wanted to assure Theo was fair-minded and thorough."

Glenn, gruff and quick both to make up his mind and to change it should new information arise, immediately became a close friend and confidant. I loved him from the start, particularly his wit and kindness. I also valued his editing eye. He was incredibly thorough, constantly skeptical, and the greatest-ever practitioner of the oft-repeated, oft-ignored journalism advice to "kill your darlings."

Tracy was the first to read the draft, and her positive reaction was better than I could've hoped for. Which is not to say she had no edits; there were lots of those. Glenn got to it soon after. I could tell when he started because the font grew six or eight points, the sign that a signature Kramon edit was underway. He immediately tore apart my structure, pushing me to be clearer and explain the exact context with as much detail as possible. Glenn, too, seemed to think the sourcing was there. By the end of the day, Tracy, Glenn, and I had come up with a draft ready for legal review. I sent our version to Sam, letting him know where we stood. "Sweet," he said. "I'll look after banquet." And I gave myself a start, because I'd forgotten I had a party to attend in just an hour.

THE DAILY BANQUET IS HELD AT THE END OF EACH SIX-MONTH VOLume, or term, to celebrate the completion of an editor's run. Sam had made the unusual decision to stay on for a second six-month stint, in large part because he wanted to see the MTL story through. *The Daily* didn't throw many events—unlike *The Harvard Crimson*, where my friend Frank had to turn away hundreds of people from its parties—but the banquet was a long-standing tradition that celebrated everyone's contributions, handed out awards, and brought the *Daily* team together. I wasn't allowed to miss it.

The party, such as it was, was sweet and lightly attended. Even the prospect of free food and merriment hadn't enticed enough people to come to fill the Daily House. But Sam and the executive editors decorated the place with string lights and tinsel crisscrossing the beams overhead, and it was cute. The awards weren't necessarily serious—one was "most likely to commit Dailycest," meaning to date another member of the staff—but they were heartfelt, handed out by Sam with a big smile.

The respite was nice, as Sam and I were already quarreling over the Alzheimer's piece. We were both insanely stressed and bickered over every minuscule decision. As two stubborn, say-what-you-think types, we tended to duke it out for hours at a time until one of us finally became too exhausted to go on, a victor was declared, and the next order of business was broached.

Sam had recently agreed to name me the investigations editor, even though I was only a freshman and shouldn't have been on the masthead. Getting there had been far more acrimonious than I'd expected, with Sam and the two executive editors tearing into me for several hours during an interview for the job, and questioning, with what I took to be some real hostility, whether I had it in me. Eventually, they relented, but I'd been shaken. I knew that they were just doing their job, but in that moment, our dynamic had become adversarial. I didn't need the editor position. But I did need the editors to support me. I needed them to have confidence in me and be on my side as this high-stakes investigation of the university's president continued, because if we fractured internally, I had nothing left to rely on. When Sam eventually offered me the post, I seriously considered not taking it, so frustrating had our fight been.

I vented to R. B. Brenner, the journalism lecturer I'd grown close to. Then I told myself to grow a spine and be a team player. As painful as working at *The Daily* could be, when I did as R.B. instructed and took a deep breath, I was reminded that I really did trust Sam. Even if I disagreed with decisions, I knew that he had the right motivations, that he was a decent person. And most important: He cared. If we were fighting, this was why. We both wanted to get it right. Sam had confessed to me a few days earlier that he was having stress dreams about MTL. I was, too.

Of course, apart from Sam and me, nobody else at the banquet had any idea what was coming. At one point, whoever was DJing began to blast a 2019 SoundCloud parody rap about MTL entitled "big daddy marc," which overlaid a catchy bass-boosted trap beat with snippets of the Stanford president's speeches and the refrain, oozing with swagger: "I'm Marc Tessier-Lavigne, you can call me daddy." I'd recognized MTL's distinctive voice from the first syllable, and immediately blanched. Sam rushed over and pulled the plug from the speaker. We'd done so much work trying to bend over backward and be fair, to treat the president with respect; I felt faint at the idea that we would then dance around and laugh at lines like "I'm Marc Tessier-Lavigne, mothafuckaaaaaah / I've got so much money mothafuckaaaaaah." Thankfully, only a few seconds of the song had made it out into the world, and as the regular music resumed, I tried to find a corner where I could make myself as small as humanly possible.

The banquet, not exactly a rager, ended not much later, and I left with Marie, another freshman *Daily* staffer I only sort of knew. Marie and I had met once a few months prior when I found her drunk outside my door in Alondra. I'd gotten her a water bottle and helped her find the friend she was supposed to be with, my dorm mate Sylvia. She came back to my door the next time she visited Alondra to introduce herself properly and return the water bottle. In the intervening months, we'd seen each other a handful of times, only in large groups. Now, though, Marie told me she was leaving the banquet to meet some friends who wanted to go to the (as always, singular) frat party that night and asked if I wanted to tag along. I was grateful for the invite.

We went back to Marie's dorm to drink first, then headed off to the fraternity, where we read the expected declaration, "Federal recognition is an embargo that starves unrecognized tribes and violates their sovereignty. The Muwekma Ohlone continue to struggle for federal recognition. I acknowledge the violence complicit in my presence here," and entered to find a predictably sweaty and unappealing dance floor.

Eventually, I ended up back at Marie's dorm, hanging out in the common room with her and a friend, Darren. We stretched out on the floor together, myself in between the two of them, and Darren slowly drifted off to sleep, mumbling something about his international beauty queen girlfriend. Tall, lanky, and with the face of a Boy Scout, Darren had been felled by a few White Claws. The weight of his head pinned my arm and I spent several minutes trying to extricate myself without disturbing him, while Marie looked on in glee. "Out like a light," she said with a cackle, while I shot back an implied shush.

Finally, I freed myself and turned on my side to face Marie, intending to make light of the bizarre turn of events. Instead, Marie and I looked at each other and suddenly found our lips pressed against each other's. I can't say how it happened, only that it did. "Do you maybe want to go somewhere else?" I asked, pulling away as I imagined what Darren would think if he woke up and saw us. Marie laughed and sat up halfway, responding in the same hushed tone. "My roommate's already in bed," she said, "but how about yours?" To this I replied with what must be the single sexiest sentence utterable on a college campus: "I don't have a roommate."

By the time we made our trek through the cold, past the empty Daily House and wide-open fields without a soul in sight, it was already around 5:00 a.m. But I didn't care *that* much. The day I'd finished the first draft of my article, less than a month after my eighteenth birthday, I would lose my virginity to another writer at *The Daily*. Not that I admitted my callowness when she proposed having sex, because how could that possibly have been the right response?

I WOKE UP THE NEXT MORNING TO POUNDING AT THE DOOR.

Outside was Sergio, my brilliant older friend and, this quarter, my SLErt (SLE resident tutor—the older student-mentor assigned to you each quarter). Apparently, we'd had a meeting scheduled that morning to talk about my paper on Dante's *Inferno*—a paper that didn't yet exist, about a text I mostly hadn't read—and instead of giving up when I didn't show, Sergio had marched to Alondra and decided to drag me out of bed. He couldn't possibly have picked a worse time.

I opened the door as narrowly as I could, but there was still no way for Sergio to miss seeing Marie on my bed, hair frizzled and clad in my backup set of pajamas. Sergio looked at me with disappointment. "I'll wait for you in the lounge," he said.

Fuck.

I threw on pants and promised Marie I'd return as soon as possible. She rolled over, seeming mildly amused by the whole thing. Sergio, on the other hand, was not. "You need to get your shit together," he scolded me. "You're weeks behind on your work and you don't seem to take it seriously. You keep saying that you want to engage, but your essay draft was due last Thursday and I didn't get as much as a message. I'm here taking time out of my day to help you when I could be doing a million other things, and you don't even have the courtesy to text me and cancel because you decided to stay up too late with a girl instead. I want to help you, Theo, but I can't do that unless *you* want to accept help." I bit my lip, nodding and just trying to get it over with as quickly as possible. He was right, of course, and I flushed with shame. I couldn't tell him why my essay was late or why I wasn't sleeping.

After fifteen minutes of dressing-down, Sergio allowed me to go. I found Marie upstairs where I'd left her, and we shared a quick brunch and a laugh over it all. Then, as quickly as she'd arrived, she was gone, still wearing my pajamas.

In a quieter moment, this tryst might've been cause for reflection—after all, it had only been about two months since Lily and I broke up. But there was no time for reflection.

A few hours after Marie left, I was showered and back at the Daily House with Sam, running through the article. This was the first time we were due to discuss exactly who all of my sources were and exactly what evidence supported each line in the piece. With the stakes of the story, I'd been hypercautious about keeping my sources confidential. I refused to put their names on my phone, where they might be accidentally discovered or even hacked. I wouldn't look them up or search for any other information that could identify them on my own Google account or while accessing Stanford Wi-Fi. I used burner phones when calling monitored lines and created online aliases and virtual machines to disguise my activity. I tried to ensure that the most important exchanges took place face-to-face, creating no written record that could expose anyone. For this reason, Sam and I had carved out an in-person block of time to run through the whole thing in excruciating detail.

It's essential for an editor to know the names and backgrounds of a reporter's confidential sources, to ensure they're real and reliable. Over the course of several hours, I briefed Sam thoroughly, sketching out on a whiteboard who each source was, what they'd told me, and how they related to the broader story. Sam asked sharp questions, and we began charting next steps for the investigation.

I knew from the beginning that it was vital to proceed in secret for as long as possible in case MTL attempted to interfere. If nobody knew that I was working on this story, I had a much better chance of reaching people independently before they could be swayed by anyone else, for or against MTL. And because this was all confidential, it was easier to ensure that my sources were giving their own recollections, not being swayed by information in the public domain.

Sam and I kept the information circle extremely tight; none of the news editors had any idea something was in the works. My sources were walled off from one another, and the whole investigation had been compartmentalized. Only I possessed all the pieces to put it together. And now Sam.

As soon as we went to Tessier-Lavigne for comment, we'd lose all control. So the whole thing had to be delicately stage-managed.

Sam and I both had midterms to take, so we cut our meeting short and I erased the whiteboard. Before leaving, Sam told me he wanted to look into the sources more on his own time, something I eagerly encouraged. "*But!*" I said. "You have to follow my rules on this one, boss." He asked, "Can you just write down their names so I can look them up later?" Feeling a spurt of creative energy, I tore a corner off a page from his notebook and scribbled the names as neatly as I could, before folding up the tiny slip of paper and hiding it inside the dry-erase marker I'd been using. I examined my work with satisfaction; unless someone was to disassemble the marker, there was no indication that it harbored secrets. We hid the marker in a drawer of the conference room, confident that the secret was safe in plain view, even if we were raided and searched—as *The Daily* had been by police officers looking for unpublished photos to incriminate protesters in 1971, leading to a case that went all the way to the Supreme Court.

IN SLE, WE WERE STUDYING MAN'S PURPOSE. FOR MUCH OF MY LIFE, I'D struggled to feel a purpose. But the closer we got to publishing the article, the more clarity I felt. This was what I was meant to be doing, this is what I *had to do.*

Glenn, Tracy, and I polished a draft efficiently, and, with the document in hand, it was decision-making time. In addition to Sam, the core team now included Andrew Bridges, a trailblazing Fenwick & West attorney who served as *The Daily*'s board chair and stalwart defender; Ambika Kumar, cochair of the media law practice at Davis Wright Tremaine; and Eric Stahl, the lawyer who had reviewed my previous stories and served as outside counsel for *The Seattle Times*. Eric redlined the new piece and came back with his questions. We consulted for hours about how to be as careful as possible.

There were a million moving pieces, none of which could be left to chance. Before the story could go out, we would need to seek comment from everyone mentioned, particularly Tessier-Lavigne, Genentech, Anatoly Nikolaev, the Stanford board, *Nature*, and Richard Scheller. Each of them needed the chance to have their say. But the timing had to be just right. Once we went out with comment requests, there was a limited amount of time we could sit on the story. It was like lighting a fuse.

To prepare, we drafted each of the comment requests and went over them with the lawyers. I also wrote a series of HFOs—hold-for-order articles, otherwise known as prewrites, which are prepared in advance so they can be released immediately when an event occurs, like an obituary of a famous person. I drafted a few options in case MTL decided to jump ahead of the article, a common PR tactic to control the narrative before damaging information emerges in full. One article could be published in the event he resigned upon receiving the comment request or was removed from office, and was effectively an obituary for his presidency. Another could be published if Tessier-Lavigne decided to step aside for the remainder of the Stanford investigation. I doubted I'd publish either, but the allegations were damning enough that it couldn't be ruled out.

We also enlisted Niko, the star photographer, to stake out MTL. Niko had already retired from *The Daily*, but I impressed upon him how important this story was—without telling him what I was actually reporting—and he leapt into action, his news sense tingling.

We settled on a final timetable: We would go with the questions on Tuesday, February 7, with a generous forty-eight-hour deadline for response. Then, on Friday, we'd publish.

I HAVE NEVER HAD SO MUCH ENERGY IN MY LIFE. I FELT LIKE I COULD single-handedly lift a train. More realistically, I feared wearing a hole straight through the carpet from all of my pacing.

Sam and I arranged to meet at the Daily House on Tuesday to set everything in motion. Just past noon, I would email a list of detailed questions to Tessier-Lavigne and immediately walk over to Building 10, the president's office, with a printed list of the same questions. I'd request to speak to Tessier-Lavigne and, if he declined to see me, as I expected, deliver the questions to his assistant to confirm receipt. Then, in quick succession, I'd reach out to everyone else.

It was a lovely day, uncharacteristically warm for the season, with the sky a bright blue speckled with wisps of playful clouds. I walked past a couple lying on a picnic blanket. Everything about campus seemed to scream stillness—*Why don't you come and relax?*—but my strides were quick and purposeful, cutting through the pleasant day with a sort of manic buzz. To passersby, I must've seemed like someone on a warpath.

Upon arrival, Sam and I ran over the plan once more. Then I made him go change. "It's the president, Sam, you have to wear something nice!"

"What, you don't like my flannel?"

"It doesn't compliment your figure," I teased. (Actually, it was one of Sam's better looks, but I felt we owed Tessier-Lavigne the respect to at least don a blazer and jeans.)

Sam returned a half hour later and the strategizing began. We wanted to reach Tessier-Lavigne in person, but Niko had been staking him out for days and the president had scarcely been to the office. In fact, our tail had only managed to snag one sighting, of MTL leaving the presidential mansion. "Did Niko show you the picture he got of MTL's car?" Sam asked.

"No, but it's the blue Volkswagen ID.4, right?"

"Yeah, how did you know?"

"It almost ran me over, remember?" I said, dryly exaggerating the only time I'd seen Tessier-Lavigne in the flesh.

At that moment, Sam walked over to the window and exclaimed, "Oh, my God, IT'S RIGHT THERE!"

Incredible as it seemed, the Volkswagen ID.4 was passing right in front of the Daily House. What the fuck were the odds of that? That thought, though, was quickly replaced by another one: RUN!

Sam and I had the same idea and bolted for the door, jumping down five stairs at a time to burst onto the street. By the time we made it outside, MTL had disappeared. Sam and I split up.

I sprinted left, and rounded the corner just in time to see the back of the VW. I shouted, "Sam! Sam! This way—he's here!" My dress shoes—infrequently worn in California—dug into my heels as I raced down the middle of the road, paying no attention to the dozens of students flowing from classrooms at the end of a period. They gawked. I ran.

Sam caught up to me on his bike and we kept up our pursuit at full speed until realizing that the car was slowing down and nearing a stop. I, too, ground to a halt, and Sam pulled a skid mark with his bike. Scarcely believing our luck, we attempted to appear nonchalant as we watched MTL get out of his car a hundred feet away and walk toward Building 10.

IF I'D BEEN HOPPED UP ON ADRENALINE BEFORE, THIS WAS SOMETHING akin to a defibrillator going off and an EpiPen being injected at the same time.

As long as we kept eyes on the car, we now had a guaranteed opportunity to approach MTL for comment. I wanted to see how he'd react, to take him in for myself.

I summoned Niko and directed him to set up camp in Main Quad with a camera trained on the door of Building 10. I didn't ask if he was in class, and he didn't hesitate. In our mad dash from the Daily House, I'd left the questions behind, along with my jacket, so I took Sam's key card and let him keep watch while I went back and retrieved them.

Then Sam and I made the short walk to Building 10 and, forcing myself to project confidence, I swept open the door to catch my first glimpse of the president's office. Or rather, the waiting room of the president's office. The two-story room, covered in dark wood and oil paintings, betrayed little information, and MTL's inner sanctum was guarded by a long desk that ran the length of the interior and the gatekeeper who sat behind it. I knew that Tessier-Lavigne was inside—feet away—but I wasn't even sure which direction to look. Upstairs? Just behind the wall against the secretary's back? The building wasn't large, but it was functionally impenetrable.

The assistant looked at us expectantly, and I approached with as serious a look as a freshman with baby cheeks freshly shaved for the occasion could muster. "Hi there," I said, "I'm Theo Baker from *The Stanford Daily* and I have some questions I'd like to ask of President Tessier-Lavigne."

"I'm sorry, but he's not available at the moment," said the assistant. "I can let him know you stopped by."

This was pretty much what I'd expected. "Do you have any idea when he might be available?" I asked. The assistant shook his head. "I'm afraid I don't know when he'll be wrapping up."

I thanked him for his time and handed over the list of questions. "Please ensure President Tessier-Lavigne gets these as soon as possible, it's fairly urgent," I said, while internally lashing myself for not having prepared a folder or letter or some other more professional method of delivery. The loose piece of printer paper seemed pathetic.

Sam and I left as quickly as we'd entered, and as I took one more peek in, I thought I could see the assistant getting up to deliver the questions. Then again, maybe he needed coffee. I wasn't sure that we—for all our exhortations of urgency—had left the impression that we had to be taken seriously. But no matter, the material would speak for itself.

WE KNEW WHERE TESSIER-LAVIGNE WAS—AND WE ALSO KNEW WHERE he had to walk to reach his car; for exactly 396 feet, MTL would be in the open and exposed.

I didn't want to ambush the president. There would be no hiding in the bushes or sneaking up on him. I would wait on a bench a respectful distance from his car. When the time came, I'd walk over in plain view, introduce myself, and politely ask my questions. I told Niko to stay put in Main Quad with his camera and alert me when the president emerged. "But keep your distance," I said. "We're not going to harass him."

In the meantime, I began to send out my other comment requests.

I emailed Aidan Ryan questions for the Stanford board and sent over a comment request to *Nature*'s press email. Because Genentech was an essential party, unlike *Nature*, which hadn't been alerted to any of the internal suspicions, I decided to call first to ensure that an email from a student reporter didn't get overlooked.

I couldn't get through to the press office, but I left a voicemail that outlined the story in broad strokes—a prominent paper, an internal review that fingered it as fraudulent, and the burying of this finding.

A few minutes later, Persis Drell, the provost, left Building 10, presumably from the same meeting as MTL. Niko said she'd passed within feet of him, catching sight of the camera and making eye contact. She'd then opened her phone and typed something while walking—a warning, perhaps, notifying Tessier-Lavigne that we were in the area?

A few more minutes passed and we began to wonder whether MTL would even emerge. Then he burst through the front door of Building 10, booking it across Main Quad.

Tessier-Lavigne was moving at an impressive clip, with giant, unrelenting strides. Niko called me. "He's on his way! He was moving so fast, I barely caught him. I'm not even sure it's in focus!" I ditched my laptop and moved to intercept, calling out politely to Tessier-Lavigne as he approached.

"President Tessier-Lavigne? Hi there, my name is Theo, I'm a reporter—"

He cut me off, clearly not surprised to see me.

"Hello, nice to meet you," the Canadian-polite president said, addressing me even as he brushed right past. "I'm in a hurry, and I did get your letter," he added, making it to his car and swinging his body into the driver's seat, "and I'll look forward to, you know, being in touch."

He slammed the door in my face before I could get a sentence out.

Richard Scheller, MTL's good friend and longtime colleague, was next on my list. I'd reached out to Scheller a number of times over two months to ask for an interview but never heard back. Several of my sources had recounted conversations with Scheller about the disputed Alzheimer's paper and called him a critical Tessier-Lavigne ally, who'd initially urged MTL to retract the study before helping him to keep it quiet.

I trooped over to Scheller's house in the so-called faculty ghetto—the one he'd purchased with his windfall from the Genentech IPO decades prior—and knocked on the door. I peered in a window and caught a glimpse of the sleek mid-century modern home's famed collection of African art, and of the portly bearded man walking over. Scheller, whom I was almost astonished to see in the flesh after having stared at his portrait for so long online, opened up, and I introduced myself. He slammed the door immediately. I let out a laugh and said aloud, to no one in particular, "Clearly this is becoming a habit."

The waiting for comments was agony. Beyond anything I'd ever experienced. I could not process anything happening around me.

I somehow typed an entire paper on Dante without registering a single word of it. (I found a copy recently and it was hilarious: I'd clearly run out of steam about two thirds of the way through and made an awkward hard pivot from the symbolism invoked by Virgil to current events, a topic I could write about without having to put in much effort.)

By nighttime, I felt like scraping off my own skin. If I'd had alcohol or weed I probably would've tried that, but I had no fake ID and no supplier, so I simply agonized alone in my room.

Wednesday I spent most of the day working on TreeHacks. We were only two weeks out now and most of the team was already in go-go-go mode. I also finally got a call back from a harried-sounding Genentech press person, asking for more details. I filled her in and sent my questions directly over email. Because it had been more than a decade since the Alzheimer's paper I was writing about, and Genentech had become a subsidiary of the international pharmaceutical giant Roche, few people were left at the company from that time, and the spokeswoman said it would take time to collect information.

By Thursday, I was a nervous wreck, bracing for impact. We had asked for comment by 2:00 p.m., though I didn't expect Tessier-Lavigne to be on time. Since he'd promised a response, I figured we would at least get something, unlike previous stories when he'd been mute.

I went to my SLE lecture—this week on Machiavelli—and did my best to focus on the tales of sixteenth-century greed and manipulation. But, halfway through the lecture, hours before I expected any word, my phone began to buzz. It was Sam.

"Did you see?"

I ran out of the lecture, scarcely able to enter my passcode, so severe were my shakes. I looked for a response from MTL. Instead, I found a letter from an attorney.

"Dear Mr. Baker, I represent Stanford President Marc Tessier-Lavigne . . ."

CHAPTER 10

THE GOOD PAPER

In the annals of fraud, Charles Keating Jr., a six-foot-five All-American swimmer turned financier who used good looks and charm to swindle countless victims, has earned a distinguished entry.

In the 1980s, Keating, brash and swaggering, cost taxpayers billions and helped set off a broader fiasco known as the savings-and-loan (S&L) crisis. Ultimately, more than a thousand financial institutions failed, and Keating became the face of the half-a-trillion-dollar scandal—considered at the time the worst since the Great Depression.

Keating bragged about buying influence with senators to keep regulators off his back and lived an opulent life. He came to be seen as a symbol of excess. The *Chicago Tribune* called him "the greediest man in America." The federal entity established to address the crisis called him an "evil mind." According to L. William Seidman, the Federal Deposit Insurance Corporation chair who helped clean up much of the S&L mess, Keating committed "one of the most heartless and cruel frauds in modern memory." He was convicted in state and federal courts, was sent to prison, and lost a $4.3 billion civil judgment, then the largest ever against a private individual.

Then something miraculous happened. His name was Steve Neal.

Neal, a Stanford-educated lawyer then at Kirkland & Ellis who, at six foot four, could see eye to eye with Keating, had begun building a reputation "as a smart litigator unafraid of unpopular cases," *The New York Times* wrote in 1991. Keating hired Neal not just to represent him but to orchestrate his bid for freedom. First, Neal went after the California conviction. He attacked the judge, and in April 1996 got the fraud ruling thrown out by an appeals court based on a procedural error. In December 1996, in front of the same court of appeals, Neal argued that the federal conviction should be negated, too, citing another procedural error. Once more, he succeeded. Suddenly, after four and a half years in prison, Keating was free.*

It was nothing short of astonishing. "Keating was saved by Steve Neal's vigorous defense," bragged Kirkland. "He's an innocent man now; he hasn't been convicted of anything," Neal told the media. Keating himself kept his comments limited. "You'll have to talk to my attorney, man. He's doing pretty good for me so far," he said, according to a 1996 *Los Angeles Times* report. The story added: "The once outspoken Arizona developer, who has been held under tight wraps by Neal, simply agreed with his lawyer that he was delighted with the ruling."

Of course, Keating wasn't absolved, merely freed. The money had still been misappropriated and the victims fleeced. Even assistance from the government couldn't heal all the wounds—college educations, marriages, homes, and even lives had been destroyed. One elderly victim who lost his life savings slit his wrists and died in a bathtub.

But Neal, for his part, was delighted at the legal outcome. He defended Keating as a man of "great dignity, wit and courage." And he made a career off it.

---

*In 1999, on the eve of a retrial of the criminal case, Neal negotiated a deal in which Keating pleaded guilty to four counts of wire and bankruptcy fraud but got off on the main charges and was sentenced solely to time served. Since the collapse had occurred over a decade earlier and most victims were elderly, or dead, prosecution was difficult. Later in 1999, Neal got the $4.3 billion civil judgment reversed, too—again on procedural grounds. A $1 billion judgment in a separate class action lawsuit filed on behalf of twenty-one thousand victims remained on the books, but Keating never paid.

After leaving Kirkland, Neal became the chairman and CEO of Cooley, the dominant law firm of Silicon Valley. He was one of the most influential lawyers in the country. He served as the chair of Meta's oversight board, the chair of the Levi Strauss board of directors, the chair of the William and Flora Hewlett Foundation board, and a director of Nvidia.

In 2017, Neal signed on to represent Elizabeth Holmes, the Theranos fraudster. He would be her lead attorney in the class action filed against her in Arizona by patients who'd relied on Holmes's unreliable blood tests. Neal attempted to have the case dismissed, arguing that the cost of the tests had already been refunded and therefore no more recompense was required, that because individuals couldn't prove their specific blood tests had been inaccurate at the time, they weren't entitled to relief, that Theranos's flagrantly false statements were merely "non-actionable puffery."* The court rejected these motions.

At the same time, Neal was assisting Holmes with the Securities and Exchange Commission. When Holmes sat down for her now-infamous SEC deposition, in which she used the phrase "I don't know" more than six hundred times, Neal was right beside her.† "I represent Ms. Holmes in all capacities," he said.

Now he was in my inbox. Representing MTL.

DARTING OUT OF MY MACHIAVELLI LECTURE, I THUMBED THROUGH Neal's letter with shaky fingers. It wasn't subtle. "Your errors are many, fundamental, and egregious," Neal wrote me on Cooley letterhead.

*Theranos had claimed, "All tests are developed and validated under CLSI, FDA, CDC and WHO guidelines," and said that the company "continuously conducts proficiency testing and participates in multiple proficiency-testing programs." These specific statements, and others, caused the judge to rule that the company had gone beyond "puffery." Neal served as Holmes's counsel until late 2019, when he withdrew. (Not for any moral qualms; she'd simply run out of money to pay him.)

†The deposition has since been viewed millions of times and became a significant plot point in Hulu's *The Dropout*.

"Any dissemination of these allegations has been and will continue to be extremely reckless."

While I'd been prepared for a denial, this was an all-out, take-no-prisoners attack. "There was no investigation," Neal wrote. My questions were "indefensible and evince a fundamental misunderstanding of the Paper's scientific work and findings." And "given that the falsehoods in your letter concern activities at Genentech and the conduct of Genentech personnel, we felt compelled to notify Genentech of your allegations." In fact, Neal had copied Genentech's general counsel on the email, implying that the corporation and its former employee were in lockstep, rejecting my reporting.

Lovely.

I forwarded the letter to my own lawyers and advisers while arranging to meet with Sam. We greeted each other with a hug that felt necessary and decided to go for a walk, trying to absorb the fact that one of the most powerful lawyers in America had now declared himself our adversary. Soon, we ended up inside Memorial Church, my first time inside the stately chapel, Stanford's most historic. It was empty, peaceful.

"What do you think?" Sam asked me.

"It's hard to reconcile with the things we know," I said.

MTL wasn't just denying fraud, he was denying even aspects of the story that seemed cut-and-dried. "Contrary to your assertions," wrote Neal, "Dr. Tessier-Lavigne's later papers did not repudiate the Paper's primary findings and a correction or retraction of those findings would have been unwarranted and inappropriate." Neal continued, "the Paper's central tenets—which reported involvement of DR6, APP and Caspase-6 in developmental axon degeneration, also known as pruning—have been validated in vitro and in vivo."

This was a remarkable claim, one that seemed to directly contradict the scientific record. In fact, the study's key discovery, the binding between the N-APP fragment and DR6, was never replicated, despite numerous attempts. Everything else in the study was based on that binding. The paper claimed that beta-secretase, essential for plaque formation in Alzheimer's, was required to cleave the APP and lead to the DR6 binding. It wasn't. The study noted that "unlike neuronal cell body apoptosis, which requires caspase 3, we show that axonal degeneration requires caspase 6," a surprise finding that was also inaccurate—caspase 3 was indeed required for axonal degeneration. And then there was the Alzheimer's piece. Because that, too, was proven inaccurate.

Tessier-Lavigne had described the paper's findings at the time in a speech by saying that "an established bad actor in Alzheimer's disease is a protein called APP," but "what this theory does is really to turn our current understanding of Alzheimer's on its head because we're focusing on a different part of the APP molecule": N-APP. "This N-APP fragment has been previously shown to be present in the Alzheimer's brain, but it's largely been ignored," Tessier-Lavigne said then. "Our model together is that this N-APP fragment binds DR6, activates caspase-6, which then triggers degeneration."

The fragment, in other words, was key.

But Tessier-Lavigne's team later performed a crystal structure analysis showing that the N-APP–DR6 binding described in the paper was impossible. Indeed, the larger protein APP—the one already central to Alzheimer's theories—did bind to DR6, but only at a site that was not contained in the N-APP fragment. Thus, the core insight of the paper—what Richard Scheller called "the most important discovery made in Alzheimer's disease in the last twenty years, maybe ever"—turned out to be wrong.

This, in and of itself, didn't mean the 2009 paper was fraudulent. Indeed, Tessier-Lavigne had been the one in the subsequent papers to walk back claims made in the original study. In 2014, he and his coauthors wrote that they revisited the N-APP–DR6 binding and found it incorrect. "This conclusion was based on use of partially purified N-terminal fragment," they explained, "but we found that the interaction was lost when it was fully purified." (Even that explanation, though, was problematic: The 2009 study had claimed to be using fully purified N-APP in the first place.)* Also in 2014, Tessier-Lavigne published a study that concluded the N-APP–DR6 pathway "Does Not Contribute to Alzheimer's Disease–Related Pathophysiology," based on further experimentation in a different medium.

Core aspects of the original paper clearly hadn't held up on closer analysis. So why was Neal trying to pick a fight on that point?

THE FULL-THROATED DENIAL MADE IT IMPOSSIBLE TO PUBLISH OUR story the next day. Frankly, we weren't sure whether we'd be able to publish at all. I'd guaranteed three of my four key sources' anonymity, meaning that I had an obligation to protect their identities even in the event of a lawsuit. If MTL sought to bury us in litigation—Neal's self-proclaimed favorite part of the job—it would be a long, difficult process. With this kind of story, even getting every fact 100 percent correct was not a guarantee of safety. Sure, we would likely win at trial, but getting to trial would upend my life and Sam's, cost millions of dollars, and become a yearslong ordeal.

That wasn't a fun prospect for someone who'd just turned eighteen.

An hour or so after Neal's letter arrived, Genentech's statement landed in my inbox. It was more professional—and delivered by a PR representative, not a lawyer—but it was nevertheless a denial. "The account of events that you shared with us is false," it said. "There have not been any formal investigations, allegations, claims or complaints regarding scientific fraud or misrepresentation involving the *Nature* 2009 paper—never to the Genentech Research Review Committee (RRC) and, to our knowledge, never to anyone else at Genentech."

That said, Genentech's statement opened a door. The company

*In his response to questions for this book Tessier-Lavigne wrote that the reagent "was described in the paper the way we understood it to be," and that he "believed the contents of the paper were all accurately presented" at the time. He continued, "The fact that the reagent was less purified than we were led to believe at the time unfortunately only came to our attention years later."

wrote that "in November 2011, the project received a regular review by Genentech's Research Review Committee (RRC)," which decided to order more experiments, and "based on the results of the genetic experiments at Genentech, the RRC terminated the Genentech research project in 2012." This was a confirmation of some of the basic facts that each of my sources had recounted.

The company characterized what happened differently than my sources, of course, saying the company's review was merely the kind "routinely done for Genentech's drug discovery projects." But in confirming the existence of the review, they had also confirmed that my sources possessed insider knowledge of the internal process surrounding the Alzheimer's study. Genentech's statement left some room for interpretation that MTL's aggressive letter had not—and it struck me that the word "formal" was doing a lot of work for them.

The story wasn't dead in the water. But moving forward with it would require us to be incredibly confident in the reporting.

MY FIRST STEP WAS TO RUN NEAL'S ASSERTION ABOUT THE "CENTRAL tenets" past an independent Alzheimer's researcher I'd been consulting for a few months.

Matthew Schrag, a Vanderbilt professor, was an expert in the field and had uncovered rampant fraud underpinning another seminal Alzheimer's study the year before. But he also had a unique viewpoint. Soon after the *Science* investigation that unveiled this fraud was published, Schrag was alerted by PubPeer sleuths to issues in two of his own papers, which he'd coauthored as a graduate student fifteen years earlier. Schrag investigated, and found that his mentor Othman Ghribi—still a trusted friend—had fudged figures in a number of studies both before and after Schrag worked with him. In an emotional phone call, Schrag confronted his fellow scientist, who admitted to the manipulation.

For my purposes, this meant Schrag was especially credible. Not only was he a subject-area expert whose ethics were unimpeachable, but he understood what it was like to be on the other side. He wouldn't pull his punches, but he also wouldn't render judgment until an overwhelming case had been proven.

I asked Schrag to review the scientific literature on my behalf and provide his analysis—without details about what I'd learned from internal sources so as not to bias him. Not long after, my phone began to buzz with a FaceTime notification. I picked it up and there was Schrag, face close to the screen—he'd clicked the FaceTime button by accident. I piped up and he swung the screen back in surprise. "My gosh, you're young!" he exclaimed. I broke down laughing, my first time doing that in a while. Schrag and I had been texting and calling since November, but this was his first time seeing my face.

It was late his time—Schrag had just put his kids to bed—but he walked me through the studies, pointing out the ways in which the initial paper was found to be inaccurate in later research. Schrag was cautious, and stressed that none of what he was telling me inherently connoted fraud, but he answered my questions and made it clear that the subsequent findings "create a problem for this paper." He agreed to provide me with an analysis in writing in a few days that I could attribute to him by name.

In the meantime, I'd already gone back to my insider sources. I made clear that if they had some sort of grudge or if they had misrepresented themselves I would be the one left hanging out to dry. They didn't waver.

I ran Genentech's characterization of the company's review past the member of the review committee I had spoken with. Was this right? Was it really routine? "No, no, no, no, no, no," he responded. This had been "a reexamination of the paper's key findings" that left little doubt, he said. By the end, the panel had been "100 percent confident that [the issues] weren't innocent."

When I went back to another source to check my reporting and asked about the assertion in the threatening letter from MTL's lawyer,

I also got a categorical rebuttal: "It is impossible for that to be a true statement."

AFTER A DOZEN EMAILS OVER THE WEEKEND WITH THE HEADING "Attorney-Client Privileged," we were stuck.

Sam asked to listen to the full recordings of all of my interviews. I worried that this would just be an excuse for him to micromanage, but I was wrong to fear. Sam came away even more confident in the story. Meanwhile, just to be sure, we'd quietly asked the top lawyers of two major, nationally renowned news publications to review the story in addition to *The Daily*'s own attorneys. Both said they were comfortable with the piece. So were Glenn and Tracy. But it was a hard call given the seriousness of the allegations and the legal firepower MTL was training at us.

Eventually, we felt prepared to send another round of questions to Tessier-Lavigne and Genentech. None of us believed that responding to Neal was the best course. After all, our goal wasn't to engage in a legal battle, but to request MTL's own perspective. I emailed questions directly to Tessier-Lavigne and the Genentech spokeswoman.

THEORETICALLY, I HAD CLASSES AND HOMEWORK AND ALL OF THOSE normal things to attend to, but I couldn't bring myself to care. I guess people were starting to notice, and I received a message from the resident director of my Stanford neighborhood:

> Hi Theo, I hope you are doing well. I wanted to reach out to you to check in, as it was shared with me via the Student Services that you had missed some classes.
>
> How are you feeling? We can also walk to the [campus psychological services] office if you need to.

Please advise.

In community,

RD Kenneth Graham

The note was well meaning, but what was I supposed to say? After all, nobody could know why I was wandering the halls late at night with a dazed expression, why I was skipping meals. The distance from my peers grew exponentially.

At the same time, the annual TreeHacks competition was scheduled to begin at the end of the week, and I had obligations that, unlike a class assignment, couldn't be put off. By now, the entire team was meeting each night, usually well into the early morning hours. This should have been an exhilarating occasion, an event we'd been planning for months. But I couldn't bring myself to summon enthusiasm. Even the fact that I'd be seeing Lily that weekend for the first time since we broke up—actually, the first time since I'd gone to college; I'd secured her a slot to participate in TreeHacks and offered to let her stay in my room—couldn't shake me from my stress.

ONCE MORE, I RECEIVED A RESPONSE NOT FROM TESSIER-LAVIGNE, BUT from his attorney. Once more, it was aggressive. "Dear Mr. Baker," Neal wrote. "I am responding to the letter you sent to President Tessier-Lavigne yesterday afternoon. Your letter is replete with flagrant and seemingly deliberate distortions and disregard of the information presented in my letter of February 9, Genentech's response to you of the same date, and the scientific record." Neal continued, "We are deeply disappointed that you appear to be persisting in the publication of a brazenly false and distorted story."

For the most part, Neal's response ignored the questions to MTL. But Neal also attached a separate letter, signed by Tessier-Lavigne himself and purporting to explain the scientific context of the paper. In the letter, Tessier-Lavigne went through each of the elements of the study and what held up, while also explaining the conclusions that had shifted. MTL stated emphatically that "the data that led to those proposals were reproducible and many were independently reproduced by other groups." Here he referenced two other studies before doubling down. "Let me underscore this: the data were reproducible."

This was an extraordinary claim, made without equivocation—and it just didn't seem to be true.

Neither of the two papers that Tessier-Lavigne referenced had attempted to replicate the N-APP–DR6 binding at the core of the 2009 study. Those who had attempted to reproduce the binding, across several institutions, had failed. At least two studies—including a Biogen paper published by *Nature Medicine*—showed a failure to reproduce the binding even prior to MTL's first paper revising the 2009 paper's conclusions, and other failed attempts went unpublished.

I tried to look at it from every charitable angle, to give MTL every benefit of the doubt, but I could find no way to square his statement with the other available evidence. And I was baffled. Why was he staking himself on this point? Why undermine his credibility so severely?

ANATOLY NIKOLAEV WAS ALSO PROVING TO BE AN UNRELIABLE NARRATOR. In an initial telephone interview, MTL's former protégé had claimed the two were "on very good terms and we speak often." He denied that any kind of review had occurred and said he left Genentech "on very good terms" in 2011. But when I asked why he had departed a lucrative position in biotech to take classes at a community college in Michigan, his only explanation was that medicine was his "lifelong dream." "Leaving Genentech was my own decision," he said, and Genentech and Ryan Watts—MTL's Denali cofounder—would be able to confirm this, he said. (Neither Genentech nor Watts would answer repeated questions about Nikolaev's exit.)

Hours later, Nikolaev emailed to recant one of his statements, writing, "I have not spoke [*sic*] with Marc since after he left Genentech in 2011." In another interview, he again amended the statement, saying that Tessier-Lavigne had invited him to a lab reunion, which he did not attend, but that they'd otherwise had no interaction.

This wasn't the only detail that seemed to shift between his accounts. Nikolaev initially had said "nothing in our paper is 'false' or 'falsified'—I can assure you that." In a subsequent interview, he said, "I can only speak for myself . . . and say I did not do anything wrong when I was at Genentech." He demurred from speaking more specifically about the paper, citing a confidentiality agreement.

In that second interview, Nikolaev also claimed that the 2009 paper "doesn't even talk about Alzheimer's disease," and said that Alzheimer's was not "even mentioned in the paper." But the word "Alzheimer's" appeared in the paper thirty-one times, including in its abstract. What was I to make of this guy?

Sam and I had long, painful conversations, rehashing every detail. If we published the story, MTL had made clear he would fight vigorously, with the help of his legal bulldog Steve Neal. But we couldn't ignore the accounts of four independent, senior figures at Genentech, with no known ulterior motives, whose recollections matched one another's and publicly verifiable details.

The strain of wrestling with this story was getting to me. As I was walking the loop I'd taken a million times from Alondra to the Daily House on the afternoon of Neal's second letter, I started sobbing. I couldn't help it. This was all so much. I texted Phil Taubman, a seasoned *New York Times* correspondent who'd retired out west and lectured at Stanford, and told him I wasn't in a great place. "Be there in three," Phil responded.

For the longest time, I'd tried to keep Phil and his wife, Felicity Barringer, an equally extraordinary former *Times* correspondent, separate from my reporting. I had met them back in the fall, when they took me out for dinner after I joined *The Daily*. Phil was particularly attached to Stanford, and knew MTL—I didn't want to put him in an awkward position. Phil had told me he wouldn't provide me information and didn't want to see my copy in advance, a request I understood and honored. But I was so alone. In that moment, I needed him—not as a source, but as a human—and he rose to the occasion.

Phil picked me up in his SUV and we drove around aimlessly for a while, my sniffling slowing and eventually stopping. We talked about his relationship with Felicity. The two had met at *The Stanford Daily*, where they served as back-to-back editors in chief. They knew something about resistance to student reporting. Felicity had been the editor when *The Daily* was raided, leading to the Supreme Court case and *The Daily*'s separation into a distinct legal entity from the university, exactly fifty years before I joined.

"I feel so small," I said to Phil. "I don't know if I can do this."

He asked me simply, "Do you have the story?"

For all the uncertainty I was feeling about publication and what would come next, my response came quickly, through a shaky but firm voice.

"Yes."

"Then you have your answer."

We drove around for another half hour, passing Cooley's offices at the Stanford Research Park along the way. By the time I got out of the car, I knew what needed to be done.

ON THURSDAY MORNING, FEBRUARY 16, 2023, I WOKE FROM A RESTLESS three hours of sleep and darted into a ridiculously cold Northern California morning. It was only 7:00 a.m., and the temperature was still in the thirties, a harsh wind magnifying the frigidity as I biked across campus to Sam's room, my first time seeing him in such an intimate environment.

Genentech's spokeswoman had asked for a meeting with her and their senior vice president for public affairs, one of the top executives at the thirteen-thousand-person-plus company. Fritz Bittenbender was traveling overseas, hence the early morning timing. I arranged to add Sam and Andrew Bridges, the *Daily* board chair, too.

As we did introductions at the beginning of the call, Bittenbender sounded surprised. "Now, Andrew, you are *not* a student, I'm guessing from the sound of your voice," he said.

"That's right," Andrew responded, noting that he was in fact an attorney and our board chair.

"I didn't realize," said Bittenbender, "that *The Stanford Daily* is a foundation or a board-driven organization."

Andrew launched into a little spiel about *The Daily*'s separation from Stanford as an independent 501(c)(3).

From that moment, Genentech's tone took a noticeable shift.

Bittenbender now took a much more collegial approach. "You're talking to people on the phone who weren't around during that time. None of our leadership was around during that time," he said. He continued, "I actually want to solicit your help, because Genentech has taken these allegations very seriously . . . and we have not been able, from the documents that we have been able to find, to substantiate some of the various allegations." Bittenbender wanted to make clear that the company was acting in good faith. "Unfortunately, the record is over ten years old. We certainly don't have access to some of the records." So, he asked, were there documents that we could share to help them in their due diligence? Could we help Genentech, please?

Clearly, they were putting some daylight between themselves and Tessier-Lavigne and trying to figure out what level of danger our potential article represented. They seemed much less confident in their denial now. Sam, Andrew, and I politely declined to provide more than we'd already given in our request for comment, which they promised to respond to by later in the day. And when their response arrived, it was, indeed, far less definitive than MTL's account or even their first statement. Genentech still rejected the accounts of my sources, but not categorically. "Given that these events happened many years ago," the company now acknowledged, "our current records may not be complete."

With this, Sam and I agreed we finally had all the ingredients to publish. That plan was to meet that night and, hopefully, pull the trigger.

A FEW HOURS LATER, I WAS JUST WALKING INTO MY SLE SECTION ON *Don Quixote* when my phone rang. It was a New York number, and I thought it might be a Genentech insider I'd been trying to reach.

It wasn't.

"Theo, this is John Darnton here with the George Polk Award committee. Are you sitting down?"

"What?" I responded, bursting out into the parking lot next to Alondra.

"Congratulations, you've just won a Polk Award!"

My heart stopped. The moment seemed to freeze in place, the trees pausing their rustling to listen in.

"Is this a prank?"

Darnton laughed.

"No, this is very real."

I put the phone on mute and let out a mostly silent scream into my arm, trying to contain my excitement even as the rest of my section could see me through the windows.

The committee told me that they'd admired my "moxie" and that I was the youngest person ever to win the award, which would be announced Monday. They were recognizing my initial investigation into MTL, as well as the follow-up reporting I'd done, and took special notice of my piece on Felix Baker, the board member with a financial conflict of interest who had initially been named to the panel investigating Tessier-Lavigne. I was in shock. What. The. Fuck.

I called my parents, on the verge of tears. They'd dropped me off in the same parking lot I was standing in just five months prior. Back then, I'd had no indication that I might get sucked into journalism, much less be in the middle of whatever this was. If you'd told me exactly a year earlier that I would even get into Stanford, I would've been overjoyed. If you'd told me that I might win a Polk Award in twenty years, I would've told you to get lost.

I grew up in a journalistic household, where the Polk was one of three awards that really meant something. In the pantheon of journalism, it was the Pulitzer, the Polk, and the National Magazine Award. This didn't feel real, especially not with the absurd timing. Right when I needed not to stand alone, some of the most important names in journalism had stepped up to back me. It was the first time the award had ever gone to someone at a student newspaper, a recognition that our work competed with the best professional journalism.

I called Sam. "Dude, that's crazy, no way!" he said. "Oh, my God."

Then he asked whether I'd heard back on the latest story draft yet.

SOMEWHAT HILARIOUSLY IN RETROSPECT, THE THOUGHT OF CELEBRATING never occurred to me. That night, I wouldn't be partying, I'd be right back in the newsroom, getting my piece out. All I hoped was that I could wrap it up in time for Lily's arrival.

Sam and I reunited at the Daily House. While we waited for our lawyer, Eric Stahl, to finish redlining the draft once more, we prepared social media posts and a whole multimedia package. The piece would run alongside Niko's incredible photo of MTL darting across Main Quad with his head bent mere moments after receiving the questions regarding the Alzheimer's paper. But my story was so long—the longest *Daily* article anyone could remember—that we needed other elements to break up the text. I put together a timeline graphic showing some of the notable events in the saga and used an iPad to trace over a picture of MTL from when he assumed office. We couldn't afford to actually license the image. We ran the illustration without my name attached because Sam worried that it would seem unprofessional for a reporter to also be doing the graphics.

Then it was time for the lawyer.

Sam and I squeezed into his cramped editor in chief office (named after Phil Taubman and Felicity Barringer) and got on a Zoom with Eric. Here was the final hurdle, after all this work. I'd written the story in as restrained a fashion as possible, and we quoted extensively from MTL's denials alongside every allegation by his former colleagues. I'd removed any mention of the word "cover-up," and we settled on a fairly restrained headline: INTERNAL REVIEW FOUND 'FALSIFIED DATA' IN STANFORD PRESIDENT'S ALZHEIMER'S RESEARCH, COLLEAGUES ALLEGE. Our headline didn't even reference the most incendiary aspect of the story, that MTL had allegedly known this and still refused to retract the study. But it still wasn't risk-free.

Eric, Sam, and I went back and forth for another two hours. Duran, *The Daily*'s affable, handlebar-mustachioed professional layout man, was starting to worry that he'd carved out a fifty-five-hundred-word space taking up most of the front page and nearly two whole pages inside for a story that hadn't appeared. Our midnight deadline for the printer loomed. Finally, we put it to Eric directly: Should we run the piece? After a brief pause, he looked both of us in the eyes through the video monitor. "If this were my paper, I would go for it."

SAM AND I SPENT THREE MORE HOURS GETTING THE STORY OUT THE door. We read through it over and over again. We read paragraphs out loud to each other. We prepared an email digest. We kept finding excuses to do something else.

Lily arrived at the Daily House straight from the airport, lugging her suitcase up the stairs to the open-floor-plan newsroom where only Sam, Duran, and I remained. I hugged her tightly, and apologized profusely, before leaving her to observe the publication drama from a couch. We'd been apart for so long, but the story had to come first.

While Sam and I had been at odds at times, on this occasion I found myself much more understanding of his agonizing in the final moments before publication. I'd reported and written the piece; it bore my name, as did the aggressive letters from Steve Neal. But Sam's name was at the top of the masthead. It was his call to publish. He hadn't asked for this—after all, he was going off into tech—but when I came to *The Daily* and began ruffling feathers, Sam stood by me. Neither of us wanted to be reporting this story, nor did we particularly like what it revealed. But we felt a sense of duty. For all our bickering, in that moment—the final seconds before we made the most important decision of our young lives—Sam and I became permanently bonded. He was my brother now, and we would brave whatever came together.

Sam pressed the button. Then he called the printers to confirm receipt. "Let's spring for the good paper," he told them.

CHAPTER 11

TREEHACKS

My checklist ran a mile long: Assemble the RFID-tag scavenger hunt. Pick up the projectors. Erect a mocktail bar. Find the magician. Greet, brief, and set up the sponsors.

With 1,700 people to take care of, the 20 of us on the TreeHacks team were stretched incredibly thin—and because the 126,000-square-foot Huang Engineering Center we rented from Stanford would remain occupied by others until just before we were to get started, the entire event had to be thrown together in mere hours.

This alone would've been stressful enough, but, of course, as I donned my bright purple organizer shirt, my focus was divided. Lily was still dozing a few feet away. We'd gone home just past 1:00 a.m. and stayed up talking for a few more hours. It feels redundant to say this, but so much had changed. I knew that I loved her—and I knew that wasn't enough. Our lives had gone separate ways.

As I looked at Lily now, I had no words to express the array of emotions her face generated in me, some combination of sorrow, joy, gratitude. Last night, we'd shared a kiss, but nothing more. It felt like a farewell. Not long before the birds began their morning chirping, we went to sleep in separate beds. Now I slipped out without waking her.

Then there was the other thing distracting me. People were starting to see the MTL story.

At 6:43 a.m., I posted my tweet with the article. Before long, "Stanford" was trending in California, and thousands of social media accounts were exchanging messages about my investigation.

A post from Bill Grueskin, a Columbia Journalism School professor and former senior editor at *The Wall Street Journal*, soon garnered millions of views:

> You can't summarize this story in a tweet, except to say:
>
> 1) The president of Stanford University is in deep, deep trouble
>
> and
>
> 2) The student who wrote this story, Theo Baker, appears to be one kickass reporter

The response was far greater than to any of my previous stories—and it wasn't close. The journalism, higher education, and scientific communities were stunned. Most gratifyingly, people seemed to be reading the entire thing, going through and pulling out their favorite quotes. "Every paragraph is a grenade, except for the ones that are 1000 pound bombs," someone posted. "Don't recall ever reading a better piece of student journalism," the editorial page editor of the *Chicago Tribune* opined.

BUT OF COURSE, IT *WAS* COMING FROM A STUDENT NEWSPAPER, AND OUR front page served only to emphasize this. Alongside my investigation, the other pieces were titled: TUITION INCREASES BY 7%, EMAIL HOAX SENT TO STUDENTS, and FULL MOON ON THE QUAD RETURNS, referencing a Stanford tradition where students meet at Main Quad under a full moon in winter quarter and all kiss each other at midnight. These were good stories, each serving the needs of the student community. But the contrast between their subject matter and seriousness made the Alzheimer's story seem all the more alien. It stood apart.

Because I had been apart.

For the months I spent working on this story, I'd given myself over entirely to the pursuit. I'd had countless low moments, invested God knows how many hours into reporting, and shouldered a huge responsibility, knowing that if I didn't do it, no one would. People online wondered how the story had come to be. Was there some sort of conspiracy? It seemed impossible to them that a student could have reported something like this. Later, when they learned who my parents were, they assumed nepotism or some other kind of backroom deal got me everything I published. The reality was so much more mundane. I'd just worked, constantly. I hustled and pushed and skipped classes and lost sleep because the story came first. Everything else about college came second.

While my peers were hanging out in the Alondra common room, making friendships that would last a lifetime, I dug through scientific papers and financial records. When Full Moon on the Quad happened, I was on the phone with an attorney. It had been exhausting and unhealthy, and I felt like I'd missed out on a once-in-a-lifetime experience. Then again, I had to remind myself, so what? At least I was doing something that mattered. Here was the proof sitting in front of me, a front page printed on the good paper that Sam had ordered.

Besides, Full Moon on the Quad wasn't all it was cracked up to be. Nowadays, the tradition representing Stanford's "freedom"-focused culture requires a signed agreement in advance, wristbands indicating level of consent, and a police presence. The Quad is barricaded so you have to queue up and show your ID for access. Alcohol is not allowed, nor is intoxication. Administrators from the Title IX office are standing feet away. And basically no one is kissing.

If I longed for a Stanford experience like the one I'd dreamed of, in part that was because it no longer existed. At least, not as it used to. The university now was something different—something bigger, wealthier, more legalistic, more carefully stage-managed.

AS THE DRONE ROOM WAS ERECTED, THE MAKER SPACES POPULATED, the virtual reality lab assembled, and the robots set loose to wander about, TreeHacks was gradually taking shape.

I was in the process of unloading prizes—hundreds of thousands of dollars' worth of them. We would store them for the weekend in the Hewlett-Packard shed: a replica of the humble wooden structure where Stanford alums Bill Hewlett and David Packard birthed Silicon Valley. Here was the mythology of Stanford, the brilliant Builders single-handedly changing the world in a garage, stacked up against its new reality, the glass-and-steel Huang Center in which the replica shed sat, now filled up by teenagers with more money than Hewlett and Packard had ever seen when they began their company.

I was just attaching a flimsy padlock when I got a call from a reporter at the *San Francisco Chronicle*.

"Hi, Theo, I was calling to see if you or *The Daily* had a reaction to Marc Tessier-Lavigne shitting all over your reporting," she said.

Huh?

The reporter told me that MTL would be sending out a statement shortly to all faculty and staff attacking my piece. The *Chronicle* had been given an embargoed copy. I told her that I hadn't been aware of the statement. Could she send it along?

Tessier-Lavigne's statement came through, and for a minute I thought I was looking at the wrong document.

MTL's email, entitled "False allegations in the *Stanford Daily*," took direct aim at the story I'd written. "Members of the Stanford Community," he wrote, "Earlier today *The Stanford Daily* published an article criticizing a paper I published in 2009 in *Nature* when I was at the biotechnology company Genentech. The *Daily* article is replete with falsehoods and betrays a misunderstanding of science and the scientific process." Yeah, it didn't stop there. "I must start by saying that I reject these allegations in the strongest possible terms," MTL continued. He called the article "breathtakingly outrageous" and "completely and utterly false."

Huddled in a corner of the Huang Center, I did my best to suppress any feelings and focus on the specific claims MTL was making.

"A first strand of the *Daily*'s criticism is, in essence, directed at the fact that we didn't get all aspects of the model right in our very first publication," Tessier-Lavigne wrote. "To anyone who knows how science works, this is a preposterous criticism."

This was in no way an accurate description of our story, which quoted the expert Matthew Schrag saying, "To his credit, Dr. Tessier-Lavigne authored several of the later studies which revised the findings of his 2009 paper." The story also quoted Tessier-Lavigne, his lawyer Steve Neal, and Genentech itself characterizing the revisions as responsible. The problem that had been raised by the other people I quoted was not that the study got things wrong, but that it got things wrong *because it had been based on falsified data*. But this got to the more important mischaracterization: For Tessier-Lavigne, this was "the *Daily*'s criticism."

Nowhere in his letter did Tessier-Lavigne mention that it was his own colleagues and prominent scientists making allegations about the paper. Instead, it was simply criticism from an uninformed student. At least, that's what he was telling all the faculty, which meant, of course, all my professors, too.

The most striking part of the statement was MTL's assertion, "I never heard claims that the 2009 paper contains fraudulent data." It was one thing to deny that the study was based on flawed data. As pointed out in the piece, this is hard to prove definitively. But to say that he'd never even heard the *claim* of fraud at all in any form was absurd. Even if he chose to dismiss any evidence of falsification as unfounded, was it really possible to believe that all four of these Genentech insiders I was quoting had independently known about the questions raised about the paper and that somehow these questions had never reached Tessier-Lavigne? I was reminded of his initial statement in November, when he had claimed that the alleged image manipulation in his papers had "no bearing" on any of their findings. This, too, felt like an over-denial.

I CONSULTED WITH SAM AND THE BOARD OF *THE DAILY* BEFORE CALLing the *Chronicle* reporter back. I explained the story as best I could and gave a short comment. MTL was entitled to say whatever he wanted, and it was my job to report on him all the same.

At my urging, Sam asked Mary, the former *Daily* editor, to write an article about MTL's denial. I felt I shouldn't be the one to do it because the story was specifically about Tessier-Lavigne attacking my reporting. This would be the only *Daily* article on MTL's research bylined by someone other than me.

Mary wrote an evenhanded story. She picked up on a detail most commentators missed: While MTL had quoted from my piece, stating, "*The Daily* article itself includes a statement from Genentech that 'we reviewed the records from that meeting and saw no allegations of fraud or wrongdoing,'" he'd omitted the next line from my article: "The company acknowledged that 'given that these events happened many years ago . . . our current records may not be complete.'" That wasn't the only place where MTL had tried to recast Genentech's account to make it sound better for himself.

MTL's public statement included copies of Neal's letters to me, but a small portion was redacted. This was the portion where MTL claimed, "I understand that Genentech has also communicated to you that [the review] did not raise issues." In fact, Genentech pointedly hadn't said this, despite all of its other denials, an omission I'd found noteworthy even before MTL's statement. I'd asked Genentech, specifically, about the "any issues" language on several occasions. Each time, the company spokespeople avoided the question. They denied "fraud and wrongdoing," but weren't willing to say that no issues had been raised. I know, I know, this probably doesn't seem like much of a distinction, but as the crime-fiction hero Jack Reacher says, "In an investigation, details matter," and the fact that there was a difference in their language that Genentech wasn't willing to bridge was interesting.

As for Stanford, the university's only comment to the *Chronicle* was to refer to MTL's statement. Even if Genentech might diverge from Tessier-Lavigne in subtle but meaningful ways, the university seemed comfortable implying that it was aligned with its leader.

THE TREEHACKS OPENING CEREMONY BEGAN WITH A HIGH-PRODUCTION sketch video, set to the Bobby Fuller Four's 1965 hit "Let Her Dance," that depicted the TreeHacks team scouring campus for a lost remote. Eventually, high up in hiking trails that overlook campus—the site of "The Dish," a 150-foot former air force radio antenna—our tech lead, Pranav, finds the missing clicker and flips the switch. As if by magic, the grand, sweeping treelike sculpture positioned squarely in the middle of Huang lights up green. The game is on.

The tree was just one of the many things constructed by the TreeHacks team. There was the main website, of course, but also the team-matching website, the scheduling website, the mentorship website, the website to access software tools and tutorials we provided, the judging website, the app. Every student was given an RFID name tag they'd use to scan into events and get food and register for awards across the weekend. The team also built a robot, a giant metal-and-LED TreeHacks sign and complementary decorations, machined lightsabers, and a million other cool projects. The scale was immense. So were the demands.

After months of preparation, we were a surprisingly well-oiled machine. We kept in touch via headpieces and traversed campus in golf carts. Our small but dedicated team was trusted to act independently. If there was an issue, you simply solved it. I loved the controlled chaos, the badass demos and excited hackers.

By Friday night, the hackers were in teams working overtime on their projects, including Lily, whom I scarcely saw. I'd been going since 6:00 a.m. but was far too keyed up to rest. Resting would mean thinking about the president of my university telling the world that I was a liar. One by one, other organizers drifted off to sleep. I volunteered to hold down the fort overnight, since someone had to be there to manage things.

At a certain point, some hackers figured out how to break into the building next door that was called, in classic Stanford fashion, Y2E2, and the university was pissed, threatening to shut down the entire event. I had to hunt down the rogue TreeHackers, eventually finding them set up next to sensitive nuclear research facilities without a care in the world. I herded them to the doors. And as I myself left, I took a moment to register what the "Y2" in Y2E2 actually stood for: Yang and Yamazaki. Yang as in Jerry Yang, Stanford's board chair, who, even as I was kicking people out of the building named after him, was fielding phone calls about my article. But then the radio beeped, summoning me to another crisis.

At 5:00 a.m., twenty-three hours after my day began, I went back to my room, but by 6:30 a.m., I was back at the event. Bleary-eyed and noticeably slurring my words, but back. There were things to be done.

We were going through pallets of supplies, and began to run low on Pocari Sweat, the Asian sports drink produced by one of our sponsors, the pharmaceutical giant Otsuka. I let them know about the extra demand and they were delighted; more would be there soon, they said. Great! I said. Yeah, I should've asked a few more questions.

A couple of hours later, my phone started buzzing.

"Hi, this is the driver, can you tell me where I'm supposed to go?"

I was confused. What driver? How did he have my number? Turns out, Otsuka had sent an eighteen-wheeler full of sugary drinks, and now he was lost, trying to drive down a twisty one-lane road mostly reserved for bicycles.

After some back-and-forth golf cart adventuring, I found the missing semitruck and, with some truly expert maneuvering, the driver was able to make it to the loading dock behind the Huang Center. This, though, led to another problem. The giant wooden pallets, each thousands of pounds, could only be moved by a forklift—and I didn't have one. I radioed for help, and, with all of us on a sort of sleep-deprived high, our team formed a human chain to break open the boxes and cart the drinks away by the twenty-four-pack.

THESE WERE THE KINDS OF PROBLEMS I HAD TO SOLVE FOR TREEHACKS, and I was grateful for them. 3D printer out of filament? Great, I'll hunt down the spares. Sponsor bailed on a workshop? Okay, I'll run it myself. Puppies missing for the puppy hour? Fine, if you really insist, I'll go look for puppies.

The volume was overwhelming, but it was satisfying to do work that wouldn't result in anyone getting sued. (Presumably.) Frankly, I think I was a bit addicted to the rush, especially amid my anxiety over everything else. Here I felt useful and part of a team. At one point, Sara the codirector and I got trapped in an elevator and laughed our asses off for twenty minutes. Vedant, the other codirector, and I had an extended lightsaber battle to test the weaponry in advance of the competitive bout for hackers later in the day. *This* felt like college, even if the surroundings and money and scale were all a bit out of proportion. Plus, having middle-of-the-night conversations about AI was way more fun than talking about NDAs and the threat of lawsuits.

On Saturday, the TreeHacks alumni surprised us saplings with a final-night tradition kept secret until each year's event: the U-Haul party. It's basically what it sounds like. A giant U-Haul rental truck is fashioned into a makeshift speakeasy, with string lights and liquor and a happy group of TreeHacks devotees waiting to fete the unsuspecting saplings. One by one, we were picked off and told to retrieve something from the truck, only to pull open the door and find a party waiting inside.

It was a blast. I was running on four hours of sleep over the past sixty-four hours. I'd walked more than fifty thousand steps and lugged around hundreds of pounds of various items. It'd been thirty hours since I'd had a proper meal. But at least I was with friends. And I really did consider these my friends. I partied for an hour and had three drinks before realizing I had to run one more workshop that night, on ethical hacking and penetration testing. I was a little tipsy but more than capable of coordinating the session. Don't worry, I told everyone, I'll be back.

Sure enough, an hour later and after a perfectly acceptable workshop, I was passing through the loading bay on my way back to the party.

Then the world went black.

I WOKE UP, ALONE, ON THE FLOOR IN MY DORM ROOM. THERE WERE electrodes attached to my chest. I had no idea what had happened.

Searching my memory provided no answers. I had a perfect recollection of everything right up until there was nothing, as if someone had popped the film out or accidentally stopped recording. I cast around for my phone, but it was nowhere to be found, nor were there any other clues.

I took stock of my body and felt . . . nothing. All was completely normal. What on earth had happened? I looked at the clock and it was shortly past 8:45 a.m. Shit! I had to get back to TreeHacks before judging started! Presumably I would find answers there, too.

Walking in, I went straight to the organizer headquarters, and Sara looked up and blanched. "Oh, my God, what are you doing here?"

"What do you mean?"

"After last night . . . Are you okay? We were so worried!"

I shamefully admitted my amnesia.

"Theo, you just collapsed," she said. Nobody could rouse me, it turned out. I'd started throwing up and was completely without motor function. The stress, the exhaustion, the lack of food, the alcohol—it had all caught up to me, and in an instant, my body had said, "Enough!"

My heart seized up. This was exactly the time I needed to be beyond reproach. I couldn't afford a mistake. And now I'd gotten drunk and blacked out on campus. How fucking irresponsible could I be? Even worse, my phone was still missing—with all the sensitive Signal messages it contained. Already dreading the answer, I asked Sara who knew about what had happened.

"We called your friend, and he and a couple alumni picked you up and carried you to his car and drove to your dorm. One of your RAs opened the door and helped carry you up. We really didn't want to tell anyone, especially because you were sort of babbling about how scared you were and, like, we know that everything with the university is tense, but the alumni were worried and called the paramedics." Apparently, they'd checked me out and pronounced me fine, just in need of sleep.

But the damage had been done. Stanford knew.

IT WAS THE PERFECT STORM, IN SO MANY WAYS. WITHIN THIRTY HOURS, I'd earned the biggest recognition of my life, made the toughest decision of my life, had the most heartbreaking reunion of my life, worked the most consecutive hours of my life, been the most stressed I'd ever been while facing the biggest risk of my life, and, at the end of it all, crumbled.

To have fully lost my memory was also a mindfuck. I've always had a good memory. My first gamertag (at age seven) was EncyclopediaB, in honor of the boy detective Encyclopedia Brown, but also a nod to the many hours I spent on the floor of my dad's office reading through volumes of the World Book cover to cover.

Now, for the first time, there was a hole. Not just a faded impression or a gap—I had plenty of those—but a yawning absence. Had I more time to think about it, this lapse in consciousness would've presented me with deeply existential questions about my own sense of self. Many people who go to college have a similar freshman year experience. If I couldn't remember it, was it really *me*? But this wasn't a blackout under the usual freshman circumstances. I still had work to do.

TREEHACKS JUDGING WAS ONE OF THE HIGHLIGHTS OF THE WEEKEND. Each team set up a presentation or demo, and we judges moved between them as instructed by an algorithm. The judging platform built by the tech team would then take all of our scores, do some statistical analysis to control for individual biases, and identify the most promising projects.

It was cool to see what everyone had built, although, with ChatGPT only a few months old by that point, in early 2023, we'd underestimated the extent to which it would be integrated in basically every project, even ones totally unrelated to AI. Some projects were obviously half-baked or half-assed. But, in just forty-eight hours, many people had displayed extraordinary creativity. There was the machine that flipped and scanned physical book pages more cost-effectively than any commercial option, the reinvention of the math behind the blockchain to create a more secure rotating wallet, the machine learning model trained to identify illegal overfishing from satellite imagery, the device that could attach to the shoes of the blind and guide them with vibrations, and lots more. It was amazing to see what people could do when given the resources, mentorship, and incentive to build.

At the prize ceremony, the winners of our grand prizes did short demos and companies proudly presented their awards. TreeHacks had been sponsored by giants like Google, OpenAI, Y Combinator, Nvidia, and more of Silicon Valley's stars. (Up until recently, Genentech had been a sponsor, too.) These companies—and the tech leaders who showed up to speak—provided some kickass perks, including drones, GPUs, SAFE checks to fund companies, 3D printers, hacking devices, a free self-driving car for a year, and dozens of other goodies. It wasn't lost on me that second place in one of the cryptocurrency categories came with ten times more money attached than the Polk Award. This was a tech bonanza. But it rewarded genuinely cool work.

Somehow, despite everything, we'd done it. We'd pulled off the largest college hackathon in the world, with a tiny team, and things had gone pretty damn well, especially given that it was the first time the event had been hosted in person since the pandemic. Andrej Karpathy, a cofounder of OpenAI and ex-director of Tesla AI, remarked, "I just love TreeHacks as an event. I think it's a very unique thing that happens in Silicon Valley—it's so much bigger and better." Ali Partovi, a cofounder of code.org and the head of VC fund Neo, took it one step further, jumping around onstage screaming, "I LOVE TREEHACKS!"

Finally, after everyone had departed, the seven of us who stayed latest cleaning up went out for a steak house dinner on the TreeHacks company card, casually running up a thousand-dollar tab on the black hole budget.

I felt ready to sleep for a month. But I still couldn't find my phone. And a lot of people were trying to reach me.

CHAPTER 12

SOLVE FOR PEOPLE

Things, surprisingly, were getting better. Catastrophe hadn't engulfed my world so far, and I'd made it through the twin trials of publication and TreeHacks largely intact.

The worst-case scenarios I'd envisioned didn't come true. I heard from my resident director about my collapse but was otherwise able to avert a disciplinary kerfuffle. Even more important, my reporting was holding up. My biggest fear—aside from a lawsuit or a major error—had been that MTL would marshal a united front to reject the reporting, pressuring those who'd been on the Genentech Research Review Committee in 2011–12 to publicly deny that there had been any investigation.

But they all kept quiet, even the one who'd cofounded a company with MTL. This, to me, was telling. If the piece had been as false and outrageous as Tessier-Lavigne asserted, his friends and coworkers would presumably say so, especially since they themselves were potentially implicated. So far, none of them would—not when I'd reached out to them prior to publication and not now, as Tessier-Lavigne tried to rewrite the narrative.

When the Polk Award was announced on Monday, only days after the Stanford president had thrown his full weight behind an attack on *The Daily*'s credibility, legions of people reached out to congratulate me. It was also the moment when everyone figured out who my parents were. None of my sources had known that my parents were also journalists, nor had the student body, nor even had Tracy or most of the people at *The Daily*. But it was out there now, for better and for worse.

With the Alzheimer's article finally published, I was able to reemerge somewhat. I started eating a bit more regularly and going to class again. Some people gave me funny looks, but mostly I tuned it out—and I even enjoyed some of my coursework.

I loved my data science professor, Jeremy Freese, whose passion for learning and kindly disposition made him a treat to be around. I'd become friends with a girl in the class—Jenny, a short tomboy lesbian with a thick Southern accent—and we passed notes and cracked jokes. I teased her about her new obsession with jujitsu—"It's like doing hot yoga, but with other people's bodies," she said—and in turn Jenny roasted my love for cars. After class, she let me tag along for dinner with her friends.

Other people in the class were clearly conscious of me. One posted on Twitter the day the Polk was announced about us being in the same section; another had blurted out in front of everyone on the first day of class, "Wait, aren't you that reporter?" Jeremy afforded me much-needed grace without requiring explanation. He let slip, too, that the class normally included a unit on data falsification citing Elisabeth Bik, the fraud-hunting scientist I had relied on for my reporting, but given my presence he thought it prudent to change topics this time.

While I found it funny that I'd unwittingly thrown off the class, it didn't surprise me that Jeremy was paying close attention to the MTL saga; most faculty members were, far more so than students. To the average undergraduate at a sprawling university, a president, especially one as distant as Tessier-Lavigne, is fairly abstract. But most faculty members have been at the school longer than students will ever stay.

Oftentimes, they've interacted with the president and had projects impacted by his priorities. Faculty members conducting research had an additional incentive to follow the case, as many of them weighed the way he was treated against their own experience.

In that sense, Tessier-Lavigne's aggressive letter appeared to backfire. A number of faculty members complained that he'd used the Stanford presidential email to disseminate his personal defense to an article about his research prior to assuming office. The harsh tone of the message and Steve Neal's legal letters were also off-putting to some, though not all.

At the first meeting of the faculty senate after publication of the article, MTL stood up to offer an unsolicited defense. "There was no fraud. There was no investigation. There was no cover-up," he said in a soliloquy that lasted several minutes. At the end, Tessier-Lavigne waited for someone to speak up or respond.

Nobody said a word.

WITHOUT THE CONFIDENCE OF THE FACULTY, THERE WAS NO WAY FOR MTL to lead effectively, and it was increasingly unclear whether he had that support.

I began reporting extensively within the university, mapping out the power dynamics in a place where many professors maintained their own individual fiefdoms. This required a phone, and despite days of searching after the TreeHacks collapse, I'd found no sign of mine. So, wincing all over again at my irresponsibility, I bit the bullet and purchased a replacement. My sensitive Signal messages were gone for good, but at least I could get back to calling around.

Most of the professors I spoke to were antsy, pinning their hopes on the Stanford board's investigation to settle things. Some rebuffed me, others were cautious, but I cultivated a number as sources. Soon, emails were being forwarded to me, and professors would hang up after their group calls to call me and recount the details.

Much of what I learned was off the record, disappointingly. But not all of it. And an especially interesting detail came a week after the article was published.

I WAS LEAVING STANFORD FOR A WEEKEND WITH MY PARENTS, MY first time off campus since the retreat after my birthday. It was Family Weekend, and I was still recovering from my exhaustion, so I gratefully accepted my parents' proposal to get away for a few days. Instead of the official planned activities on campus, we headed to the house of my mom's best friend from college, about an hour and a half away.

Just after we arrived, I got a voicemail from an unknown number. "Give me a call. You're going to want to hear this," the voice said. I recognized it as a professor I'd recently begun speaking to, and I knew that he kept his ear close to the ground.

I locked myself in the guest bedroom and dialed the number. The professor wasted no time. He had been forwarded an email written by another professor. An email to Jerry Yang, the Stanford board chair. An email corroborating my reporting.

The author of the email had told Yang the account of "a Genentech employee of 15 years, VP level" who confirmed what I'd written about the 2009 Alzheimer's paper and added a story about "how Genentech became convinced that Anatoly . . . had falsified data." According to the professor, "Researchers at Genentech were having trouble replicating the results from the 2009 *Nature* paper. Apparently they then asked Anatoly to repeat a key experiment from the paper himself, but when he did his data seemed too perfect to be true. They then switched the reagents they were giving him to use in the experiment but didn't tell him—when he came back with the same result again, they knew he was falsifying the data."

This was an intriguing account, although my own sources didn't recall that detail. Still, that it was alleged to the board was newsworthy, as well as confirmation by a fifth high-level source that there had been concerns raised about the paper. After just an hour of digging, I figured out who the original source of the email to Yang was from details revealed by the professor—which was, on the one hand, useful for reporting purposes, but also a reminder of how dangerous it was to come forward, even "anonymously."

The email also mentioned a separate allegation that each of my four original sources had raised but that I hadn't felt was pinned down enough to publish. The email had been forwarded to a few faculty, including the professor showing it to me now. It also gave Yang a list of names to contact. "These can provide the fire and can say there was discussion of fraud/fakery and MTL knew."

I was grateful to have independent corroboration. No other reporters were seriously pursuing the story, which made me feel deeply uncomfortable. The MTL saga straddled two particularly challenged areas of media coverage—higher education desks on national papers are understaffed, and science reporters struggle to overcome a Next Big Thing bias, often favoring stories about promising studies without following up if they collapse. While there have been improvements in recent years, the lack of aggressive science journalism has, frankly, allowed research misconduct to fester.

So I kept at it. And, having developed a broad source network, I was collecting more information than ever.

Now that the TreeHacks event was over, the fun began. We'd spent just about as much money on the competition as we could imagine but found plenty left for shenanigans. The black hole budget financed parties and dinners and movie nights and general revelry. We were flash-bonded by the adrenaline-packed experience of running the event and soon forged a tight social circle.

We went out for hot pot and got milkshakes and did shots of

Jägermeister in someone's room, leaving all of us drunk and ridiculous. (One of the other saplings proposed that he and I jokingly make out in front of the group. He was straight. He said he enjoyed it.) Still, there were reminders that this wasn't quite a standard college experience.

First, there was the lack of oversight. The flat structure of TreeHacks meant that money was floating around basically everywhere without anyone to check what happened to it. Not the sponsors, who typically gave it without restriction, or the organization, which emphasized individual trust. This made it easy to fuck up in major ways. For example, the failure to send a single email resulted in our losing sixty thousand dollars in free API credits, and nobody noticed until after the event. The lack of oversight also made it incredibly easy to pilfer money. Over margaritas one night, past codirectors told us about the former TreeHacks organizers who created a fake limited liability corporation and took tens of thousands of dollars for themselves.

Thankfully, none of that happened my year, but there was still some moderately shady behavior. We forgot to return a five-thousand-dollar device to a company that never asked for it back. Some leftover prizes that hadn't been awarded became property of a TreeHacks organizer. It was "just a little bit of fraud," Sara said jokingly.

Soon after the event, we had the first of our VC dinners, hosted by a firm to get to know us organizers. In an upscale Italian restaurant, the head honcho explained his fund, saying, "We began with the audacious mission of identifying the next great talent young." They aimed to "break down the barriers that separate us." To meet our TreeHacks team, the VC firm brought a few partners and a handful of CEOs whose companies they'd funded.

I found myself sitting between one of the partners and the head of a major AI firm. During small talk, I asked the VC investor why she'd joined. "I always wanted to solve for people," she said. And now this was her job, wining and dining the future. All of us were encouraged to start companies. As the AI guy put it, "AI is going to fundamentally shift the balance of power between labor and capital, so only capital will matter. Now is the time to secure your time-slice of the universe."

Also, by the way, he was looking to "circumvent the traditional acquisition matrix," so "if you know any cool small companies, we're totally down to acquire them."

The TreeHacks vibe was markedly different from my journalism life. Arthur, one of the most brilliant members of the team, was working on commodities trading with a couple of friends. They called their group chat "The Neo-industrialists." Arthur had already built an algorithm for corn futures that modeled ethanol demand, gasoline prices, and something to do with Chinese pigs. What was his edge? "If you have all the private data, you're just winning," he said. Wasn't that problematic? "There's no insider trading in commodities," he said with a wink.

When I was talking with another TreeHacks organizer, expressing my desire to travel to Belize, he exclaimed, "Oh, I have a shell company there!" A moment later, he added, "Never been, though."

As the timeline for selecting next year's copresidents grew tighter, I was repeatedly asked whether I was going to run. For a while, I considered it. But ultimately, I realized that I wasn't the right person for the job and it wasn't the right job for me. At a crossroads—one road filled with lucre and bleeding-edge advancement, the other, well . . . not that—I chose journalism.

STORIES BEGET STORIES, AND, AS I HAD BEEN AFTER THE INITIAL MTL piece, I was in hard-core "fucking menace" mode.

I was encouraged by a strange constellation of allies cheering me on from afar, none of whom I'd ever met. There was Ed Tufte, the legendary pioneer of data visualization, the man *The New York Times* called the "Da Vinci of data," who even put me in one of his textbooks; an attorney from Chicago named Philip who emailed me every week; and the Reddit College Football Twitter account—yes, really—which regularly went to bat on my behalf. It was all a little bit mystifying, but I was incredibly grateful.

Holden Thorp, the editor in chief of *Science*, had also become a somewhat unlikely interlocutor. While he had initially seemed to regard me with wariness when the first MTL story broke, Thorp and I had begun to speak more regularly.

From him I learned that the Stanford investigation had only just reached out to *Science* in late February, and hadn't even scheduled an interview to assess Tessier-Lavigne's account of the unpublished corrections. This was shocking—surely that was one of the first steps any inquiry would take? The Stanford board investigation had been opened three months earlier, and it was unclear what, if any, progress had been made. My sources also reported that the committee had yet to reach out to any of them. And, while the committee said they were working with an image analyst, they refused to identify who.

So, was someone slow-walking here?

I was getting maddeningly mixed signals. I spoke to one person who recounted a meeting with Jerry Yang about the matter in which they "got the feeling from Jerry that unless they proved MTL was directly involved in the falsification, they would be unlikely to take action." But that was speculation, of course.

More concretely, I learned that Yang had a call with Kenneth Schultz, the chair of the faculty senate, who relayed concerns from a number of professors about Tessier-Lavigne's ability to lead. When I asked Schultz about this, he confirmed that he'd spoken with Yang but wouldn't elaborate. This was the second time I'd reported about Schultz's communications with the board, having seen emails he exchanged back in December, and Schultz wasn't happy. He called me, clearly agitated. "My role really depends on being able to talk to people and not having it appear in the paper," he said. "As a faculty, we can't function if we worry that conversations we're having are going to appear in *The Daily*."

Maybe that was the standard Schultz and Stanford were used to—but he held a position of authority, and that made him fair game.

THE BOARD ITSELF WAS BASICALLY IMPENETRABLE. DESPITE MURMURS here and there, nobody would speak to me, no matter how many times I called their cell phones or popped up in their inboxes.

Were they defending MTL? Were they defending themselves? Were they defending the institution? Was something else entirely afoot?

MTL, I was learning, held immense sway over the board. A trustee recalled a meeting, years earlier, in which a vote had been held over a specific policy, with Tessier-Lavigne's side clearly in the majority. Then, halfway through the vote, MTL abruptly reversed himself. The board then voted unanimously for his new position.

I couldn't tell if this was an accurate portrait of what the board members were feeling now, though. They were obsessed with privacy, focused on avoiding leaks and presenting a united front. "We were all sworn to secrecy," another trustee told me later. "They threatened our firstborn children."

The discipline was impressive. And completely unlike the other side of Silicon Valley that I was starting to encounter.

IT WAS CRAZY TO ME HOW WILLING SOME PEOPLE WERE TO BLAB TO A reporter. A little later, I was invited to join a secret society started by a famous billionaire to bring together powerful people in tech, finance, government, academia, and other fields to discuss "non-obvious ideas." While the organization prides itself on secrecy, repeatedly emphasizing that it is off the record and bragging about never appearing in the press—the organization "strives to remain out of the public eye, so that participants feel free to share what they really think"—when I asked for clarification, I was told that I could refer to things people said without attribution. And, wow, people in this "community of leaders" were willing to tell some *wild* shit to an eighteen-year-old they'd just met.

A billionaire told me about the birthday party he held for himself on a private island, where he paid top professional tennis players to stage a private tournament and gave all his guests LSD. Speaking of private islands, one woman—whose boyfriend was a crypto billionaire; they met at one of the secret society events—spent our first interaction complaining that "living on a private island is really hard." As she put it, "We were rolling around in bed making love and I realized I wanted French toast." But on the private island, she couldn't get it. Why did they stay? "It's a tax dodge," she explained. One senior official at a major AI firm confessed that they liked to go to "*Iliad* wrestling parties," where the participants would "drink wine, read passages of the *Iliad*, get naked, and wrestle."

And then there were the takes.

"Peanut butter allergies are woke," a CEO told me. "Mass shootings are caused by antidepressants," said an investor. "We drastically under-incarcerate," said an elected public official. Somehow, almost all of these conversations would inevitably turn to pro-natalism, and the shockingly pervasive belief among this crowd that those with superior genes need to repopulate the earth. "In one hundred years it will be considered barbaric" if you don't, one tech bro told me. All of this at a retreat at a sprawling luxury resort closed to the public by the secret society.

I was most struck by the organization's self-description: "Although [the society's] public-facing secrecy is purposeful, we value transparency among the inner circle."

Was this not a perfect description for the entire Valley? Was this not what I was experiencing—from the other side—in my reporting process? The constant teeter-tottering between insider and outsider was relentlessly odd.

I WAS IN SUCH A DIFFERENT PLACE THAN A YEAR EARLIER, WHEN I APplied to college.

Tour guides at Stanford were now telling their groups that *The*

Stanford Daily had just won the first-ever Polk Award for a college newspaper. (Shocker: They didn't mention the content of the reporting, just the prize. Somehow, Stanford always comes out on top.) There were lengthy threads on various forums trying to figure out my major. (I didn't have one yet. This became the lede of a piece at *BuzzFeed News*.)

One of our SLE lecturers started talking about me and my work during class, without knowing I was in the room. I came up to him afterward and we had a pleasant chat. I was nothing like he'd expected, the professor said. "I'm here thinking in the movie version of this, I wouldn't cast you as you," he said. In what way? "You're much less brash than I expected." The cartoon version of me had nothing to do with reality. But more people seemed to be familiar with the character than the person.

Within the next year, at least seven stage shows put on by student groups would parody me. Law school students wrote a musical in which a character based on me sang a song called "In *The Daily*," set to the tune of "In the Navy," with hunky backup dancers. The marquee undergraduate production, a tradition since 1911 called *Gaieties*, which most of the student body attends, also depicted me reporting on the president—"I heard back from our sources. The allegations against our president are true. Let me see here . . . [checks notes] He claims to be six foot on Stanford Profiles, quote, 'if that matters' . . . and . . . [flips page] oh yeah, there was data manipulation in his research"—and included a scene where actors playing Sam and me kissed. I hated watching that.

As a journalist, I wanted to do my reporting in peace, but because I lived in the place I was reporting on—and because I was such a recent arrival—my relationship to Stanford was colored by the commentary of others. The "story" didn't take a break, because the story was everything around me at all times. Every step was being watched. I went on a podcast for the first time a couple of weeks after the Polk, talking about my grandfather and falling in love with journalism, only to have Steve Neal later cite some of my comments in one of his long letters seeking to block more material from coming out. (I hadn't said anything there that wasn't already in my pieces; I wondered whether he cited it solely to remind me that I was being watched.)

WHEN I WENT TO MTL WITH NEW QUESTIONS ABOUT THE DETAILS I'D learned about his wavering faculty support, I again heard back from his lawyer. We had a routine by now, where I'd directly email the president, who never acknowledged or responded, allowing Neal to do so instead—after which I'd staunchly refuse to address my questions to Neal, going back to Tessier-Lavigne.

In this letter, Neal quoted *Stanford Daily* policy to me about how individuals facing specific assertions should receive notice in order to respond. That, of course, was the exact purpose of my emails to Tessier-Lavigne. But even as Neal again declined an interview on MTL's behalf, he asked at the end of his letter, "Are you including comments from faculty members who have confidence in Marc's leadership?"

In my next email to the president, after providing more questions and additional detail about what my reporting had found, as requested by Neal, I wrote: "We are including comments of all types made by faculty in interviews with *The Daily* and in private correspondence. Feel free to provide faculty members who are willing to speak in favor of your leadership, we'd be happy to speak with them."

The next day, an email appeared in my inbox from Garry Gold, a professor of radiology, with the heading "Support for MTL." He wrote, "I wanted to reach out and offer my support for Marc's leadership. The following is a quote from me you can use, if you like." Tessier-Lavigne, Gold continued, "has done a terrific job as the President of Stanford University. Setting up an independent investigation into the allegations that have been raised is an example of transparent and responsible leadership."

I responded to Gold: "Hi Garry, thanks for emailing! A bit confused by your statement—are you saying that you support Tessier-Lavigne's leadership because he set up the investigation into himself?" Because, well, he hadn't. Gold emailed back several times before I could respond, saying he hadn't realized the board had opened the investigation, not Tessier-Lavigne, and tried to change his statement. "Please confirm you will run my corrected quote if you quote me at all," he wrote.

Politely, I had to tell him *The Daily* didn't allow quote alteration, but "if I quote you I'll be sure to note that you amended your statement." Gold went ballistic in several additional emails. "You clearly intend to misquote me here. If you do that, I will take legal action," he threatened.

I couldn't help but laugh. MTL was trying to show that he had support, and the person who jumped to his aid did so by citing something Tessier-Lavigne hadn't actually done, before trying to take back an unsolicited statement made on the record in writing—and threatening to sue me.

Ultimately, we didn't print the back-and-forth over the comment, not because we couldn't or because it was wrong to, but because the story was already too packed and Gold was just a distraction.

TESSIER-LAVIGNE DID HAVE SUPPORTERS WHO WEREN'T QUITE AS abrasive. Neal provided me with a list of three professors, all of whom told me some version of "Let the process play out."

Much more interesting was the email I got from Richard Scheller.

Tessier-Lavigne and Scheller had been deeply intertwined for two decades. Their families were close, their careers were enmeshed, and they'd been working behind the scenes to combat this story since it started coming out in November. Multiple people had recounted direct conversations with Scheller about the Alzheimer's paper in which he had expressed concern that it was fraudulent and should be retracted. So I'd tried to reach him. First I emailed him in January. Then I visited him in February, only to have the door slammed in my face. Now, finally, he showed up in my inbox.

After all this time—more than a month since I'd first given him the opportunity to comment and weeks after our Alzheimer's investigation story came out—Scheller's statement, aside from laying out his CV, was just a single line: "I do not recall any discussion at the RRC," the Genentech review committee, "or anywhere else at Genentech, that Dr. Nikolaev, Dr. Tessier-Lavigne, or anyone associated with the APP/DR6 study falsified data that were reported in the 2009 *Nature* paper, or that they behaved improperly in any way."

Scheller was the first and only person with knowledge of events to back Tessier-Lavigne publicly. But "I do not recall" was the best he could come up with? Unsurprisingly, Scheller did not agree to an interview or respond to further questions. Nevertheless, it was an important detail, adding to the on-the-record denials of the other interested parties, including MTL, Nikolaev, and Genentech.

As for Tessier-Lavigne himself, the president had all but disappeared in the wake of the Alzheimer's investigation. Sam, Niko, and I kept up a running watch of Building 10, but MTL scarcely seemed to come into his office.

What was the president up to?

CHAPTER 13

FREE TO SPEAK

When spring unleashes its splendid rays, Stanford's campus breathes a sigh of relief.

The turn is marked. Floaties and beach balls appear in the fountains, shirtless men with glistening abs and perfectly tanned women in the tiniest of bikinis are everywhere. Professors assign less material, meetings start a little late, and urgent emails seem a little less time sensitive. It's just too lovely to be bothered with much of anything.

The mid-seventies weather was alluring after a winter of record-breaking rain. I longed to be sunbathing at the Oval next to the bright red-rose Stanford *S* or traipsing through the cactus garden or playing beach volleyball.

But goddamn it, I had work to do.

THE FACULTY SENATE MET IN A DUNGEON ABOUT AS DETACHED FROM the splendor of spring as possible, a dreary, windowless classroom of the law school with nondescript desks arranged in a tiered semicircle, drab beige carpeting, and aggressively artificial lighting giving everyone a pallid yellow tint. I snuck in just as the action was about to begin, accidentally entering through the wrong door so that I emerged right in the well with too many eyes on me as I hurried to the back. Marc Tessier-Lavigne saw me. So did Condoleezza Rice.

A fight had been brewing for some time, and I'd been warned in advance that it was about to erupt. So I came to watch.

Two professors had prepared a faculty senate resolution advocating the removal of Rupert Murdoch and Rebekah Mercer from the board of the Hoover Institution, Stanford's influential conservative think tank. Their resolution quoted Tessier-Lavigne, who'd stated, "Out in the broader world, we see too often the effect of misinformation, oversimplification, and, especially, demonization in public discussions. Social media, cable news, and political discourse can be home to taunts, personal invective, and even the rule of the mob. We must collectively reject such corrosive conduct at Stanford."

The faculty senators advocated that this standard be applied to Mercer and Murdoch for their role in promoting baseless conspiracy theories about the 2020 election, which led to the January 6 insurrection and a $787 million settlement paid by Murdoch's Fox News to Dominion Voting Systems. The resolution also cited the Great Replacement Theory, a racist conspiracy theory routinely peddled by Mercer and Murdoch's companies. The senators said they had attempted to broach the topic with MTL several times over the past year and never heard back.

The first person to respond to their proposal was Tessier-Lavigne, who came out hard against it, arguing that "free expression of ideas is the lifeblood of the university" and "the Senate would be setting itself up as a thought police," which would have a "chilling effect on our intellectual community."

Seconding him was the director of the Hoover Institution, Condoleezza Rice, the former secretary of state, known universally as Condi. She said she wished to "join President Tessier-Lavigne in his concerns" over "free speech and freedom of the press," then went on a tear, aggressively defending her turf and passionately roasting her opponents. She called the motion "insulting" and said she would quote from a message one of the authors of the bill had privately sent a different professor "because it revealed the true reason for this motion." The authors of the bill had slimed their colleagues as "being in the thrall of extremists," Rice said, adding, "This has been an attack on Hoover."

At this point, her impassioned monologue had already lasted more than five minutes, and the senate chair, Ken Schultz, attempted to get her to wrap up. Rice would have none of it, barreling through and continuing on, accusing the bill's authors of ill motives.

Joe Lipsick, one of those professors, attempted to respond. Addressing Rice, he said his comment was being mischaracterized. Then he pointed at me. "I will ask the student newspaper to publish the entire conversation," Lipsick said.

Rice piped up again. "Context or no context, to say that the Hoover Institution would accept financial support, even if it came from extremists, is simply beyond—"

Lipsick butted in. "You *do* accept financial support—" he started, and then he, too, was cut off, and suddenly five people were yelling at one another on the floor of the faculty senate.

Soon, the session was dissolved without a vote, and I followed Rice as she went up to another of the bill's proponents. "*You* have been a *problem* this *entire time*," she told the offending professor.

THE INCIDENT WAS QUITE SOMETHING TO BEHOLD—COLLEAGUES, SENATORS, academics at each other's throats. Rice was terrifying. I couldn't imagine being on the other side of her withering glare.

As to the bill itself, it was never going to pass. The faculty senate had no purview over Hoover, much less authority to remove Murdoch or Mercer. This battle was purely an intellectual one, a reflection of the self-seriousness with which some academics viewed their squabbles. As Henry Kissinger, himself a Hoover fellow, famously put it, "Academic politics are so vicious precisely because the stakes are so small."

The interesting bit was watching MTL navigate these politics.

In trying to save himself, Tessier-Lavigne was attempting to find a constituency and seemed to believe, at least to some extent, that a public pivot to the right might help. In this Hoover brawl—and in his reaction to a troubling incident the month prior, when law school students shouted down a judge over his anti-LGBTQ views, disrupting the talk—Tessier-Lavigne had positioned himself as protector of free speech and academic freedom. Later, he would link to an opinion piece absurdly claiming that the investigation into the integrity of his research was all a plot by lefties going after him because he was unafraid to buck orthodoxy and align with the right wing.

Not even two weeks earlier, I'd received yet another letter from Steve Neal, this time demanding retraction of all my articles about the president because, he claimed, they'd been categorically disproven. "*The Daily* has done significant harm to Dr. Tessier-Lavigne's reputation through its irresponsible reporting," he wrote. The evidence he cited consisted entirely of the denials of interested parties, all of which I'd duly reported in the articles he wanted retracted, and in some cases they contradicted his own arguments. Neal also took issue with characterizations made by sources that were statements of opinion and obviously impossible to disprove. At this point, given that he'd actively requested retraction, we felt obligated to have our own lawyers respond. Even after that, Neal sent another attacking letter to me, despite the fact that the California Rules of Professional Conduct governing attorneys state that "a lawyer shall not communicate directly or indirectly about the subject of the representation with a person the lawyer knows to be represented by another lawyer in the matter." This from a lawyer for MTL, who was telling audiences that he was all about freedom of speech and the press.

Tessier-Lavigne's newfound political posture was somewhat at odds with his own record. A registered Democrat, MTL wasn't exactly some right-wing hero or proponent of institutional neutrality. He and his family had only ever donated to Democratic candidates. During Donald Trump's first term, MTL had signed several open letters criticizing the president on immigration and Islamophobia, overseen the removal of the names of controversial historical figures from Stanford buildings, and written, like many, about the painful murder of George Floyd and the need to "advance racial justice at Stanford." He allowed a large "K(no)w Justice, K(no)w Peace" banner to be draped over the face of Stanford's signature library. He condemned Russia's invasion of Ukraine and allowed Hoover Tower to be lit up blue and yellow, the colors of Ukraine's flag. And, during the pandemic, when this same faculty senate had voted to censure Scott Atlas, a Trump adviser and Hoover fellow, for spreading COVID disinformation, MTL had approved the action. Tessier-Lavigne said he was "compelled to distance the university from Dr. Atlas's views in the strongest possible terms."

In that sense, Tessier-Lavigne's record differed little from that of every other normie liberal university president during the first six years of his tenure, at least in terms of politics. What was extraordinary now was the idea that Tessier-Lavigne was somehow a victim of political correctness "bucking leftist orthodoxies," as the opinion piece he shared had stated, rather than a scientist whose research work had come under investigation by his own board of trustees.

SO, DID MTL ACTUALLY HAVE A CONSTITUENCY?

The funny thing was that many people who publicly defended his stance on academic freedom confessed to me in private that they believed he should be removed. But they weren't saying that in public. In fact, that spring few Stanford figures were willing to publicly say that.

Some professors with whom I wanted to engage as a student, not a journalist, now told me they supported my work but "can't be seen with you in public." Despite having tenured posts, many were afraid to speak their minds. Not just about MTL, but, for example, about Sam Bankman-Fried and his connection to Stanford or other issues that might suggest problems within the institution.

Besides, many faculty members were focused on their particular lanes—and many of those lanes revolved around making money.

Stanford's faculty is the richest professoriat in the world, reaping immense rewards of their own from students' ventures. One computer science faculty member was known as Professor Billionaire. The moniker actually undersells it. As a full-time professor for decades, David Cheriton amassed a fortune worth more than $20 billion, much of it by investing in the companies of Stanford students. He cut the first check to Google in 1998. He also cofounded several companies, including Granite Systems (acquired by Cisco for more than $200 million in 1995) and Arista Networks (market cap $176 billion), all while teaching full-time—exactly the kind of arrangement Stanford encourages.

One department chair is known to brag about having "a Ferrari for every day of the week," and, according to one of his mentees, funnels a large share of the hundreds of millions of dollars his lab has received in grants to his personal consultancy company, allowing him to be paid significantly more than his Stanford salary. The former chair of the genetics department, Michael Snyder, has cofounded seventeen companies that he says have a combined value of more than $6 billion—and claimed to have found a technique he calls "Theranos that works." He's also rubber-stamped the pseudoscience techniques of Tony Robbins, whose "Date with Destiny" claims a "100% remission from depression" with "no drugs, and only 6 days of time," based on "scientific study" by "the Snyder Lab of Genetics at Stanford University." Robbins—who charges thousands of dollars for his alternative medicine, subjects people to fire walks that have injured dozens, and has been accused by multiple people of sexual misconduct—has become entangled with Snyder and his various commercial ventures, with one smiling image showing Snyder's lab members posed with Robbins next to his private jet.* (Worth noting: One of Snyder's colleagues in the genetics department was Stan Cohen, the professor levied with the fraud judgment totaling $29 million.)

The way that most faculty—or rather, those in such potentially lu-

*Robbins denies accusations of misconduct.

crative areas as engineering and medicine—become rich isn't through fraud, it's through the commercial pipeline allowing them to monetize the work they or their students do at Stanford. A 2007 study on faculty entrepreneurship quoted a professor saying, "It's an almost unwritten rule that you have to start a company to be a successful professor at Stanford." And even professors who don't start companies become involved with students who do.

A good example is the startup called Clinkle, the brainchild of the Stanford undergraduate turned founder Lucas Duplan and two classmates. With initial resources provided by Stanford's StartX accelerator, the university's in-house venture capital program; guidance from current computer science chair Mehran Sahami; funding enabled by Stanford alumni like Jim Breyer and Peter Thiel; and the approval of then-President John Hennessy, who signed on as an adviser, the students raised more than $30 million from a who's who of investors. Duplan and Richard Branson took a picture of themselves lighting fake hundred-dollar bills on fire. But soon after, the entire company would go up in flames. It turned out Clinkle never had a real product, and Duplan was, charitably, a poor leader. But with the Stanford access and hype cycle, nobody looked too closely. Just give the cash to the twenty-one-year-old—what could go wrong?

Stanford is awash in money. In 2003, it became the first university to establish a corporate partnership program, which functions, as two sociologists wrote in their analysis of the subject, by "selling students." Stanford has dozens of corporate partnerships now. It is surely the most commercial major university in the world. Yet it also houses some of the best humanities and social science programs in the world—ranked number one in psychology, political science, sociology, and economics and in the top five for English, history, and philosophy.

Ken Auletta, in a landmark 2012 article in *The New Yorker*, "Get Rich U.," memorably described the university as "a giant tech incubator with a football team." For years, Stanford has fought the idea that it would become a purely engineering-focused school feeding talent directly into Silicon Valley. But over the last decade or so the lure of the tech business, with its billion-dollar payoffs, has changed who comes to the university and why. Stanford today has more professors in the philosophy department than it does graduating seniors majoring in philosophy. As recently as 2008, the history department graduated more seniors than the computer science department. Now there are *sixteen times* as many graduates in CS as in history—341 to just 21 in 2025. Symbolic Systems, a unique-to-Stanford major that combines CS with other interdisciplinary work, graduated a further 102.

The professors in the humanities are still excellent, producing remarkable scholarship and teaching great classes. But demand has fallen off a cliff, and cultural conflict over the mission of the university—is this a place to learn or a place to get rich?—has been profound.

Suffice to say that the professors Tessier-Lavigne had to appeal to were a dizzyingly fragmented bunch.

MY OWN ENCOUNTERS WITH MTL WERE FRAUGHT, FOR OBVIOUS REASONS. After someone drew swastikas and an image of Hitler on the door of a fellow Jewish student in my dorm who'd discussed his heritage for the first time that day—a horrific hate crime that I found shattering—Hillel called an event to discuss antisemitism. I was standing outside with close friends who were Jewish, just chatting, when, suddenly, MTL appeared, walking up to our semicircle. He introduced himself to each person, asking their names, going around the group. I was the last person.

When he got to me, he froze. I did, too. Normally, I'd have asked a question, but this wasn't an appropriate venue, so I just sort of awkwardly nodded. MTL didn't say a word, not even summoning his Canadian-polite affect this time; he just stared at me, his ice-cold gaze boring a hole in me. I have never faced a look of pure hatred like that one. For the first time, I truly understood what people had meant when they told me that Tessier-Lavigne could be intimidating—he towered over me, and his rage was palpable. Then it was over, and we went inside for the event, where he said a few words and slipped out before I could find him.

AT THE SAME TIME, I WAS BUSY LEARNING MORE ABOUT GENENTECH. The more I looked, the more information I found that complicated the company's image. In 2009, the year the Alzheimer's study was published, Genentech was pursuing a $46 billion acquisition deal with Roche that would make its stakeholders wealthy. In conjunction, the company was engaged in a secret lobbying campaign in DC to the tune of tens of millions of dollars, seeking a legal monopoly for its drugs. Genentech recruited dozens of members of Congress—Democrats and Republicans, many supported by Genentech campaign contributions—and ghostwrote their public statements, pushing for a twelve-year legal monopoly, seven years longer than what was allowed for the rest of the pharmaceutical industry.

When *The New York Times* documented forty-two nearly identical statements entered into the *Congressional Record* in 2009 by lawmakers whose talking points had been secretly authored by Genentech, a proxy delivered the company's defense: "This happens all the time. There was nothing nefarious about it."

That wasn't the end of it, though. Luke Mullins of *Politico* and his brother, Brody Mullins, a Pulitzer Prize–winning reporter for *The Wall Street Journal*, revealed in their excellent 2024 book *The Wolves of K Street* that Genentech had engaged in "a masterstroke of corporate influence peddling" that had until then gone unreported: the campaign to exploit Avastin. One of the company's most profitable drugs, Avastin had been given an emergency authorization by the FDA in 2008 to treat metastatic breast cancer, but subsequent research had shown that it was not effective for that use. Given the host of risks associated with

Avastin—including heart attack, high blood pressure, and internal bleeding—regulators were planning to revoke this temporary authorization.

Genentech knew it was only a matter of time; scientifically, the matter was closed. But because a year's supply of the drug ran ninety thousand dollars per patient, the company was determined to protect its profits for as long as possible. Genentech employed dozens of lobbyists in a "black ops" campaign that remained almost entirely secret for two decades. These lobbyists laundered their backgrounds by creating credible-sounding advocacy groups like the Patient Care Action Network that made it appear as if patients and medical professionals—not the corporation itself—were rallying grassroots style to save the drug. Cynically, Genentech also drummed up the threat of approval being revoked as the "first step toward death panels," latching on to an unfounded right-wing conspiracy theory at the time that President Barack Obama's Affordable Care Act would empower bureaucrats to decide who was "worthy of medical care."

Genentech successfully delayed the final FDA decision to revoke authorization until 2011, by which time countless breast cancer patients had invested their hopes and savings in a drug the company already knew to be ineffective for that use. Genentech's lobbyists bragged that they'd saved the company $1 billion by ensuring the lackluster, potentially dangerous drug had remained on the market for as long as possible.*

AGAINST THAT BACKDROP, TESSIER-LAVIGNE'S RESEARCH WAS AN IMportant economic asset for Genentech.

During negotiations in 2009, Genentech's executives urged shareholders to reject Roche's proposed purchase price, arguing that their company was undervalued by roughly $4 billion. To bolster their argu-

*Avastin, first approved in 2004 for metastatic colon cancer, is effective at treating other forms of cancer and retains approval for those uses.

ment, they gave a presentation to shareholders. In it, Tessier-Lavigne was introduced by Richard Scheller, who made the comment that the *Nature* paper was "the most important discovery made in Alzheimer's disease in the last twenty years, maybe ever." In turn, Tessier-Lavigne made the case that "when we decide to enter an area, we enter in full force with the aim of making a difference very rapidly." His research was an example of that, he said, and an example of why the company was worth more money. In a slide listing Genentech's "key scientific discoveries," the Alzheimer's study was the only entry highlighted in blazing blue.

But executives at the time already knew the research was, at best, unreliable.

ON APRIL 6, 2023, GENENTECH ANNOUNCED THAT IT HAD "COMPLETED its due diligence" regarding my reporting, putting out a precise five-page statement on its website.

Essentially, the company admitted only what it clearly felt it had the legal obligation to acknowledge, yet in the process it ended up confirming several important elements of my story. "After Dr. Tessier-Lavigne left Genentech for his new role at Rockefeller University in March 2011, at least one senior leader in gRED learned that scientists outside of Genentech also were having difficulty reproducing the binding of DR6 and N-APP," the statement said, referring to Genentech's Research and Early Development division. "Also following Dr. Tessier-Lavigne's departure, one senior leader in gRED urged that the 2009 *Nature* paper should be retracted or corrected in light of the inconsistent binding results." MTL, who would later insist in response to my reporting that he had never even known of any concerns about the paper, declined to do so.

Genentech also revealed a few things I'd known but hadn't yet felt comfortable publishing, including a 2010 complaint "alleging scientific misconduct by another postdoc working in Dr. Tessier-Lavigne's laboratory." In this separate incident, a handful of people in MTL's lab had spoken up, and "the complaint led to a formal investigation by the company, resulting in withdrawal of that manuscript and termination of the postdoc's employment in August 2010."

Most important, the company confirmed that its own staff had serious scientific questions about a study it had promoted as a game-changing blockbuster for Alzheimer's research. "Genentech scientists and research associates had difficulty reproducing certain results reported in the 2009 *Nature* paper, in particular, the binding interaction between DR6 and N-APP," the statement said. And here was the critical part: "Prior to publication of the paper, employees other than the authors performed binding experiments that showed inconsistent results." Yeah, you read that right: "*Prior to publication*."

In the next paragraph, Genentech stated, "Senior leaders at Genentech including Dr. Tessier-Lavigne knew of the inconsistent binding results." No suggestion of inconsistent results was included in the final paper, nor in the public comments drumming up support for this extraordinary new Alzheimer's theory, nor in the campaign to bolster Genentech's share price.

This was, in some ways, a stunning rebuke of the Stanford president, who had stated unequivocally in his aggressive response to my story, "Let me underscore this: the data were reproducible" and insisted "the review raised no issues."

Still, Genentech's statement was couched as a rejection of my reporting. "None of the current or former employees who were interviewed reported observing or knowing of any fraud, fabrication, or other intentional wrongdoing in the research leading to and reported in the 2009 *Nature* paper," the statement said. It seemed like a masterpiece of lawyerly wordsmithing, especially when I learned that one person who'd spoken to the Genentech team after my article told them the study was fraudulent, and Genentech omitted this account in its statement. But I knew that MTL's team, already out to undermine the credibility of my work, would seize on it anyway.

Steve Neal emailed that same day to demand retraction of my articles and the "heresy" contained within them. But my sources didn't waver, and, in fact, I'd begun hearing from more people with contemporaneous knowledge of the internal Genentech review, verifying their accounts.

I wrote an article reporting the Genentech statement, highlighting the parts favorable to MTL as well as those contradicting him. I also reported that *Nature* had now issued a formal expression of concern for the Alzheimer's study stating that "readers are advised to use caution when using results reported therein."

Despite the support of my journalistic advisers, I was conscious of the *Stanford Daily* label, nervous about not being believed. I hated the contentious posture MTL had taken. I wanted to report the story aggressively but also fairly. When other news outlets would misreport details, saying that Tessier-Lavigne had himself been accused of falsifying research—which wasn't true and not something I had ever reported—I reached out to get them to correct their stories. I wanted to bend over backward to stick to the facts and reflect MTL's point of view. Indeed, my original story on his Alzheimer's paper had quoted twenty-seven separate denials from Tessier-Lavigne, Neal, Genentech, and Anatoly Nikolaev.

But no matter what I did, I was aware my reporting was standing on its own. And being on your own is an uncomfortable way to be.

CHAPTER 14

NO ROOM FOR ERROR

The day of the Genentech report, I learned that my other grandfather had died. My Pappouzi.

Eleftherios Peter Baker was born to impoverished Greek immigrants in West Virginia who turned off the lights at night because they could not afford the electricity. His parents spoke little English at first, but his mother referred to him as her "little teddy bear" and the name stuck. For his entire life, E. P. Baker would be known as Ted. He truly was a teddy bear. I never once heard him raise his voice—nor did my dad, who worshipped him. Even when Alzheimer's robbed him of his memory, my grandfather remained unfailingly gracious, unfailingly kind.

I called him Pappouzi, a childhood distortion of the Greek word for grandfather, *pappou*. He had a wise, gentle sensibility that was irresistible. He was brilliant, too. Neither my dad nor I could ever beat him in a game of chess. Although raised in modest circumstances, my Pappouzi earned a place at Harvard Law School, working as an elevator operator to help pay tuition. To the extent that there is an American dream, he lived it.

I had sleepovers a lot with Pappouzi when I was younger, always insisting he stay in the same room with me, long after I actually needed the supervision. One time he arrived to pick me up for the weekend and I was so excited to see him that I ran into our back door and smashed the glass. As I lay on the tile floor, glass shards all around me, some crisscrossing my diminutive arms, Pappouzi was stuck on the other side of the iron bars, unable to reach me. Still, he calmed me down and kept me steady. That's what he always did.

Now he, like Gramps, was gone.

I'd had three terms at Stanford, and each had begun with a death. I'll be honest, I was a little tired of the routine.

I was bereft, surrounded by people but utterly isolated. The strain of the MTL investigation, compounded by the ordinary stresses of being a college freshman, was made only worse by grief.

Thankfully, I was already scheduled to fly back to the East Coast for the Polk Awards ceremony, where I would see my family. I would stay with my grandmother in the house my mom grew up in outside New York, my first time returning since Gramps died. It was tough to be back. Gramps's absence loomed large, and, as I cried into my dad's shoulder, so did Pappouzi's. Too many feelings.

The Polk ceremony was held in an ornate Manhattan club, stuffed with journalism's highest-powered leaders. Sam had flown across the country for the ceremony, too, and wore a cute bow tie. Andrew Bridges, *The Daily*'s endlessly supportive board chair, and Tracy Jan, my indispensable editor, also came, and I loved introducing my parents to our team.

Each of the winners gave a speech, and I was saved for last, a prospect I'd been stressed about all morning. There were incredibly important people in the room, and I was painfully self-conscious. I'd bought my first-ever suit for the ceremony. The winner who spoke immediately before me was Lynsey Addario, arguably the greatest photojournalist of her generation, and she spoke movingly about a wrenching image she had captured of a family killed by an air strike in Ukraine just a few feet from her. Obviously, that was a lot more important than anything I'd done.

As I took the stage, I was already teary eyed, both from Lynsey's speech and from what one of the Polk jurors had just whispered in my ear, likely the kindest thing anyone has ever said to me: "You won before we even knew who your parents were." Needing to fill the silence as I felt eyeballs on me, I quipped: "If you're wondering why I'm up here, don't worry. So am I." The audience laughed.

I thanked my team profusely and spoke about Gramps's devotion to his student paper. Then I embraced some of the absurdity:

> The last few months have been a real crash course in journalism. I've had doors slammed in my face and been hung up on too many times to count. I've been yelled at and had high-powered lawyers—plural—threaten me. I've had anonymous letters show up on my doorstep and people break their NDAs to talk to me. I've even been in a car chase. Well, I was on a bike. After all of this, I just have one question: How the hell do you guys do this for a living?

I USED THE REST OF MY SPEECH TO TALK ABOUT THE IMPORTANCE OF student journalism and the thousands of young people who make difficult choices to hold their own communities to account every day, even though it is often unsung, demeaning work. (Not to mention unpaid.) I made it through without breaking down, although I'd come close when talking about Gramps. It struck me mid-speech that the last time I'd spoken in front of a crowd this large was at his funeral.

The day went well, but it was overwhelming. Ben Pauker, another colleague of my mom's whom I'd been close to growing up, hugged me at the end and said, "Blake would've been so proud." That sent me over the edge all over again. I felt so much gratitude, and indeed joy, but so much pain, too, so much uncertainty, so much . . . confusion.

THAT NIGHT, I NOTICED ONE OF GRAMPS'S PILL BOTTLES LYING NEAR my bed. He'd had congestive heart failure for a decade, so pills were all over the house, even eight months after his death. This bottle read "Oxycodone." I knew what opiates were, and I'd read Patrick Radden Keefe's devastating *Empire of Pain*, about how the Sackler family fueled an epidemic with precisely the same drug I was now holding. I knew it was dangerous. But I was so tired of feeling things, and curiosity got the better of me.

I popped a few of the pills and a wave of crashing warmth washed over me, replacing the world with a pleasant buzz. I'd smoked weed a handful of times before, but this was nothing like that; everything was quieter. Those pesky feelings I couldn't handle simply packed up shop and took themselves elsewhere.

I spent the rest of the weekend in Boston with Frank and Lily, and it was nice to see old friends. Frank was increasingly being sucked into student journalism at his college, too, which we both found hilarious. And Lily was up to her usual eighty-million-things-at-once ways, rattling off projects like an overcaffeinated auctioneer announcing prices.

For a long time, I'd continued to hold out a secret hope that Lily would join me at Stanford next year and maybe our relationship would resume. She'd gotten into Stanford but, in the end, chose MIT. I was overjoyed for her—she'd made the right choice for herself and would thrive. There was no question we still had chemistry and cared for each other, but both of us seemed to have accepted the new boundaries of our relationship. Something new had taken its place—a real friendship.

By the time I flew back to Stanford, I seemed to have stabilized somewhat. But I'd brought the bottle of pills with me.

A WEEK OR SO LATER, SOME OF MY STANFORD FRIENDS CONVINCED ME to go to a jazz night at the coffeehouse near my dorm.

I wasn't doing great, honestly, and I thought the night out would be nice.

I didn't really know what or who to trust. At one point, a person I considered a friend accidentally butt-dialed me from a bar and I overheard him and someone else trashing me. At first, I thought it was a joke. But they just kept going, discussing how "nauseating" and "disgusting" they found me. I stayed on the line for half an hour, wondering if they'd ever realize, but they didn't. All of this from someone who had actively sought me out, someone who had pretended to like and respect me.

For all intents and purposes, the only people who could understand what I was going through professionally were decades my senior. There just wasn't another student journalist in similar circumstances. But, of course, adults couldn't relate to the other half of my college experience, namely the still-being-a-dumbass-teenager part.

And then there was the story itself. I worried that I would be branded a liar. I cared whether people believed in the truth. Increasingly, I feared they didn't. As I saw it, I was all alone—no other reporters, no support from my own school, no peers who understood me, no grandfathers to find solace in.

So, I made the incredibly poor decision to take a handful of the opiates on my way out the door to the coffeehouse, double what I'd taken last time.

WE WERE ONLY A HALF HOUR IN WHEN I BEGAN TO SLUR MY WORDS. Soon, I wasn't able to speak at all. I felt my heart slowing down, literally halting its pumping. Even with my mind scattered, surrendering to the buzz, I knew what was happening: I'd overdosed.

Okay, okay, I told myself. Breathe. I had Narcan in my room a couple of hundred feet away, part of a friend's going-away gift package to me for college that I'd assumed I would never need. Now I did. I had to get back to my dorm as quickly as possible. Time was critical—soon

I would lose control of my limbs entirely. I knew that most people suffering an opioid overdose fall unconscious before they realize the danger and call for help. The kind of medicine I'd taken was extended release, so I might be able to make it.

If I didn't, I'd probably die.

I stumbled out of the coffeehouse, lurching toward Alondra. It was getting worse. So much worse.

Ripping open the Narcan package once in my room took my last remaining strength. I got the container to my nose and squeezed the trigger, but I'd never done this before and had no idea if I'd gotten it right. I collapsed to the floor, all but paralyzed, skin clammy and cold. Either I'd saved myself and in three to five minutes I would start recovering, or . . . I wouldn't. The edges of my vision curled toward black.

MY FRIENDS, WORRIED BY MY SUDDEN DEPARTURE, SHOWED UP OUTside my room. "Hey! We brought you your coffee!" Ilana said.

I was powerless to respond. I couldn't make a sound. They were just outside my door, separated only by an inch of flimsy wood, yet the distance was unbridgeable. My breathing was impossibly shallow. After a little while, they left, and I felt my body continuing to power down.

I HUNG ON A KNIFE'S EDGE, BEGGING MY HEART TO MOVE, TO SHAKE me from my terror. I felt myself receding and fought, desperately. I didn't want to die. But I could feel my grip weakening, my consciousness slipping. How pathetic. What a stupid, stupid way to die.

I thought about what I would leave behind, and was horribly dissatisfied with the answer. How would I be remembered? Would I be known for my faults, my insistent insecurity, my uncompromising stubbornness, my obliviousness of the world? Would I be remembered as kind? I wanted to be kind. But to die this way was unkind—stupid, selfish, cruel.

I thought about how I didn't have time to clean my room. How they'd find me next to a pile of unfolded clothes, books strewn about, a shiny black award still wrapped in its packing paper, tucked beneath my desk. I thought about how my friends would hear the news—and let out a bitter, inaudible laugh realizing that Marc Tessier-Lavigne would be the one to send out the email announcing a "campus tragedy" or something dumb like that.

Most of all, though, I thought about my parents. I could picture my dad trying to put on a brave face, my mom squeezing his hand, and it broke my heart. In the span of a year, my mom had lost her father and then one of her best friends; my dad had lost his father. Now this? They'd struggled to have me—my mom had had several miscarriages and even a life-threatening ectopic pregnancy requiring her to be air-lifted out of Russia for emergency surgery. But she made it, and in a nod to this unlikely triumph, they'd named me Theodore—"gift of God," in Greek. What a shitty gift I'd turned out to be.

THEN THE NARCAN KICKED IN, AND MY HEART BEGAN TO BEAT AGAIN. Slowly, raggedly, but steadily. I spent the rest of the night alone, knowing that I would survive, but still suffering the results of my incredible idiocy. I threw up for hours, and felt like my brain had been sucked out of my head with a hose. It was hideous. Finally, shaking, crying, I let myself go to sleep a few hours later.

The next morning, I hurled the remaining pills into the dumpster. Utterly ashamed, I told no one, apart from a doctor, what had happened.

CHAPTER 15

MONEY IS A RUSH

The resignation was sudden. Persis Drell, Stanford's provost, was out.

After six years in the role, Drell announced that she was stepping down on May 3, citing no specific reason. "This is the right time," she said simply. It was the second major resignation in as many months—Dean of Research Kam Moler also stepped down after my Alzheimer's article for what she said were unrelated reasons. Both Moler and Drell were distinguished physicists, so this meant that both of the top scientists in Tessier-Lavigne's administration had resigned.

But then came a bigger shock: MTL couldn't replace his own provost.

The official Stanford news release said that Drell would continue serving until "a successor appointed by President Marc Tessier-Lavigne can be in place." But the board quickly agreed that Tessier-Lavigne would not be allowed to appoint Drell's successor unless he was cleared by the investigation, leaving the administration's fate in doubt. It was the clearest sign yet that MTL's tenure was in peril, despite his repeated insistence that the allegations didn't affect his ability to lead.

Drell's statement said nothing about the investigation. And sources told me that her decision to retire had been in the works for some time. Drell and MTL hadn't gotten along particularly well, and she'd felt bruised by the tumultuous COVID period.

Stanford's provost serves as both the chief academic officer and chief budgetary officer of the university, making the role highly influential. As Condi Rice, who once held the job herself, said in an interview, "the Stanford provost is the most powerful provost in the country." Indeed, it was former Stanford Provost Frederick Terman who is generally credited as the creator of Silicon Valley, establishing the Stanford Research Park after World War II and dramatically expanding the school's science and engineering wing.

Drell and MTL, though, were never close, and seemed to have different styles. Tessier-Lavigne was known as a micromanager. "He was a very meticulous person, and he needed to see everything and put his stamp on everything," one trustee later told me. (Which, of course, made the notion that he'd overlooked so much falsification in his labs all the more remarkable.) The reality that Tessier-Lavigne was under a cloud of suspicion didn't help their relationship. Said one of Drell's confidants: "The fact that there were any allegations about the accuracy of the president's research was like a horrendous stab in the heart to any pure-minded researcher."

What was most striking was that Tessier-Lavigne had been unable to convince his number two to postpone her announcement. Drell couldn't actually step down from the role until he was either cleared or removed anyway, so the only effect was to underline that he was not in full control.

As all this was going on, the impostor Will Curry suddenly showed up back on campus for a night, returning to one of the dorms he'd lived in the year prior. He had a beard now and went by the name David. But because he'd become such a high-profile object of interest after my initial reports, two of the dorm's residents recognized him and immediately notified the university.

According to the two residents, Curry had holed up in the dorm's common room, wearing Stanford in Government merch. The three talked for a while and bonded after Curry expressed his love for the TV show *Suits*—a show predicated on the conceit that the main character, Mike Ross, a whip-smart, lovable attorney, pretends to have a Harvard degree despite never having gone to the university. Talk about layers!

More disturbingly, though, the two witnesses said Curry kept bringing up his ex-girlfriend, the one who'd alleged harassment to the university's Department of Public Safety, which had not followed up. Curry shared with the residents details about the woman that weren't public, including her current residence, allowing me to corroborate their accounts. I also obtained geographic location data from, of all places, Tinder, which showed Curry in the area within the past day.

Thus, when I went to the university for comment, I was surprised to hear a spokeswoman claim, "Upon receiving reports that William Curry was seen in our residences, we undertook a review of the situation to ensure the safety and security of our students. Our preliminary findings strongly indicate recent sightings of Curry were unsubstantiated."

Unfortunately for Stanford, Curry himself freely admitted to the visit when I reached him. He told me that he was going by David because it was his middle name, "so technically it's not a lie." It had been, he said, "a fun first day on campus, but now I guess I'm just too recognizable to be making my visits."

The students I spoke to hadn't even been interviewed by the university, leaving me to wonder what the supposed "review of the situation" was. Denying something without actually looking into it—by now, I was familiar with the playbook.

IT WAS STRANGE TO REVISIT THE STORY OF THE IMPOSTOR AT THIS point, six months later. Stanford clearly hadn't changed, and Curry hadn't, either. But now when I reported on him, Curry seemed a lot less like an anomaly. The impostor's philosophy of the world was eerily reminiscent of the "high-agency" belief set espoused by the likes of Justin and his Rulers, the idea that those endowed with particular skills could supersede pesky, traditional rules. As Silicon Valley relentlessly intones, "You can just do things."

Truth was something to be defined by confident assertion. The high-agency man could simply say what he believed and the world would accept it, succumbing to his "reality-distortion field." "True agency," as one Stanford insider turned Y Combinator founder put it, "is being able to bend the universe to your will." Anything less than complete certainty was for chumps.

LIKE CURRY, MANY OF STANFORD'S HANGERS-ON WOULD SAY THINGS without seeming to understand, or seeming to care, that their words might not reflect well on them.

At a VC dinner for a handful of Stanford students the day after Curry's return, I was encouraged by the organizer to chat with one of the firm's partners. "I think you two will get along great," he said.

This famous VC partner began opining on the state of the university. "Stanford's biggest problem is that it admits too few white men," he said. I was about to laugh before I realized he was serious. "Did you see the picture of the med school class the other day? I mean, come on, it's ridiculous," he said.

To be clear, white men weren't exactly lacking for opportunities at Stanford. While the undergraduate population was certainly more diverse than a few decades earlier, Black people accounted for only 4 percent of the most recently admitted class and Hispanic or Latino students 15 percent, even though California (which supplies half of Stanford's admitted students) is roughly 40 percent Hispanic or Latino. Before Stanford took its diversity dashboard offline, it showed that there were only 28 tenured Black faculty compared with 983 tenured white faculty.

Two thirds of professors are men. And Stanford is the only school in its peer group to have never had a woman or person of color as its president. Also, if you just look around at the Stanford students invited to these VC dinners, they're almost always white or Asian men.

The picture the VC then pulled up for me was of the thirteen-person group that had just matched into surgical residency internships at the medical school two weeks before. It's true, none of the thirteen was a white man. But even this was a silly complaint—in both the year before and the year after, four of thirteen matches to the program were white men.

BUT IT WAS MY NEXT VC-STUDENT GATHERING THAT TRULY CAPTURED the Silicon Valley philosophy I'd come to understand between my first impostor piece and now.

I was introduced to the general partner of a sizable firm, who seemed to be cycling through a series of rehearsed power poses. "Big fan of your reporting," he said, offering to connect me to people he thought would be helpful. In fact, he said to reach out "if there's any way I can be helpful at all" and slid me his contact information.

I figured I'd ask the man about himself.

"Chips on shoulders put chips in pots," the VC said, as he told me the story of his life, peppering it with asides that included "I only date Latina women." (He was not Latino.) This guy seemed to endorse one of Silicon Valley's most sacred philosophies: The more fucked you are, the more damaged, the more money you should have. Some firms are literally founded on the premise. Hummingbird VC, for example, pitches its team as "supporters of unconventional genius," seeking to "back founders on a mission to prove others wrong." Their whole business model is finding people who are angry and out to prove themselves.

I asked the man why he did what he did—what had driven him to the top of his industry with such relentless passion—and he looked me square in the eyes.

"Money," he said. "Money is a rush."

HONESTLY, PEOPLE ARE LESS SHY ABOUT THIS THAN YOU MIGHT THINK. "I'm only attracted to people who make money," one young AI executive said in the private room of a restaurant in downtown San Francisco later that year. People nodded their heads. At a gathering at another tech figure's mansion, one startup founder told me during idle chitchat that "I just want to get, like, filthy rich." He then invited me to a sex party. I declined.

If the Hangers-On suffered from can't-keep-your-mouth-shut-itis, their protégés in the Stanford inside Stanford were certainly picking up the habit.

"People don't like making money enough," Lyle, who served as class president for his year, told me. "It should be celebrated." He was working for a VC firm for the summer—no surprise—and said he was "going to climb the chain" and do what it took to make it big. He said he was "class president because it sounded good."

Lyle was one of the biggest hustlers of his grade, constantly trying to outdo himself. In the winter, he'd released a new AI invention with two coauthors, claiming "comparable performance" to the top large language models from Google and OpenAI "with a 100x smaller model." Unfortunately, it was a scam. Sleuths quickly discovered that this fantastic new model had actually just stolen the work of a previously published paper. Lyle and his fellow Stanford student coauthor admitted the plagiarism, blaming it on the third author and saying they'd actually done none of the coding but simply slapped their names on to promote it. (In other words, gift authorship.)

This, however, had no repercussions for them professionally, and they remained Builders in Good Standing.

STANFORD DIDN'T HAVE TO BE LIKE THIS.

I found that out definitively when I got involved in an extracurricular student club that called itself the Stanford Highly Incompetent Team (S.H.I.T.). S.H.I.T. was an amateur race team that had started when a group of friends decided that they should build a race car together. I'd loved cars all my life, and for the first time at Stanford I found a group of people who felt the same way. I'd known of S.H.I.T. since the beginning of the year—and was there to witness the reveal of the team's second car project in the fall—but I was now spending more time with the group in preparation for our race at the end of spring. It was the complete opposite of the Stanford inside Stanford in almost every way. As one team member joked to me, "A balloon would be above our budget."

S.H.I.T.'s mission was to compete in the 24 Hours of LeMons, a riff on the famous 24 Hours of Le Mans but with cars expected to cost less than five hundred dollars. The tagline: "Racing shouldn't just be for rich idiots. It should be for ALL idiots!" Laboring in the lowest level of Stanford's underground garage, hoping not to be discovered by campus police because none of this was exactly sanctioned, the team had fashioned two race cars out of beater 1990s hatchbacks barely clinging on to life, and decorated them with bright, vibrant bodywork courtesy of an art-major assistant.

Of course, working on cars was not the only activity. We would go for long, liberating drives to idyllic little towns untouched by modernity along the breathtaking Pacific coastline, or through the redwood forests so thick with foliage that we couldn't see the sun, or high up in the hills, facing miles and miles of gorgeous, rolling scenery. Northern California is made for car people. Just a few minutes away from campus we would find ourselves on some of the greatest driving roads in the world, with empty switchbacks and hairpins and sweeping corners to test ourselves. Never in my freshman year did I feel freer than on those drives.

The characters in S.H.I.T. were motley and personable. There was Nathan, a rapscallion Shakespearean actor with a love for old BMWs. There was Helen, a Native American architect working to aid Indigenous communities with her designs. There was Mick, a tall, bearded, muscular man who was always covered in motor oil and possessed a wonderfully secure masculinity—his brother was a drag queen, after all. And then there was Cole.

Cole was my year and had already bought and sold dozens of cars, flipping them to make a profit. His depth of automotive knowledge was intoxicating. He'd owned some crazy vehicles, from a retrofitted Mercedes once part of Saddam Hussein's fleet to a supercar that was one of only 750 of its kind ever made, which he scored for seven thousand dollars from a shady but oblivious guy who thought it was wrecked. Seemingly every week, Cole would tell me some new wild story, and every time I'd ask myself, Can this really be? Then he'd prove his claim. Every single time.

Cole hadn't started from money, but through smarts and force of will, he'd bootstrapped himself into the car business, identifying undervalued rare vehicles and facilitating their sale to excited owners. He was a knot of contradictions—a gun-loving, beer-swigging car guy with a Salvador Dalí tattoo, a fondness for musical theater, and, he casually volunteered one day, an 1800 Elo chess rating.

By the time we got to the race in late May, one of our cars still wasn't running. Unfortunately, we realized at the last minute that we still needed a part we didn't have—and the only store that carried it was in Reno, Nevada, 180 miles away. Two teammates and I jumped into a car at 4:45 a.m. and drove straight there and back, traversing the breathtaking Donner Pass at sunrise to arrive at the parts store right when it opened, then returning to the racetrack just in time for the start.

The whole thing was magical. We were camping—and by that I mean sleeping uncovered in a field. One of our team members had to weld an exhaust system from scratch behind a porta-potty, the only place to find electricity for the welder lent by a friendly competitor. And we were enjoying the whimsical eccentricity of LeMons, which attracts an iconoclastic crowd and encourages teams to have a "theme" each race weekend. For its last race, S.H.I.T. had gone with a Greek theme, with everyone wearing togas. This time, we mostly focused on getting both cars out on the track. Which, miraculously, we did! (No thanks to me—I love cars and can explain how they work in minute detail, but I'm a blundering mechanical idiot. I screwed up several of the tasks I was given.)

The burly Mick and I went on a quest in his pickup truck to find baby carrots—he really wanted them, for some reason—and, also for some reason, talked about dictators like Turkey's Recep Tayyip Erdoğan and Serbia's Slobodan Milošević. At night, people took breaks from working on the car to watch lectures about fluid dynamics and computational biology. One team member discussed his work as a volunteer wildfire fighter. And then on Saturday night, after taking a brief reprieve from the oppressive heat to swim in a giant reservoir, we all sat on top of the most functional team car, passing around a bottle of tequila, as a sober teammate drove us around the pits at five miles per hour, singing songs and embracing the spirit of the LeMons pit-lane party.

With no budget, no profit incentive, and no shits to give, S.H.I.T. represented the Stanford I had longed to find. The Stanford of brilliant, scrappy, hardworking kids building something for the hell of it, solving a million problems along the way. And yet, within six months, the group would splinter, in part over money disputes, as it operated without school funding, and many of its members would stop speaking with each other.

A WEEK AFTER THE S.H.I.T. RACE, I KEPT THE BUSES WAITING TO DEpart for a yacht party because my class on ethical coding went long.

It was the TreeHacks alumni reunion. The group rented a 150-foot pleasure craft for the night to sail around San Francisco Bay and chartered luxury buses to take us from Stanford to the pier. "A yacht party is, like, a central Stanford experience," Anya, one of my friends, had told me. The TreeHacks yacht party, in the context of central Stanford experiences, was fairly middle-of-the-road—we rented a three-deck, well-equipped vessel at exorbitant expense for the sake of getting lit. (And networking.)

With a stunning view passing beneath the Golden Gate Bridge, TreeHacks-engraved champagne flutes, a live band, and custom 3D-printed arrangements on each table featuring the various logos the hackathon had had over the years, the TreeHacks yacht party was life in the fast lane. It was hard to believe this was a club for teenagers. I listened to one former codirector brag to another: "I beat you by a hundred thousand dollars!"

There were TreeHacks mugs and shot glasses and shirts and self-cleaning water bottles. Supposedly, one year the team had even gotten TreeHacks condoms. Only a week after the yacht party, the TreeHacks team would go on its spring retreat, at a mansion in the countryside. We'd have a white-water rafting trip and another big, blowout party, where Vedant taught me to shotgun a beer. The week before, we had "Special D"—a special dinner, a staple yearly tradition of Stanford clubs—renting a house at Stanford for a night of celebration. The amount of alcohol was insane, but, Sara confessed, "It's easier now that our financial officer is in-house." They'd had to create a slush fund in the past to hide expenses. "Now we can be more unethical, it's nice," she said with a laugh. Unlike in S.H.I.T., nobody batted an eye when I spent five hundred dollars on groceries to cook for us, expensing it to the TreeHacks company card.

Several students who'd started the year on the team had by now dropped out of Stanford, including Vedant, who went to work at OpenAI, and a sapling who won the Thiel Fellowship. Another TreeHacks teammate, John, later told me about his friend, a freshman, who'd participated in rush week for fraternities. He'd gotten into a frat, but changed his mind because, he told John, the world needed him too much. "If I join this, I'm delaying a cure for millions of people," he told John, who in turn raved to me about his friend's new technology that was 1,000 percent going to cure cancer. "It's not Theranos, don't worry," John said. "Although I guess it could be. I don't really know how it works."

Still, despite the surroundings, despite the wealth, despite the absurdity of it all, we were, at the end of the day, just teenagers. I watched as my friend Chris finished his CS homework assignment on board the yacht, signing the "Declaration: I did not use ChatGPT," with ChatGPT open in a split window right next to it.

I WAS HALFWAY TO CLASS, WALKING ACROSS MAIN QUAD, WHEN I GOT a message from a friend. MTL had just shown up at an event with the visiting president of Colombia. Immediately, I started sprinting.

Tessier-Lavigne still went to public events like the one at Hillel after the hate crime, or the faculty senate, but not frequently and usually in a carefully orchestrated setting where he was unapproachable. He had closed his office hours after my first article back in November and scarcely seemed to interact with students. I learned that he'd been removed from an earlier event with major donors. "In the wake of the MTL controversy, he will no longer be a speaker at this event," Stanford's own fundraising team wrote to the donors.

This meant that MTL had never been publicly asked about his research, despite more than a dozen interview requests I had made. His lawyer's responses tended to ignore or bluster through many of the questions I sent, meaning there were notable gaps in the record. MTL himself preferred to communicate through the long missives he continued to post on his website, but, as any journalist will tell you, a written statement is far less valuable than someone's direct response. So I kept trying to get it.

I couldn't get into the Colombian president's event itself, but I spied a familiar vehicle in a parking lot: the bright blue Volkswagen. There was only one path from the auditorium to the car, so I knew which way MTL would be walking. And it was a long stretch of pavement, too—enough time to walk alongside him and ask a few questions.

Sure enough, when MTL came out of the event, he made his way toward the path. I wasn't hiding. In a clear area with no trees or other obstructions, Tessier-Lavigne saw me before I approached him. But there was only one path, so his only option was to come toward me.

"Hello, President Tessier-Lavigne, how are you?" I asked.

"Very nice to see you," he responded, in a perfectly even tone.

I hadn't really thought about what to ask him, so I decided to focus on the Genentech report specifically. "Why did you choose to publish Alzheimer's research you knew wasn't reproducible?" I asked. We were walking quickly at this point, and I struggled to match his pace while appearing dignified.

"I—" he started, then closed his mouth and changed his mind.

I tried again with something different. "What was the decision process behind not retracting that paper?" But he just kept walking.

I let the silence hang, not wanting to badger him. Finally, I tried to give him the opportunity to at least say something general. "Do you have anything to say to people who are wondering why there are so many allegations of research misconduct coming from your lab?" At this point, he was known to have collaborated on at least a dozen papers with suspect images, and as senior author signed off on five pretty definitively fraudulent studies from several underlings at several different institutions. How did he explain that?

"It's very nice to see you," he repeated, "and I look forward to corresponding."

I attempted to appeal to him once more, since he'd opened the door to further engagement. "I appreciate that, and I know you've said you want transparency," I said. "Why won't you do an interview?"

But the Stanford president just said, "Thank you," and drove away.

Among the questions Tessier-Lavigne had never answered were whether concerns about his research had come up when he was being considered for the presidency by the board of trustees and when they'd first been informed. Also, why hadn't he issued a public statement or responded to the PubPeer comments in 2015, despite apparently trying to submit corrections that went unpublished? Why hadn't he followed up in the seven years since submitting them? And in light of the image aberrations in the 2009 paper, did he still believe the data to be "accurately reported," as Steve Neal had claimed in his initial letter to me?

We didn't know when the Stanford board's investigating committee would issue a report or even really what they were investigating. And the school was getting hit left and right by real challenges. There was the MTL investigation, sure, but also Elizabeth Holmes, Do Kwon, Sam Bankman-Fried, the ongoing War on Fun controversy, universal discontent over the neighborhood housing system, the fight over Hoover's board, Stan Cohen, Katie Meyer, disenchantment with the foundering football program, and even a national furor over the IT department's internal "Elimination of Harmful Language Initiative" guidance, which recommended the expunging of words like "American," "brave," and "grandfather" because they were offensive.

As I sat in on the faculty senate one more time at the end of the term, I listened to two senators gossip.

"It's just so much bad news, every day," one said, shaking her head.

CHAPTER 16

FINIS ORIGINE PENDET

I believe you have presented convincing evidence," said the man.

I was speaking to one of Stanford's most recognizable scientists, a biologist with a senior position and guaranteed funding. He belonged to a small category of Stanford figures who could voice their thoughts without ramifications. He wasn't involved in any of the Tessier-Lavigne research. But he believed, based on the evidence, "that Genentech did in fact have an investigation and likely did conclude that the data published in the *Nature* paper on N-APP were incorrect and probably involved fraud by the first author." This left him with some concerns.

"What bothers me most," the scientist told me, "is that in my opinion, the entire administration should show more moral courage, exhibit an explicit orientation on values more than anything." He couldn't understand Tessier-Lavigne's refusal to "clean all of this up."

So, would the famous researcher desperate for moral courage actually say this on the record? Would he offer his advice to the board or urge others to speak out?

Of course not.

THE SCHOOL YEAR ENDED WITHOUT A RESOLUTION TO THE TESSIER-Lavigne affair, and I bade adieu to the palms and pines with little idea of what would happen by the time I returned in the fall. A small part of me wondered if I would return.

Stanford's committee announced that its investigation would be "substantially complete" by midsummer, when everyone was off campus and, perhaps, paying a little less attention.

I flew off to Berlin, where I'd arranged to volunteer for some of the Russian dissident Alexei Navalny's exiled investigators as they tracked down oligarchs evading sanctions. They were hugely impressive, with a worthy mission I admired, but I quickly found that I was just as wrapped up in reporting as ever—only in a time zone nine hours ahead. As much as I wanted to help the Navalny crew, I was effectively useless, unable to escape Stanford. It turned into just one more commitment I'd fallen down on during my journey into journalism.

BY EARLY JULY, I WAS READY TO WRITE AN ARTICLE I'D BEEN WORKING on for some time—investigating the investigation.

I'd spoken to more than a dozen people, including seven who'd been interviewed by the committee and several who, intriguingly, had not been. In fact, it seemed the investigation hadn't sought out several key witnesses. More important, though, I learned the reason that witnesses weren't opening up about what they knew: Stanford said it couldn't promise them anonymity. And for many of them, that was a nonstarter.

Some witnesses declined to be interviewed because of their concerns with the investigation. Others went through with the interview but limited their testimony. Curiously, some of the investigators' questions seemed narrow in scope.

Still, everyone seemed to feel that the scientists conducting the investigation were making a good-faith effort. The Kirkland lawyers had tried to assure people their accounts would be protected as much as possible. But who would have access to their testimony? Would it just be the lawyers and scientists? What about the board's special committee? The whole board? Would they list the names of those they'd interviewed? Even if just the scientists and lawyers had access to their testimony, that still required placing faith in a fairly large group. And in the event of, for example, a lawsuit by Tessier-Lavigne, their names would be coughed up in an instant, they were told.

For the Genentech sources especially—those with nondisclosure agreements, careers to protect, and intimate knowledge of MTL's retributive side—this was a tough pill to swallow. Effectively the only reason sources decided to speak with me was because I swore I'd protect them come hell or high water. Like any good journalist, I'd sooner go to jail than reveal confidential sources. The Stanford investigation didn't offer the same protections.

When I described what was happening to some outside experts, they voiced concerns. Jeffrey Flier, a former dean of Harvard Medical School who'd overseen a number of investigations, said the failure to assure confidentiality to witnesses was "extremely unusual." Anonymity, he told me, was highly important "for the purposes of improving the access to information that is viewed as relevant." Elisabeth Bik said that not having a guarantee of anonymity "would make several witnesses or sources very hesitant to speak."

I APPROACHED AIDAN RYAN, THE SPOKESMAN FOR THE BOARD, FOR comment on the story on July 12. At first, he promised to get back to me the next day. But when the next day arrived, a statement did not.

Stanford was playing hardball.

Ryan asked me not to publish the story. Or rather, to hold off publishing it. The investigators were almost done with the report, he said, and in exchange for holding my article until the report was published, they would offer me an embargoed copy in advance of its public release and an interview with Mark Filip, the Kirkland & Ellis lawyer overseeing the inquiry. That would be invaluable, because the report was expected to be lengthy and this would give me the chance to dig through it before having to type. But if we published our story on the anonymity policy, the embargo would be off the table—given to other outlets, not us.

I hated the thought of someone else controlling any of our editorial decisions. I knew their plan was to bury my story by forcing it to share a news cycle with coverage of the report itself. But it didn't seem like we had much choice. Losing the embargo would put me at a huge disadvantage and mean that the final result of the story that had been mine from the start would be reported first elsewhere. Aside from that, Ryan said they'd provide a response to my story on their anonymity policy, but only after the report was released. And I wanted to hear their explanation.

With some trepidation, I agreed to the embargo, and to additional terms they imposed. "One important note I want to address in writing: all journalists are agreeing not to tell anyone else that they have the report and not to communicate with any sources/parties to ask questions based on the contents of the report" until the embargo lifts, Ryan wrote. That would mean our initial story would be published without reactions, letting the committee's words stand on their own. I tried to negotiate, but Ryan politely shut me down. "We will not be giving any outlet special treatment," Ryan wrote me, and "these are the terms that all reporters and editors have agreed to." I caved.

When the day arrived, the report was set to be sent at 2:15 a.m. my time in Berlin. But 2:15 a.m. rolled around and no email arrived.

I counted the seconds, heart racing. I knew nothing about what the report would look like, no idea what tone it would take, no idea, even, who had written it. The scientists? The lawyers? The committee? The board? All of the above?

I don't think I've had a more jittery half hour. I felt as if I were in a sort of rigor mortis, every muscle clenched at once. I was alone in the dark, in an unfamiliar city, with nothing to distract me from the impending news.

Finally, at almost 3:00 a.m. my time, I received the report—on a secure website that didn't allow me to download the document and send it to my editors. Ugh. Not stopping to read, I took screenshots of each of the ninety-five pages as quickly as I could and passed them along before scrolling back to the top to dig in.

The cover letter was written by Mark Filip, addressed to the special committee, and as I started reading it, an impression began to form: MTL had survived.

Filip took an oddly deferential tone toward MTL, mentioning several times in the first few pages how willing the Stanford president had been to participate in the review, and stating that investigators "have been aware both of Dr. Tessier-Lavigne's distinguished scientific career, including his substantial contributions to neuroscience, as well as his service as president of both Rockefeller and Stanford universities."

The investigation, Filip said, had reviewed tens of thousands of pages of documents, and involved "thousands of hours" of work. (Kirkland can charge upward of twenty-five hundred dollars per hour.) More interesting, Filip said the investigation "included more than fifty meetings with individuals with knowledge pertaining to one or more aspects of the investigation, including seven meetings with Dr. Tessier-Lavigne." First of all, fifty meetings was, actually, quite a small number, especially given the breadth of the investigation (twelve papers, four institutions, and twenty-four years), and that allowed for multiple meetings with an individual. By that definition, I'd certainly conducted more meetings in connection to this investigation than they had. But even more intriguingly—seven of those meetings were with MTL. Was their primary witness in an investigation of Marc Tessier-Lavigne . . . Marc Tessier-Lavigne?

Filip stated that "it was not always possible to meet with everyone.

For example, some individuals with knowledge or potential knowledge of matters pertaining to our work refused to speak with us, often despite multiple overtures." He didn't specify why they'd refused. Plus, "while most individuals and institutions—and certainly Dr. Tessier-Lavigne—cooperated with our requests for documents, a small number of them did not cooperate either through direct refusals or indirect conduct amounting to the same." Still, he wrote, the work of the scientific panel had been "thorough, methodical, diligent, and independent," and here were its conclusions:

> For the seven reviewed papers where Dr. Tessier-Lavigne was a non-principal author, the Scientific Panel has concluded that Dr. Tessier-Lavigne did not have actual knowledge of any manipulation of research data, did not have a material role in the preparation of the data and/or figures that have been publicly challenged, and was not in a position where a reasonable scientist would be expected to have detected any such misconduct.
>
> For the five reviewed papers where Dr. Tessier-Lavigne was a principal author (sometimes referred to as the "primary papers"), the Scientific Panel has concluded that Dr. Tessier-Lavigne did not have actual knowledge of the manipulation of research data that occurred in his lab and was not reckless in failing to identify such manipulation prior to publication. Nonetheless, based on the available research record and other factors, each of the papers has serious flaws in the presentation of research data; in at least four of the five papers, there was apparent manipulation of research data by others.

And then the whammy:

> For one of the five primary papers, published in 2009 in the prominent scientific journal *Nature*, we have also assessed allegations reported in the media that Genentech previously con-

> ducted a fraud investigation and made a finding of fraud as to that paper. . . . The allegations of fraud related to the paper appear to be mistaken, as Genentech also has stated publicly.

In sum, Filip's letter appeared to present the kindest possible interpretation for Tessier-Lavigne—acknowledging that several papers were based on manipulated data, but otherwise seeming to absolve him of all responsibility. Filip even went out of the way at the end to thank "Dr. Tessier-Lavigne, who was cooperative and professional throughout his interactions with us." (Not thanked: the volunteer sleuths who identified issues in the first place.)

AS I READ FURTHER, THOUGH, I REALIZED THAT THE REPORT, SPIN aside, was far more damning than Filip's cover letter had implied.

While the cover letter had tepidly suggested "that there may have been opportunities to improve laboratory oversight and management," the content of the report itself was more explicit. Tessier-Lavigne had created a dynamic "that tended to reward the 'winners' (that is, postdocs who could generate favorable results) and marginalize or diminish the 'losers' (that is, postdocs who were unable or struggled to generate such data)." It was this dynamic that helped to explain the "unusual frequency of manipulation of research data and/or substandard scientific practices."

In addition, while Tessier-Lavigne had not known about or ordered fraud, the panel said, "at various times when concerns . . . emerged—in 2001, the early 2010s, 2015–2016, and March 2021—Dr. Tessier-Lavigne failed to decisively and forthrightly correct mistakes in the scientific record." The panel, relying on documents from MTL that I didn't have, was able to show that he'd been made aware of issues in his papers on several occasions, and said he had "not been able to provide an adequate explanation" for why he didn't correct the scientific record. Based on their investigation, the scientists recommended all of the studies be retracted or substantially corrected, and Tessier-Lavigne agreed to retract three and to issue corrections for two others, the Alzheimer's paper and a separate 2004 *Nature* study.

The scientists concluded that the 2004 *Nature* paper was falsified, just as the 1999 *Cell* paper and the two 2001 *Science* studies were. They also noted that Tessier-Lavigne's "explanations are not fully responsive to the range of publicly expressed concerns given the available forensic evidence." They concluded something similar about the two *Science* papers. In their conversations, the panel wrote, MTL had accepted the evidence of manipulation in each of those papers.

On the Alzheimer's study, the scientists wrote that "the mistaken narrative of fraud in certain reporting may stem from a conflation of various events," citing the 2010 withdrawn manuscript that Genentech had previously disclosed in its public statement and speculating that the two had been mixed up. "The Panel also finds that it is possible that accounts on this topic may have been hampered by an incomplete understanding of Genentech's regular business processes (namely, that the Research Review Committee reviews various research at the company as a matter of ordinary course)."

This was a strange conclusion. For one, my sources had independently recounted the 2010 incident as well as the review of the Alzheimer's paper prior to the publication of my investigation, providing details of each. They were not mistaking one incident for the other. Also, the report appeared to mischaracterize or misinterpret some of their statements. The Genentech executives I quoted had not claimed that the Research Review Committee itself conducted an investigation—and, given that I'd spent significant time interviewing two members of the committee about the 2009 Alzheimer's study, it seemed strange to suggest that their recollections represented a case of someone not understanding how the committee worked, as they were actually on the committee and named in internal documents as key decision-makers.

Still, the scientific panel wrote that the Alzheimer's paper, while not fraudulent in their view, "fell below accepted scientific practices, let alone Dr. Tessier-Lavigne's self-described standard of scientific excellence." Ouch. The report stated that Genentech had generated internal experiments prior to the publication of the study showing "inconsistent binding results" of the central N-APP–DR6 binding. In addition, the panel concluded that the "decision to neither retract nor directly correct the *Nature* '09 paper was suboptimal, particularly given the attention the paper originally received."

Steve Neal, in his blistering attacks on my reporting, had insisted that a correction or retraction of the paper "would have been unwarranted and inappropriate." The panel was now saying he was wrong and recommended retraction, or at minimum a robust correction, "in the interest of the scientific record and consistent with his own self-described standard of scientific excellence."

The report, with everything said and done, ended on this note: "Finally, the Panel expresses its appreciation to Stanford University President Dr. Marc Tessier-Lavigne. He was open, cooperative, and professional throughout these proceedings."

BY THE TIME I FINISHED READING, IT WAS NEARLY 5:00 A.M., AND IT was time to begin writing. I was careful to highlight the places where the report broke new ground—for example, disclosing for the first time a 2001 incident where Tessier-Lavigne had been made aware of an issue with a paper within weeks of its publication and never followed up. I wanted to make sure I presented a balanced portrait, and I led my piece with the fact that they'd confirmed manipulation of data in several of his papers—clearly the most significant news—and their affirmation that he had not manipulated anything himself, been aware of falsification in any study prior to submission, or instructed people to fudge the data. (To be clear, no one had ever said he had. They were absolving him of allegations that had never been made, either by my sources or by my articles.)

Pulling together all the details in so little time was madness. The report included an incredibly thorough appendix compiled by forensic analysts who confirmed the findings I'd reported from volunteer sleuths and even found a few other manipulations they hadn't.

The report's level of detail, I figured, would overwhelm some journalists just coming to the story without being immersed in it for ten months, meaning they were likelier to rely on the cover letter's more positive framing than the actual findings; that made it all the more important that my piece include the parts that might be overlooked. But I expected the news to leak before the official embargo broke, and we couldn't be caught flat-footed, so I also had to be done as quickly as possible. Plus, I wanted plenty of time for Glenn, Tracy, and the lawyers to look at the article.

Just as I began typing the third paragraph of my story, however, my trusty laptop conked out, overheated. I spent ten panicked minutes trying to revive it. I had no idea what to do if it didn't spring back to life—it was desperately early in the morning in Germany and I had no alternatives. Thankfully, the laptop listened to my prayers and powered up again.

I was in a flow state, my fingers a flurry as I worked on the two stories—the main story about the investigation findings and a sidebar about the anonymity limitations. Sam was busy coding a new website layout so that we could feature both on the homepage with a banner headline. At exactly 9:01 a.m. my time in Berlin, I turned in my lead story. By 3:22 p.m., I'd finished the editing and legal review for both pieces. Although I'd already been awake for twenty-nine hours, there was no time to sleep—my interview with Mark Filip was in an hour. I jumped in the shower, trying to prepare for what would come when all of this became public. But when I got out, there were two messages waiting from editors at two national publications. Both asked me the same question: What did I think now that MTL was resigning?

What?

Whaaaaaat?

I called one of the editors immediately. "Yeah," he said, "I have a statement here from the board announcing Marc Tessier-Lavigne is stepping down, 'in light of the report and its impact on his ability to lead Stanford,' and someone named Richard Saller will be interim president." I learned that the other publications had been given a different embargo than the one I received, that Stanford had tried to fuck me over one final time in the eleventh hour by withholding the real news. (So much for "no special treatment.")

This changed everything.

Immediately, I called Sam announcing the news, and began typing up a new top to the story even as I pressed the phone to my ear. I didn't really feel anything in that moment except astonishment—the most I'd felt probably since the last time the board shocked me, when it opened its investigation based on my reporting in the first place.

When it came time for my interview with Filip, I confronted him with what I'd learned and he tacitly confirmed that, yes, MTL would be resigning. Aidan Ryan called me up soon after and offered me the additional embargoed documents that the others had already gotten, as long as I agreed to the same terms. That was fine, I said. I didn't give him shit for shafting me in the first place, but I admit I was pissed. Not just because they'd attempted to screw me over, but because they thought I somehow wouldn't hear about it anyway. Even now, at the end of a ten-month investigation triggered by my reporting, they were still underestimating me.

But it didn't matter. After all, I *had* heard, and I managed to get my stories together just in the nick of time to publish the second someone else broke the embargo, about an hour early.

At 10:06 a.m. Pacific time, on July 19, 2023, exactly 232 days after I unwittingly triggered a series of events nobody could have predicted, the saga reached its conclusion. Marc Tessier-Lavigne was out as president of Stanford University.

ONLY, IT WASN'T ON JULY 19 THAT THE HAMMER FELL. THE REAL DENOUEMENT, as I would later discover through more reporting, had come a month prior, at a high-stakes meeting of the board that excluded MTL. And even now, not everything was quite as it seemed.*

While Tessier-Lavigne wrote publicly that he himself "made the decision to step down" for "the good of the university," this was not wholly accurate. Instead, I learned, the board had received an update from the special committee in early June to assess the findings of the investigation. They were provided preliminary conclusions along with a public relations presentation led by Charles Bakaly, a former spokesperson for Kenneth Starr, whose investigation into President Bill Clinton resulted in impeachment.

Trustees were given a slate of plausible outcomes. They could conclude that there was no falsification whatsoever by anyone but still fault MTL by declaring that "he's behaving in an unpresidential way," as one person close to the process described it to me. They could find "something worse, say, actual falsification" by MTL. Or they could choose a finding "in the middle—there's some level of misconduct and a pattern of concerning issues and lack of accountability." What to do based on that?

The trustees were presented with slides predicting the reaction, including one that listed the likely headlines about the report in different publications: *The New York Times*, *The Washington Post*, *The Wall Street Journal*, *Science*, and *The Stanford Daily*.

"People got the picture really quickly," said one participant. "And honestly his comportment had a lot to do with it." The board discussed Steve Neal's aggressive letters to me, concluding that Tessier-Lavigne's admit-nothing, deny-everything approach "did not reflect well on him and, by extension, the institution," as the participant put it. And there was another incident, too, that influenced the trustees—one omitted from the public report. "There was an instance of a younger, female colleague who had work that challenged some of the conclusions of MTL's

*Stanford, Marc Tessier-Lavigne, and Jerry Yang did not respond to questions about MTL's resignation.

work, and he sidelined her," said a source familiar with the investigation, calling it "a misuse of power." Another person recounting the June meeting said the episode "was a confirming factor," revealing to the trustees what Tessier-Lavigne had been like behind closed doors.

At the end of the day, according to four participants in the process, the vote by the board of trustees was unanimous: Tessier-Lavigne had to go. In fact, "there was no pro-MTL camp" by the end, one of the participants told me. The report's findings, MTL's aggressive public posture, and particularly his failure to correct the scientific record when presented with opportunities to do so meant that Stanford's president had lost the support he once had. "Very quickly the conversation moved on to who would be the interim."

It had been a grueling meeting, with trustees required, as one participant put it, to "think existentially about Stanford."

IF MTL WAS SURPRISED BY THE FINDINGS OF THE INVESTIGATION, AS he reportedly was, he should not have been. When the scientific panel arranged to interview him for the first time over the previous winter, he "came out of those meetings thinking he did a great job," but the panel "had not bought any of his excuses," according to one person close to the process. In fact, this person told me, the members of the scientific panel emerged "genuinely crestfallen-level disappointed to see somebody of that stature just utterly fail to take accountability."

Over the course of the next few months, the scientists, the lawyers, the board members, and the public relations representatives would meet constantly, at all hours of the day and night, on weekends and holidays. Everyone I've talked to inside the investigation has spoken highly of the others involved. They took their jobs seriously and recognized the pressure they were under.

There were differences of opinion, to be sure, and the scientists reflected a generational divide, with the youngest member having a much harsher opinion of Tessier-Lavigne than some of the older ones who sympathized with the plight of a leader. How to frame the report became a point of contention. But by and large, each of them committed to the investigation.

The bigger problem was something else.

AS I SPOKE TO ONE PERSON ON THE INVESTIGATION WHILE REPORTING this book, I raised the issue of access. "Was there a concern that MTL's response would sort of chill people from coming forward, as in the more aggressive he was, the more people might fear retaliation?" I asked.

"No," this person responded. "I don't remember that being voiced, and that may just have been because of the faith everybody had. . . . Like, who wouldn't want to talk to this panel? Even though we can't guarantee anonymity, I don't think anybody thought there was really very much risk in talking to the panel."

This was a shocking response. For such sophisticated researchers, the scientists had a real blind spot. Even if the panel couldn't see it, potential sources of information did perceive real risk in speaking up. The scientists seemed not to fully grasp the strength of the omertà in place at Stanford and Genentech. There was fear. Genuine, palpable fear, which I routinely encountered.

And the risks weren't purely imagined, either. At least one person who requested confidentiality in fact had their testimony leaked to someone outside the investigation.

BY SPRING, EVEN AS THE STANFORD INVESTIGATION WAS PICKING UP steam, many of the trustees lost trust in MTL amid the drip, drip, drip of bad news I'd heard the faculty senator bemoaning. At the start, they'd underestimated how far the case would go. "We didn't know back then," one trustee told me later. "He seemed like a stand-up guy." And, yeah, it didn't go unnoticed that it was a seventeen-year-old writing about this.

The continuing slew of allegations, though, "really undermined his ability to lead the faculty. Really undermined it dramatically," MTL's predecessor, John Hennessy, told me. "As that became more public and more obvious, I think the trustees were surprised." They "basically didn't understand the issue," and had no choice but to figure it out.

IN THE NEGOTIATIONS OVER HIS FORCED RESIGNATION, TESSIER-LAVIGNE asked for "the sun, the moon, and the stars," according to one person privy to the discussions. He wanted to stay in the presidential mansion for six months, pushed for a significant amount of money, and, in what was the most offensive demand to some trustees, asked for guaranteed lab funding. They negotiated him down. Ultimately, he would receive a seven-figure payout.

Until the end, trustees worried that MTL would go rogue and blow up their carefully crafted plan. They strategized for what to do if Tessier-Lavigne decided to issue a statement along the lines of some of his earlier, more bombastic letters that didn't take responsibility or went on the attack. Jerry Yang himself delivered the directive to withhold the announcement from *The Daily*.

It was all a series of calculations—how to present the right face. And the trustees knew what they were doing. As I learned more about the events preceding MTL's removal, I went back and rewatched the tape of his commencement address in mid-June. "Thank you, Provost Drell, and on this occasion of *your* final commencement," Tessier-Lavigne began, emphasizing the *your* part, "please accept my thanks for your service to the university." I looked at the trustees sitting behind him onstage. They already knew what was coming, knew that this would be *his* last commencement speech, too. That in exactly one month to the day it would be announced. But none of the rest of us could have known.

As Tessier-Lavigne stood, tall, smiling, bedecked in glorious red, the board calmly observed him from behind. They could see the knives in his back, the ones we couldn't. If they had any regrets, they didn't show.

And if the robot bled, his Cardinal regalia concealed the damage.

GRAMPS, THE MAN WHO'D INSPIRED ME TO BECOME A STUDENT JOURnalist in the first place, used to sprinkle Latin phrases into his conversation, and as I contemplated the fall of MTL, one came to mind. It was a phrase I'd last heard a year earlier, at my high school graduation, back when both of my grandfathers were in the audience and I'd never dined with a Nobel laureate or been feted by a VC or interviewed to be a Ruler.

Finis origine pendet. The end depends on the beginning.

It was this notion that captured the whole affair of perfidy and struggle, captured the sacrifice of MTL to a higher virtue. "We couldn't claim to be the nation's top-rated research institution," said one of the trustees who ousted him, "while we had this going on." And that, at the end of the day, was the only thing that counted.

Stanford is supposed to look perfect.

CODA

Opposition is true Friendship.

—WILLIAM BLAKE

When I arrived for my first day of sophomore year, I didn't bother to unpack. I took an Uber from the airport to my dorm, dropped my suitcases in my new room, and immediately set out on foot.

My destination was Building 10, the president's office in Main Quad. It was a perfect afternoon, and the golden face of Memorial Church reflected beams of light back toward Palm Drive, the iconic bridge to the outside world that I'd driven down exactly one year and four days earlier to begin my Stanford journey. Seeing it again now, I broke down.

I began crying, then laughing, then crying some more. It was only in that moment, as I stood in front of the president's office, that it all became real. The strange enormity of everything that had happened in the last year hit me at once. And for the first time, I was finally able to feel relief. It was over. The stress and isolation and uncertainty that had pushed me to my limits—I could let them go.

One week later I was inside Building 10 for the first time, whisked past the waiting room I'd visited while dropping off questions in early February and into the inner sanctum I'd wondered about for so long. I was there to interview the interim president, Richard Saller, a classicist who'd previously served as dean of humanities and sciences. Roughly a full foot shorter than Tessier-Lavigne, and wearing a button-down but no suit, Saller cut a striking contrast to the man he'd replaced. Of MTL, he said, "Everybody's eager to move on."

Turnover was remarkably swift. Between my freshman and sophomore years, Stanford replaced its president, provost, dean of research, head of undergraduate education, and head of student affairs. Both the football coach and then his successor were pushed out within two years, as was the director of athletics.

A presidential search committee was launched to find a permanent replacement for Tessier-Lavigne, with cochair Gene Sykes promising to "conduct due diligence in a way that was not done in the previous search." And everyone seemed more or less ready to put the previous guy behind them.

Within six months, the page dedicated to the board's investigation into MTL would be scrubbed from Stanford's websites as if it had never happened.

FOR MY PART, I STRUGGLED TO MAKE SENSE OF IT ALL. MY FRESHMAN YEAR brought me face-to-face with impostors—one literal, many metaphorical—and would-be Rulers. I'd dwelled in the weeds of neuroscience research while witnessing firsthand the ludicrous behavior of people with money to burn.

As I discovered, there is a system that embraces "just a little bit of fraud," in the memorable phrase of my TreeHacks colleague. The relentless Duck Syndrome pressure to dominate and appear perfect, the Hangers-On looking to "pluck" those they deem worthy, the Stanford inside Stanford awash in money and lacking accountability—none of it was what I had expected. I caught a glimpse of the life I'd thought I wanted, then quickly realized it wasn't for me. Ruling the world was much less appealing than uncovering how others did it.

With the changing of the leadership guard, Stanford pledged to address many of the issues I'd reported on freshman year. In his first speech as interim president, Saller called out "fake-it-till-you-make-it culture" and defined Stanford's "fundamental mission" as maintaining "excellence with integrity," requiring "education and research done with both high ethical and scientific standards, and deserving of trust." And he promised to end the War on Fun.

When Saller handed the reins to Jonathan Levin, the dean of the business school who was appointed Stanford's thirteenth president a year after Tessier-Lavigne's ouster, Levin also assumed these priorities. To Stanford's credit, some things improved. The despised neighborhood residential system was all but scrapped and a few bureaucratic processes were simplified.

Still, it would be a mistake to think everything healed.

Today, business is booming for the Stanford inside Stanford. The AI rush kicked off in winter 2022 has only exploded further, making it easier than ever for insiders to profit. The guy who used to pour me shots of cheap overproof whiskey in his dorm room freshman year, who tossed me fully clothed into a pool with the carefree exuberance of a child, dropped out and raised tens of millions of dollars for his startup. Within months the company of fewer than twenty employees was valued at over a billion dollars. Plenty of others have ridden the tidal wave of funding to similar success. And there remain vanishingly few safeguards in place discouraging bad behavior.

The school is at something of a crossroads. AI has made the most valuable researchers and entrepreneurs far more valuable than ever before—recently, Meta paid $14 billion effectively just to acquire Alexandr Wang as its new head of AI; other top researchers have garnered $200 million signing bonuses—but it also threatens to replace many of the entry-level programming positions that Stanford computer science graduates once claimed. As one Stanford insider put it: "It's easier now to raise money for a startup than to get an internship." Will CS continue to be as valuable a degree? And will people even want to stick around?

Temptations are perhaps higher than ever to decamp to industry, where all the money is. One of the great strengths of this country since World War II has been the public-private-university partnership that enabled basically every major technological and scientific innovation for decades. Yet AI is breaking that compact, requiring so many resources that only the private sector can lead the way. Both Fei-Fei Li, who created the field of machine vision and directed the Stanford Institute for Human-Centered Artificial Intelligence, and Christopher Manning, who pioneered much of the technology underpinning today's large language models and directed the Stanford Artificial Intelligence Laboratory, have taken leave to work in the private sector in the past year.

Like other campuses, Stanford struggled to deal with the aftermath of the Hamas attack on Israel on October 7, 2023, and the resulting war in Gaza, and has tried to navigate Donald Trump's war on higher education. All this is a lot for Stanford's new leader to tackle. I've sat down with Levin three times since he became president. He's definitely smart and seems to have the right priorities, but he was guarded. He took enormous pride in Stanford's many strengths and sounded in awe of its top place in rankings even as he acknowledged they should not matter. But he reflected on the ways Stanford's modern culture puts so much pressure on today's students, pushing them to think about career from the minute they arrive on campus. "I don't think it's particularly healthy, and I think having more space at the university for just calm and fun, for that matter, is a good aspiration."

John Hennessy, who ushered in the modern Stanford during his transformative presidency, expressed concern about some of the changes. "When I look at what I've seen in the last, say, twenty years, students have become much more focused on career," he told me. Stanford's symbiotic relationship with Silicon Valley has come to define the university. "We live in this environment, which, of course, we helped create," he said. "It's very hard to separate that out."

I'M TWENTY YEARS OLD NOW; BY THE TIME THIS BOOK COMES OUT, I will be about three weeks away from graduation. My feelings about Stanford still haven't settled. People today tend to ask me why I stayed—and why I still, even now, recommend that others attend. The truth is, I continue to love Stanford. There is so much good here, and many people here really do change the world for the better.

It is precisely because I love Stanford that I wish it to be better.

This university has made a Faustian bargain with Silicon Valley, one that has enabled its meteoric ascent and allowed for its corruption. As Justin teaches in his secret class, success out here is all about "extracting value from people." The money, the talent rush—when it works, it really works. But too often the integration of the university and the tech world has proven exploitative and tolerant of misdeeds. Stanford's most singular attribute is also its gravest flaw.

Can those elements even be separated? I asked Condi Rice about this. "The flipside of opportunity and progress is risk," she said. "This is one of the things you learn as you get older, that there's always a balancing act." Rice brought up an example from her time as George W. Bush's national security adviser to demonstrate: "You have to go after a terrorist nest, but you know it's sitting inside of a village. There are going to be civilians that are going to be killed. If I don't go after the terrorist nest, you're going to have thousands of people killed. And so it's competing values." Rice then applied this logic to Stanford. "If you're going to have a big research enterprise, and you're going to have a big commercialization arm, and if you're going to encourage people to take risk, you will have some bad actors."

Perhaps it's just that I'm young, as Rice pointed out, but I have a less fatalistic view. I think you can inculcate innovation without enabling fraud. If Stanford is going to claim credit for its success stories, it must also shoulder responsibility for its failures. Even now, the university trumpets Stan Cohen's recombinant DNA research in press releases about the school's research enterprise while ignoring his ethical lapses. Both emerged from the same Stanford lab.

AS FOR TESSIER-LAVIGNE, HE WAS FORCED TO RETRACT THE 2009 ALZheimer's study in the end anyway, despite his refusal to do so for more than a decade. This was, in effect, an admission that the paper should never have been published. Extraordinary claims require extraordinary evidence, and they'd never had it.

Even when Tessier-Lavigne resigned, he tried to hold on to the Alzheimer's paper, insisting a correction would do. But with the number of visible issues, the inaccuracy of its findings, the false portrayal of reagents used, and the lack of any original data to back the study up, there was just too much against it. Five months after his ouster as president, the study was formally purged from the scientific record.

Ultimately, my reporting and the work of volunteer sleuths resulted in nearly a dozen studies receiving post-publication notices. Tessier-Lavigne was forced to retract four papers on which he was senior author and pledged to correct a fifth. This was a rare act for a researcher of his stature; across scientific publishing, just four studies are retracted for every ten thousand published. Papers that had sat for years with unaddressed issues were finally cleaned up. The process continues even now. In January 2026, *Nature* appended an Editorial Expression of Concern to another study Tessier-Lavigne oversaw in 1999 after Elisabeth Bik uncovered apparent photoshopping in that paper, too.

The resignation of Tessier-Lavigne as Stanford's president brought national attention to the problem of research misconduct, engendering a broader reckoning over the responsibility of authors and journals. Holden Thorp at *Science* announced that all six journals under his purview would now use forensic tools to detect the kind of manipulation I'd reported on; a number of studies have already been withdrawn as a result.

Still, although MTL was the first president in the history of Stanford to be ousted by the board, this wasn't the end of his story.

Four days after his resignation was announced, in mid-July 2023, Tessier-Lavigne closed on a 7,600-square-foot mansion in Atherton, the most expensive zip code in America. "Tucked away in a private oasis, this Atherton estate offers a secure and quiet location," a listing website proclaimed, advertising the estate now valued at roughly $10 million. It came with a Dolby movie theater, nine bathrooms, and a sauna, and was purchased under an LLC created a few weeks before the resignation.

Nine months later, MTL announced that he was cofounding a new company, called Xaira, and that he would serve as CEO.

To get started, Tessier-Lavigne's new company raised $1 billion.

BY PROMISING TO BRING ARTIFICIAL INTELLIGENCE TO BEAR ON DRUG discovery, Tessier-Lavigne had pulled off the largest seed round in biotech history. It was a remarkable comeback, and it wasn't just the enormous dollar amount that caught my eye.

Tessier-Lavigne debuted Xaira on April 23, 2024, with an interview in a friendly industry publication, his first of any kind since November 29, 2022, when my first *Stanford Daily* article reporting questions about his research was published. The matter of his ouster as the president of Stanford was left until 1,400 words into a 1,500-word piece, when the reporter asked him what he'd learned. Tessier-Lavigne said it was important not to take data at face value. "That's certainly a lesson I've taken to heart," he said.

But was there anything he actually planned to do differently in his next big job? Were there any different controls he would put in place?

MTL wouldn't say.

Two of the VCs leading the investment in Tessier-Lavigne's new business turned out to be ones I'd spoken with during my freshman year—the racist one and the "money is a rush" guy who'd been such a fan of my reporting. Even after announcing their investments in MTL, both of their firms continued to be friendly with me. One invited me to a private event a few months later, with an investor texting me, "Theo when you aren't knocking university presidents off their perches into the hands of VCs willing to fund them for a $1B, you should join ;)"

Then a partner from the other VC firm reached out—unsolicited—to offer me funding, too, if I wanted to start a company.

I was surprised, but I shouldn't have been. That's how this place works.

ACKNOWLEDGMENTS

This has been a pretty weird way to do college. I spent freshman year living through the improbable and utterly strange events described in this book, then immediately began the process of writing about them, without a pause in between. In that way, then, *How to Rule the World* has been with me through every second of my time at Stanford.

The first seeds of this book grew out of a conversation in late 2022, when I was still in my first quarter of freshman year. Rob Reich and I were discussing the Stanford inside Stanford and my experience with the Therac-25 incident in CS107, when none of my peers raised their hands to say they cared about ethics. Reich told me I should write a book about this place. So thanks to him, and, needless to say, all culpability for the resulting text falls squarely on my shoulders.

I couldn't have asked for a better agent, ally, and friend than Rafe Sagalyn, who immediately saw the potential in this project. I trust Rafe without reservation, and to have him as a guide to the world of publishing has been invaluable. The whole CAA team has been fabulous, and I owe special thanks to Tia Ikemoto, Matthew Snyder, and John Ash.

Ginny Smith has been a close collaborator for the past two years, joining this project before a single word of the manuscript had been written, and before its ending had even taken place. I am enormously grateful to her and the rest of the Penguin Press team, including Ann Godoff and Scott Moyers, who took a chance on an eighteen-year-old first-time author. Without the faith they placed in me, I'm not sure I could've written this book. Ginny has supported me throughout, and our partnership has been deeply meaningful. I'm also delighted to have worked with the team at Allen Lane, especially Tom Penn.

Amy Pascal is the coolest person ever, and I'm grateful to her, Rachel O'Connor, and Kevin McCormick for our thoughtful conversations over the past few years, as well as to the rest of the Warner Bros. team, including Mike De Luca, Pam Abdy, and Jesse Ehrman, for the interest they've shown in this story.

Andy Young has saved me from countless embarrassing errors. Yuki Hirose and Louise Carron ensured this manuscript was precise and protected. It was a delight to work with Elena Seibert to get the author photo for this book. Julia Whelan gave me so much more confidence than I otherwise would've had in reading for the audiobook. So many people, from copy editors to art directors to marketers, have believed in this project, and I'm grateful for all of their efforts.

This book is based on hundreds of interviews. Many of those who participated cannot be named, but you know who you are. Thank you for entrusting me with your stories.

Elisabeth Bik, my first fearless source, deserves special praise. Very few people of any profession are as dedicated, principled, and talented as she is, and the scientific world is infinitely better off for having her. To all the scientific sleuths and writers who have been doing difficult, unsung work for years to bring matters like this to light: I am so impressed by you, and grateful that you do this work. A few shout-outs go to Matthew Schrag, Ivan Oransky, Adam Marcus, Charles Piller, and Carl Elliott.

At *The Stanford Daily*, I was incredibly fortunate to find supporters, friends, and advisers who made this work possible and never backed down. Andrew Bridges, Ambika Kumar, and Eric Stahl have my undying gratitude. Tracy Jan is a gem of a human being in every way. Glenn Kramon is the greatest mentor a boy could ever hope for. And then there's Sam Catania, who put himself on the line when it mattered most because he believed in the importance of this work.

There are so many Stanford friends I'd like to thank—people who kept me going when I reached my lowest moments. For the sake of preserving the anonymity of characters in this book, I've made the decision not to name any students here who aren't already named in the text. But those of you who have shared in the past few years of crazy ups and downs mean so much to me.

This is a book, ultimately, about education. I wouldn't be here if not for the teachers who believed in me and pushed me to achieve my dreams. Rina Chakrabarty, Johnny Miles, Tina Hudak, Ted Haley, Kelly Castellanos-Evans, Daniel Finer, Colleen Dunn, John Velosky, Keith and Nikki Mills, Donna Denise, Carrie Friend, Chris Jones, Clara Isaza-Bishop, Emma Staffaroni, Kiran Bhardwaj, Corrie Martin, Andy Housiaux, Nick Zufelt, and Abbey Siegfried are among the passionate educators I've been fortunate enough to learn from. My relationship with Melissa and Randy Hollerith has meant so much to me. Michael Hansen is single-handedly responsible for my love of computer science and has done so much to shape the course of my life. Taylor Ware is probably the most empathetic person I've ever met. David Gardner is utterly brilliant and, whether dissecting Russian literature, gossiping, or bantering about the world, I'm grateful for every minute we've gotten to share.

And then there's Tracy Ainsworth. From the minute I set foot at Andover, Tracy became my guardian angel, and I couldn't imagine a more caring, thoughtful, and undeniably wonderful person. She deserves the world.

Far and away the best part of Stanford has been the professors I've grown close to. In every respect they have blown my expectations out of the water. Rob Reich has been a confidant and friend. Marietje Schaake is principled, brilliant, and inspiring. Joshua Landy has been a scintillating raconteur ever since our thirty-minute coffee became a four-hour discussion back in freshman year. Fred Turner cares for his students deeply and has shown me profound compassion. Larry Diamond is among the greatest humans I have ever had the good fortune of knowing. R. B. Brenner can light up a room like no one else and has always been there for me. Steve Zipperstein is the definition of a mensch. Becoming close with Michele Dauber has easily been one of the highest privileges of my life.

I first reached out to Jennifer Burns a few weeks before enrolling in college, having enjoyed her first book. Ever since, she has been a sage mentor and adviser through thick and thin. Jody Maxmin represents Stanford at its very, very finest. I don't think that any professor of any kind at any institution in the history of the world has devoted themself more to their students, and I love Jody dearly.

Since I came out west, Heather, Elliott, and Somerset Grant have done so much to make this place feel like home. Glenn Kramon and Lauren Grossman have become family in everything but name. Phil Taubman and Felicity Barringer have provided support and encouragement from the beginning, no questions asked. Jessica Kirschner is a genuine, caring person who has helped me find my bearings here.

Writing this book was beyond difficult for me. I was fortunate to spend a few months in residence at Yaddo, where I was able to clear my head and get going. A huge thank-you to Meena and Liaquat Ahamed, Ayad Akhtar, Elaina Richardson, and everyone else who made that possible.

Michael Lewis, Kara Swisher, Alec Berg, and David Grann provided early advice that helped me get going. Frank Foer and Leon Wieseltier reassured me when I needed it most. And the esteemed members of the Scribblers Society—David Maraniss, Rick Atkinson, and Rafe Sagalyn—were so generous with their time, talking me through thorny structural issues and giving me the confidence to "get on with it." Thank you also to Mike Grunwald, who provided crucial feedback on the manuscript.

Bill Grueskin has become a good friend whose piercing wit helped me get through sophomore year. Any time spent with Griffin Gaffney leaves me energized and excited for the future of journalism. John Smith and Jan Eckendorf are fantastic people who have gone above and beyond for me, even when I haven't deserved it. I have gained so much from my unlikely friendship with Brian Zeger, who has provided mirth and good counsel in spades. Frank is my best friend and I don't know what I'd do without him. Lily, though that is not her real name, was generous enough to review this manuscript and give her thoughts; she remains very important to me.

As I write in this book, the permanent cast of characters in my life have had a huge influence on me. I'm particularly grateful to Jane Mayer and Bill and Kate Hamilton; Gary Bass; Nicole Rabner, Rick Long, and Andie Kanarek; Heidi Crebo-Rediker and Doug and Charlotte Rediker; Susan Ascher and Paul and Audrey Kalb; Rajiv, Julie, Max, and Leo Chandrasekaran; Mike, Max, and Lina Grunwald and Christina Dominguez; Indira Lakshmanan and Dermot, Devan, and Rohan Tatlow; Valerie Mann and Tim Webster; Michael and Caitlin Shear; Sabrina Tavernise and Rory MacFarquhar; Julia Ioffe; Bruce and Marilou Sanford; and John Olson and Tom Kim.

Bill Cohan and Deb Futter have kept me sane. Every moment we're together is a joyful one. Jeff Mays is a singular man—wise, kind, hilarious, and damn good at tennis. I treasure our relationship. Martina Vandenberg and Alan, Marshall, and Max Cooperman are my village; I would do anything for them.

This book is dedicated, in part, to my late grandfathers, Steve Glasser and Ted Baker. I miss them every day. I'd also like to recognize the rest of my family: Martha Baker; Karin Baker and Kait Nolan; Linda and Keith Sinrod; Lynn Glasser; Laura Glasser, Emily Allen, and Will and Ben Allen-Glasser; Jeff, Diana, Caroline, and Elizabeth Glasser; Jennifer Glasser and Matthieu, Alex, and Oliver Fulchiron; Tiffany Hudson and Chris Sebastian; Larry and Amy Corey; Daniel and Elizabeth Corey; Jordan Corey and Katie Gutman; and Linda Allderdice.

Rosamaria Brizuela has made me into the man I am today. She has been with me at every step and exudes care for others. Abby, te quiero con todo mi corazón.

Finally, and most importantly, my parents: Peter Baker and Susan Glasser. I have woken up every single day of my life proud to be your son. You have shown me an extraordinary example to live up to while affording me the independence to go off and make my own successes and failures. No one could possibly be more supportive, encouraging, and loving. You have included me in your life from the start, and I cherish our bond more than anything. (Aside from Ellie, the best dog ever.) I love you to bits.

NOTES

This book relies upon hundreds of sources, including many original interviews conducted for this book, as well as reporting previously published in *The Stanford Daily*. Throughout my freshman year, I published thirty-six articles in the student paper. Only after Marc Tessier-Lavigne's resignation did I begin contributing to other outlets, ultimately publishing in *The New York Times*, *New York* magazine, *The Atlantic*, and *Air Mail* during my sophomore year.

Wherever possible, my recollection has been checked against contemporaneous notes, diary entries, images, videos, or, in the absence of confirming documentation, other witnesses. An independent fact-checker was employed to comb through the manuscript, in addition to the editorial review and legal vetting performed by the publisher.

These notes are intended to give further background about my reporting process. Additional citations for secondary sources are available at https://theobaker.info/rulenotes.

Marc Tessier-Lavigne, Stanford, *Nature*, Richard Scheller, Justin, and Jerry Yang were provided detailed questions for this book. Stanford, *Nature*, and Scheller declined to comment. Justin and Jerry Yang did not respond to requests for comment. Tessier-Lavigne declined to answer the majority of the questions he was provided, but, through his lawyers, did respond to a select few concerning his scientific work. Where relevant, his responses have been noted in the text of the book and in further detail below.

Chapter 1: Drafted to the War on Fun

My account of the War on Fun is largely drawn from reporting conducted between October 10, 2022, and October 24, 2022, which culminated in the

Stanford Daily article "Inside 'Stanford's War on Fun': Tensions Mount over University's Handling of Social Life." My piece drew on more than a dozen interviews with students, faculty, and administrators, as well as internal emails, training materials, and publicly accessible Stanford policies. More than fifty people declined to comment during the reporting process.

Chapter 2: The Impostor

Reporting on the impostor, Will Curry, is largely drawn from four articles I published in *The Stanford Daily* between October 28, 2022, and November 3, 2022. In total, I conducted around thirty interviews with Curry's friends, fellow residents, people whose rooms he broke into, a former romantic partner, his high school principal, and Curry himself. Other details, like my Woodside conversation and the Codex-Pitbull story, are drawn from contemporaneous notes, text messages, and images.

Fizz started at Stanford but expanded to other universities. Each university has its own Fizz group, each one only accessible if you have the requisite school email. Many other communities have reported similar issues with toxicity. The Stanford Marriage Pact has also expanded to other universities.

Chapter 3: Coupa Circuit

This chapter is based on real-time experience supplemented with additional material subsequently reported. My portrait of Ivan is based on six interviews over the course of a year, while I render Julian based primarily off our more casual interactions in class and one-on-one conversations at Coupa. All elements of TreeHacks relayed in the book have been corroborated through multiple sources. In assembling my portrait of the Stanford inside Stanford, I have interviewed numerous students as well as instructors; members of ASES and BASES, as well as Friends and Family and the Venture Capital Club; recruiters; investors; engineers; and more.

Chapter 4: Binary Bomb

My reporting on Marc Tessier-Lavigne began primarily with open-source investigation—anyone could've started where I started in 2022 back in 2015. I received the first tip pointing me to PubPeer on November 1, 2022, and published my first article about the allegations on November 29, 2022. Three independent forensic image analysts reviewed the figures at my request. While I'd already begun to assemble some behind-the-scenes reporting, interviewing several former colleagues of a postdoc suspected of having falsified some of the results, I chose to base my first piece primarily on the open-source, verifiable allegations I was reporting. The reporting I'd already gathered would be published later—including an email I obtained from MTL calling the postdoc a "deeply troubled person" who "needed help."

Citation counts for papers are taken from Google Scholar. When citation percentiles are cited, they come from Clarivate's Scopus database, which computes normalized percentiles based on field.

Chapter 5: A Fucking Menace

This chapter is largely based on a series of nine articles I published between November 30, 2022, and January 2, 2023. I spoke with journal editors, leaders at other prominent universities, scientific sleuths, principal investigators, colleagues and peers of Tessier-Lavigne, lawyers, and others. The board announced an investigation on November 29; on December 2, members of the special committee to investigate were announced; by December 5, after I began asking questions about a potential $18 million conflict of interest, one of the members of the committee had stepped aside; on December 6, *Cell* reopened an inquiry into a 1999 paper and MTL sent his first statement directly to faculty; by December 15, three MTL studies were issued editorial expressions of concern, validating the severity of the allegations.

The details about Stan Cohen in this chapter are taken directly from court documents. Cohen appealed the verdict, and in late 2024 an appeals court reversed and remanded the decision based on procedural error. In January 2025, the two parties reached a settlement to reinstate the original decision from 2022 finding Cohen liable for negligent misrepresentation. Cohen agreed to pay back the original investment with interest and the right to a further appeal was waived, finally ending the nine-year legal saga less than a month before the Stanford legend's ninetieth birthday.

Chapter 6: Rule

My account of Rule is based on significant original reporting, including interviews with six students in the secret class, whom I slowly convinced to talk over the course of nearly two years, as well as conversations with several other people in Justin's vicinity, including the cofounder of his company. The portrait presented of the Stanford inside Stanford is based on more than fifty interviews conducted exclusively for this book, including students, dropouts, investors, and CEOs.

From the minute I heard about the How to Rule the World class, I knew I would be writing about it; the only question was when. I was first referred just after my TreeHacks rollout and had my interview a month later, on

December 3. I heard back on January 9 from Justin: "Unfortunately, I can't offer you a spot in the cohort this quarter. That being said, you were a strong contender, and as such I'd be happy to go for a walk and discuss any topic of your choosing." Justin is, after all, a networker.

Derek, in a fluke of timing, first reached out to me on December 3, *while I was in my interview with Justin*, writing that he ran "a pre-IPO software company" and asking if I would be "up for grabbing coffee sometime on campus" because he was interested in my potential. We first met on February 5, 2023, for coffee and a hike (in the rain), and the Rosewood brunch—our first meal—took place sometime later. I'm still not entirely sure why the state senator was there, but the three of us have a group chat and continue to be in touch.

My interviews with Steve Blank and Sam Altman both took place in 2024, and my interview with John Hennessy in 2025. That said, while the chapter is populated with many details obtained in subsequent reporting, its chronological spine is accurate to my own journey through the Stanford inside Stanford.

Chapter 7: Duck Syndrome

The majority of this chapter is sourced from personal recollection, diary entries, text conversations, and videos, as well as reporting done by others and publicly available data. The lawsuit over Katie Meyer's 2022 death has yet to go to trial as of fall 2025. Her story is tragic, and I encourage you to seek out the full version. It also ties into another issue I didn't have space to touch on: Stanford's abysmal record with sexual misconduct.

At Stanford, advocates say just two students have ever been expelled for sexual assault or rape. (Stanford gives a slightly higher number, but it includes students who voluntarily withdraw and thus don't have expulsion marked on their permanent records.) This is despite the fact that one in three undergraduate women at Stanford report that they have been assaulted at the school. That number comes from an external study in which 63 percent of undergrads participated. Most damningly, the study found that fewer than 2 percent of sexual assaults at Stanford are reported to the school, in no small part because students don't trust the system to work for them. Frequently it doesn't.

Stanford's unusually laborious process can extend years and, of course, often results in scant sanction against an offending party anyway. The university has repeatedly made promises to reform its approach and failed to live up to them—for example, pledging to bring full rape kit access to Stanford Hospital in November 2018, a promise that was not kept until an audit by the Santa Clara County Board of Supervisors and sustained pressure from students and faculty forced Stanford's hand in mid-2023. Several professors found to have violated

Title IX protections teach freely without consequence, and, though the school experienced a national reckoning over sexual assault with the Brock Turner case in 2016 and subsequent revelations that year, the problem is far from solved.

I reported on this during freshman year on a few occasions, most directly in January 2023, when I learned that Stanford had stopped reporting some Title IX data without explanation. When asked about it, Stanford provided several contradictory and two outright false statements.

Chapter 8: Harriet the Spy

This portrait of Marc Tessier-Lavigne is based on extensive interviews with colleagues, friends, and collaborators from each stage of his career and every institution where he worked—from Columbia as a postdoc, to UCSF as a fledgling principal investigator, to Stanford for a two-year stint, to Genentech, to Rockefeller, and then back to Stanford as president. I interviewed those who interacted with MTL as a scientist, as well as those who knew him as an administrator; I interviewed people who reported to him, those who were peers, and people to whom he reported.

Much of this material was collected as I examined the president's research during my freshman year, but some details—like the story of the reagent that scientists in a collaborator's lab thought had been stolen—were only unearthed as I continued reporting for this book. The shift in MTL's lab oversight in the late nineties that was described by my sources was also hinted at in the Stanford investigation's final report, which noted that accounts of "Dr. Tessier-Lavigne's commitment to scientific mentoring and rigor" came "particularly during the earlier years of Dr. Tessier-Lavigne's career in his UCSF and original Stanford labs." In response to questions for this book, MTL's lawyers forwarded two public statements by former postdocs in Tessier-Lavigne's labs, Andy Plump and Nick Hertz, praising their former boss. "Marc Tessier-Lavigne is a remarkably good and ethical person," wrote Plump, whose company is partnered with Denali Therapeutics. "As a scientist and leader, he has contributed at the highest level, at or above any peer of this era."

I first received the anonymous letter cluing me in to a story at Genentech on December 3, 2022—the same day as my interview with Justin and the note from Derek, because that's just how absurdly overlapping my freshman year really was. My "jackpot" interview took place in late January.

Chapter 9: [[Not for Distribution]]

The account given here of the 2009 Alzheimer's paper is a slightly fleshed-out version of my February 17, 2023, *Daily* article, "Internal Review Found 'Falsified

Data' in Stanford President's Alzheimer's Research, Colleagues Allege." In reporting this book, I obtained several corroborating accounts that backed up my initial piece and added some new context—for example, the detail about the Research Review Committee's highly edited minutes.

Ultimately, I collected the accounts of seven well-placed sources who each had knowledge of the internal review at the time to piece together what happened. This includes two members of Genentech's Research Review Committee—the body of the company's most senior scientists.

Chapter 10: The Good Paper

This chapter is based primarily on my own personal recollection, supported by texts, Slack messages, emails, notes, and videos. It also details Tessier-Lavigne's defense. Steve Neal sent his first message to Sam and me on February 9, 2023, with the email subject line "February 7, 2023 Letter to Mark Tessier-Lavign [*sic*]" and ultimately sent a further ten letters over the next few months. In addition to Neal and another Cooley attorney—senior counsel Marty Schenker—MTL also retained two separate public relations firms. He created a dedicated web page on his Stanford lab site to defend himself in response to my reporting, ultimately sending out more than 10,500 words to the Stanford community.

Even after his forced resignation, Tessier-Lavigne continued to go on the attack. In a January 8, 2024, message on his lab website, MTL preposterously claimed, "At the time of publication [of the 2009 *Nature* paper], I was not aware of any binding experiments . . . showing results inconsistent with those we presented in the paper." But the Stanford scientific panel, whose results Tessier-Lavigne said he accepted, wrote in its final report, "In October 2008, that lab generated results which showed 'much weaker' binding against four different N-APP preparations" and that "Dr. Tessier-Lavigne was aware of these results." While he dismissed those specific experiments as less important—and insisted to the scientific panel that he was unaware of the more clearly inconsistent binding results—this still flatly contradicts the unequivocal statement that he was unaware of any evidence that the binding was inconsistent. (In response to questions for this book, Tessier-Lavigne claimed that his statement was "fully accurate and consistent with the Stanford report." He then claimed that he had only been referring to evidence of inconsistent binding in mammalian cells as opposed to fruit-fly experimentation. The "any binding experiments" language in the statement, however, did not contain such a distinction.)

MTL's 2024 statement on his lab website also made the claim that prior to "the Panel's review" in late 2022–early 2023, "there was no falsification that was brought to my attention that I could have corrected. What had been brought to my attention in prior years were other types of issues that were not thought to involve data falsification." This is incorrect. While MTL attempted to explain away the PubPeer issues from 2015 as "tiling" anomalies—aka innocent errors—the scientific panel concluded, "In fact, tiling does not explain the underlying image manipulations in at least some of the figures to which the explanation was intended to apply." Even if MTL did not believe the issues constituted falsification, they did—and in 2015, in 2016, and again in 2021, the scientific panel found, MTL did not fully address the problems.

Chapter 11: TreeHacks

This chapter relies on contemporaneous notes, images, and videos to corroborate my own recollection. Full Moon on the Quad restrictions are taken directly from an email announcing policies for the event.

Of the 1,696 students admitted to compete at TreeHacks, 866 came from other universities, comprising forty US states and several other countries. More than 5,500 applied.

Chapter 12: Solve for People

In addition to a ream of communications between faculty, this chapter is based on more than two dozen interviews with professors, tech figures, and students. There are three separate chronologies at play in this chapter. The ground covered by the MTL investigation extends from February 21, 2023, to March 5. The TreeHacks timeline is more extended, broadly covering events from February 21 to March 18. I received my invitation to the billionaire's secret society only near the very end of spring quarter. "The Nominations Committee has selected you to join" read a mysterious email inviting me to a resort in New Mexico on June 3. "Retreat is 3 days of deep, off-the-record conversations with leaders from across the globe," and "we intentionally keep a low profile." The Nominations Committee listed four names—a world-famous economist, a Supreme Court litigator, a leading libertarian activist, and one of the most powerful investors on the planet. I decided to go.

Details of *Gaieties* are taken from a version of the script I obtained. The organizer of the law school musical later sent me a recording. Details of board conversations are new reporting for this book. All TreeHacks dialogue is taken directly from contemporaneous notes. The VC dinner took place on March 2, 2023, but some exchanges were reconstructed using additional notes from the 2024 event. (It is a yearly dinner between the TreeHacks team and a particular VC firm, and the lead investor makes the same speech each time.)

Chapter 13: Free to Speak

Much of this chapter is based on publicly available materials. The faculty senate scene is rendered from my personal notes as well as the official Stanford minutes. Details of Tessier-Lavigne's governance on political issues are taken from various public sources, as are his voting and donation records. Professor Billionaire, the Avastin campaign, Clinkle, Get Rich U, and Michael Snyder's alliance with Tony Robbins have all been publicly reported elsewhere. Statistics on Stanford majors are public. My account of MTL's appearance at Hillel is drawn from contemporaneous notes, my own recollection, and corroboration from other witnesses.

U.S. News & World Report ranks Stanford number one for economics, political science, psychology, sociology, statistics, physics, environmental sciences, and biological sciences. Stanford Law School earns a number one nod, too. English is ranked number five. Because *U.S. News* doesn't rank history programs, I relied on Niche, which ranks Stanford number four for history and number three for philosophy. Stanford's Graduate School of Business is almost always in the top three of rankings lists.

College rankings are a terrible business and, frankly, do little to measure the true value of a university. Individual experiences vary widely and the metrics these lists rely on are often quite detached from reality. Regardless, I rely on rankings here solely to show Stanford's cross-discipline ambition.

Chapter 14: No Room for Error

This chapter is the most personal of the book. I still rely on additional documentary evidence and corroborating accounts where possible. The overdose took place on April 28, 2023, seemingly around 10:00 p.m. Several of my friends noticed I was looking off. "Hey you ok?" texted one at 9:55 p.m. "You look like you're sleepy." Another friend texted at 10:13 p.m., "just making sure you're okay?" A third friend an hour later: "Hey—hope you feel better 🫶" These are the same friends who brought the coffee to my door while I was inside, on the floor, unable to respond.

I should note that the description of my overdose is my subjective lived experience. I am not a doctor, and some of the terminology I use may not be technically precise. But this is how I experienced it.

On a lighter note, the Polk speech ad-lib is taken directly from a recording. The detail about the "car chase [where] I was on a bike" actually refers to an incident on March 13, 2023, that was cut from the book due to space constraints. It wasn't a successful bike chase anyway.

The details about my grandfather are corroborated by family records, and the quotes trashing me from the butt dial by a person I thought was my friend are taken from a full transcript of the call.

Chapter 15: Money Is a Rush

The events of this chapter took place in April and May 2023. Further reporting supplemented public knowledge about the provost's resignation. Each VC encounter was recorded in contemporaneous notes; reporting on Curry revolved primarily around the accounts of two direct witnesses, Curry himself, and interviews with his former romantic partner; details about the stolen AI research were documented publicly.

My portrait of S.H.I.T. is largely drawn from notes, images, and videos taken during the weeks leading up to the event—as the team toiled away in an underground garage late at night—and from race weekend itself. Additional interviews were conducted to corroborate and expand on certain details.

The TreeHacks events described in this chapter took place in the following order: Special D party on April 8; yacht party on May 17; spring retreat spanning May 19–21. Wherever possible, specific details have been confirmed through several additional sources, including contemporaneous communications, images, and internal documents.

Chapter 16: *Finis Origine Pendet*

My investigation of the investigation relied on more than a dozen interviews with people who'd been interviewed by the committee and several who'd refused.

The true story behind MTL's resignation was assembled only in reporting for this book, for which I conducted interviews with several people involved with the Stanford investigation—including two of the scientists on the panel—and collected testimony from trustees.

Interestingly, one of the scientists told me that he'd informed the Kirkland lawyers that his "prior relationship [with MTL], although it was not intense, was long-standing" and that he believed "it constituted a conflict of interest." The scientist was asked to join anyway. "I'm always afraid that the most treacherous conflicts are not the ones that are out in the open," the scientist said, "but the ones that you don't even know you have, and I think we were all—at least I was—positively, very positively, predisposed to Marc." This scientist and all others involved with the investigation believed that, despite "the initial false start," it had been carried out thoroughly and without bias.

As of fall 2025, one of the *Nature* papers that Tessier-Lavigne agreed contained manipulated data remains without correction or retraction more than two years after the Stanford investigation concluded that "a thorough correction which adequately addresses all issues is required and appropriate for the paper," and stated that "Dr. Tessier-Lavigne is seeking" said correction. The study bears an Editorial Expression of Concern, which, *Nature*'s policies note, is a step "typically superseded by publishing another amendment—such as a correction or retraction—once the investigation is complete." Tessier-Lavigne wrote in response to questions for this book that it "serves as a de facto Correction."

During the fact-checking process for this book, Elisabeth Bik discovered new concerns in several additional papers for which Tessier-Lavigne served as a coauthor that were not previously identified. These fresh concerns, which are not analyzed and discussed in the text of the book, point to the inherent incompleteness of the Stanford-commissioned investigation, which limited its scope solely to the papers that had already been publicly flagged at the time. One of the studies Bik identified in fall 2025—a 1999 two-author paper in *Nature* for which Tessier-Lavigne served as corresponding author—has already been marked by the publisher with an Editorial Expression of Concern advising "readers to interpret the results and conclusions of this article with caution" due to several issues with "two panels [that] are meant to be illustrative of the key result."

Details of my own experience in Berlin are derived from contemporaneous notes, text messages, and videos.

Coda

My sophomore year was dominated by everything that happened after October 7. Campus was torn apart at the seams, and students were at each other's throats. My interviews with interim president Richard Saller, and dozens of hours of interviews with pro-Palestinian and pro-Israel protesters, students, professors, and others, ultimately became a six-thousand-word feature in *The Atlantic* about how discourse had broken down.

Over the course of my sophomore year, I would be attacked as a leftist hack in the opinion pages of *The Wall Street Journal* and as a right-wing maniac by places like *The Intercept*. The right and the left each took turns embracing and attacking me. Nobody seemed quite able to make up their minds. *The Nation* wrote one article about how great I was, then followed it up a couple of months later with an article about how evil I was.

By spring of my sophomore year, I couldn't leave my dorm room without being harassed. I received numerous death threats, had events canceled over nebulous "security concerns," and eventually had to leave campus altogether for a spell. Someone threatened to waterboard me, but with gasoline, and then set me on fire; another threatened to gas me like my relatives who died in the Holocaust. I'd spent part of the summer after my senior year of high school volunteering with the World Central Kitchen to feed refugees on the border of Ukraine; when one of my former colleagues was killed distributing aid in Gaza in the spring of 2024, I received a number of messages saying, "Good. He was friends with you."

Still, while all of this was going on, I had to actually do the reporting for this book.

I began working on this project just before the start of sophomore year and spent the next two years writing it. I tried to keep the book mostly secret, but wasn't entirely successful. News of the book deal leaked in fall 2023, and not long after, a lengthy letter from Steve Neal showed up on the doorstep of the CEO of Penguin Random House, before I'd actually written a word of the manuscript. A subsequent letter was sent in January 2024. Together, Cooley's letters comprised sixty-four pages, alleging my reporting had been "false, misleading, and disproven."

Yet another legal letter arrived in fall 2025 after my fact-checker reached out providing Tessier-Lavigne the opportunity to comment on detailed questions. In it, Cooley senior counsel Martin Schenker complained: The "inquiry is certainly not what we intended" when they asked that the book be "subjected to a review by an experienced and independent fact-checker." (Indeed, my fact-checker was both independent and experienced, a veteran of the *New Yorker* fact-checking department who'd checked books for Ronan Farrow, Jonathan Eig, Susan Sontag, and Joan Didion, among others.)

Finally, after more than three weeks, Tessier-Lavigne's lawyers provided a response, ignoring twenty-three of the thirty-one questions we posed. MTL did not dispute the account of his forced resignation, nor the story about the younger colleague whom he purportedly sidelined after she contradicted some of his published research. He denied that he had referenced the Alzheimer's study when fundraising for Denali, but did not deny asking Richard Scheller to reach out to witnesses after the initiation of the Stanford investigation.

After failing to prevent publication of this book through his lawyers at Cooley, Tessier-Lavigne then retained the aggressive anti-media firm Clare Locke as his "defamation counsel." Clare Locke is known for its representation of Russian oligarchs, the Sackler family, and James O'Keefe's disinformation outfit, Project Veritas. Its founders have a stated goal of overturning press protections in the United States and the firm features prominently in the 2025 bestselling book *Murder the Truth: Fear, the First Amendment, and a Secret*

Campaign to Protect the Powerful. Clare Locke began sending letters on Tessier-Lavigne's behalf to Penguin Random House in November 2025, saying my reporting was "false, highly damaging, and defamatory per se" and that the publisher "should not" proceed "with publishing any of these negative claims about Dr. Tessier-Lavigne." Another letter alleged that Penguin Random House "is creating serious legal risk for itself" and threatened "resulting litigation."

* * *

The coda is based primarily on publicly accessible reporting. A lot of material had to be condensed into very little space—for example, I ultimately spent several hours with current Stanford President Jon Levin while working on this book, and had to fit that into just a couple of lines. Many stories I wish I had space to tell had to be cut, like the athletics program collapse.

Marc Tessier-Lavigne had two papers retracted on his first day out of office. The Alzheimer's paper was officially withdrawn on December 18, 2023. Out of all the news publications that wrote about the study when it originally came out in 2009—out of all the outlets that heralded this revolutionary theory—not a single one wrote about its being retracted. When MTL launched Xaira, few mainstream publications wrote about it, either. One that did included this line: "Tessier-Lavigne himself was cleared of wrongdoing."

To no one's surprise, Richard Scheller was added to the board of MTL's new company.

Stanford has taken an active approach in trying to manage me. Levin, Provost Jenny Martinez, Hoover Director Condoleezza Rice, and former presidents John Hennessy and Richard Saller all made themselves available for interviews and were always solicitous. This was obviously a contrast from before; in fact, the very day MTL's resignation was announced, I reached out to Saller for an interview, and within ten minutes he'd emailed back, assenting.

It seems fairly clear that this was part of a calculated strategy. After all, at one point in spring 2025, I had four additional trustees who'd agreed to interviews—then, on the same day, all of them stopped responding to my emails. But I do give the administration credit for engaging and appreciate the time Stanford's leaders have spent answering my questions.

I don't know exactly how the university will react to this book when it comes out, but I have done everything in my power to chronicle the institution fairly, studying its history and its present and gathering the perspectives of those at every level. Hopefully I still get to graduate!